D0398717

The Life
of a
Children's Troubadour

The Life
of a
Children's Troubadour

* * *

AN AUTOBIOGRAPHY

RAFFI

HOMELAND
PRESS

Canadian Cataloguing in Publication Data
Raffi
Life of a children's troubadour
Includes bibliographical references and index.

ISBN 1-896943-44-6

1. Raffi. 2. Singers–Canada–Biography. I. Title.
ML420.R137A3 1998   782.42'083'092   C98-910470-2
Printed and bound in Canada

★ ★ ★

A word about pronunciation:

The English spelling of Armenian names and words is something of an art, but the
pronunciations needn't be. Here is a guide for some of the names in this book.
Except for Namin, the accent is usually on the *last* syllable; with the English usage
of my family name, however, it is customary to accent the second syllable.

Cavoukian	ca - vook - yun	Papazian	pa - paz - yun
Mayrenie	my - ren - ee	Asadaour	ah - sa - dour (oor)
Ohannes	o - han - ness	Mardig	mar - deeg
Harootune	ha - roo - tune	Barooyr	ba - ruir
Onnig	ohn - neeg (silent *h*)	Namin	naw - min
Anahid	a - na - heed	Minas	mee - nuss / as in *bus*
Hagop	ha - gop / like *hope*		
Jano	with a soft J , like the s in *measure*		
Aghavnie	a - ghav - nee / *gh* is softer than gutteral *kh*		
Echmiadzin	etch - mee - a - dzeen / *dz* is softer than *ts* in *its*		

To Arto and Lucie
with great love

troubadour

The name given to a class of poets which appeared
in Provence, in the south of France, near the close of
the 11th century, but later spread to Spain and Italy.
They engaged in the production of lyrical poetry,
chiefly of the kind complicated in meter and
rhymes, and devoted themselves to the musical art
rather *for the love of it* than to secure monetary profit.

(Author's italics)

The New Teachers' and Pupils' Cyclopaedia
Holst Publishing Company 1915

CONTENTS

PREFACE

THE DEPARTURE OF MY PARENTS FROM THIS WORLD WITHIN twelve hours of each other, on October 26, 1995, brought to life an unending round of family stories among my brother, my sister and me, and our relatives and friends. In the telling of these stories and the reflections that followed, I gained new perspectives on my life and its roots.

For years I had wanted to write about my journey of self-discovery, a process which unfolded as I learned about children and their way of being. My search for selfhood involved a long struggle with my parents that gave me, after considerable effort, understanding and acceptance of their lives as well as mine.

With my parents' passing into spirit, it occurred to me to combine our stories. Theirs began with exile, branched into my grandfather's black-and-white photo studio in Cairo in the 1920s, and evolved to my father's internationally renowned career in color portraiture. My story involves the inner life of a contemporary troubadour and the quest for meaning that colored and shaped my musical career. After many articles written about me and my work, I felt it was time to give my own account of the events I experienced.

In addition, I wanted very much to speak to the issues of children and society in these unparalleled times.

At the start, I had no idea this would entail such an intimate portrayal of my emotional life. However, given that I have no children of my own, I realized as the work progressed that, as well as drawing on over twenty years of focusing on children and related issues, my views pertaining to childhood needed to be based largely on how I had experienced my early years.

I am fully aware that when we touch on child rearing we tread on sacred ground. Let me therefore say that with my writing I have sought only to shed light, and not to injure. Any failings along that line are completely unintended and come with my sincere regrets.

The interwoven themes of this narrative meet in the emotional realm of growth and transformation, for it is the inner landscape that governs how we move in the world. Indispensable to this process is our experience of childhood and the way we as adults see children and thus ourselves. In the end, it is my hope that these pages will promote a renewed look at the luminous subject of my heart's lens: the child.

Raffi
July, 1998

There are children in the morning,
they are leaning out for love,
they will lean that way forever . . .
                Leonard Cohen

OVERTURE

CHILDREN ARE THE MOST REASONABLE PEOPLE I KNOW. THEIR DAYS
are spent trying to make sense of the world, searching for meaning,
figuring things out. Their perception is magical, and their questions
are intelligent quests for understanding.

A mother in Ontario once shared a story with me about her five-
year-old, who was very excited about my upcoming concert and
counting the days until she would "see Raffi." But on the big day,
when mother and daughter walked into the crowded auditorium,
the child became very upset. When her mother wanted to know
what the matter was, the girl tearfully asked, "What are all these
other people doing here?" In the child's mind, "going to see Raffi"
had meant a private visit, and not the scene that confronted her in
the concert hall.

At the end of one of my concerts in California in 1985, when I
walked back on stage for an encore, a child near the front called out
in a loud voice, "Why is he coming back?" The audience erupted in
laughter. Knowing that the child had asked in earnest, I took a
moment to say to the audience that this was a very good question.
Perhaps it was the child's first time at a concert. Before my closing
song, I had said that it was to be my last one, and then I had waved
good-bye during the applause and left the stage. Now suddenly, there

I was walking back! No wonder he was confused. I then explained to the child what an encore was and why I had returned to the stage.

One question that children often asked me over the years was "Raffi, how did you get out of my tape?" (In the days of vinyl it was "How did you get out of my record?") My usual answer was that it was only my voice that was on the tape, not all of me. Luckily, the reply seemed to satisfy, and I loved to watch my young fans intently weighing the implications of this explanation.

* * *

Since 1976, I have had a unique career entertaining young children, an audience who often does not know what a concert is or how cassettes make sound—people who are still trying to sort out what is real and what is not.

I started singing professionally as a folksinger, a self-taught guitarist and singer-songwriter playing in coffee houses, college campuses and occasionally in bars. My wife, Debi, and I did not have children, and when I started singing in schools in the mid-'70s, I scarcely knew who children were. Although I was good-natured with those I met, mostly I was oblivious to them because I really didn't see them as people.

That changed one day in 1975, when I had a startling revelation in front of a class of first-graders I was entertaining.

For about a year, I had been supplementing my meager folksinger's income by appearing in elementary school classrooms as part of a music-in-the-schools program run by the Mariposa Folk Festival in Toronto. I used to prepare my repertoire of songs based on the grade I was to work with on a given day (mostly it was kindergarten to third grade), and routinely thought of the children as a group of a certain age. While some kids were more noticeable to me than others (and some needed the teacher to sit close by), I generally had a group portrait that I related to while holding the class's attention.

On that memorable day, I was seated in front of about thirty kids and, as I prepared to sing the first song, a light went on in my head:

I suddenly noticed that each member of the group was a single, individual person. It was a profound wake-up call for me to see who I was with. Astounded and very moved, I held that moment and stretched it to include every face. I asked every child to say his or her name out loud while I gazed into each pair of eyes.

For me that moment was pivotal: I never again missed the individual child within the group, and it was this experience that kindled my desire to understand the childhood years more fully.

Books on child development and stimulating conversations with Deb (a kindergarten teacher) and our primary teacher friends Bonnie and Bert Simpson gave me an ongoing forum in which to process my early music sessions with kids.

I came to understand how children were by observing their play and general behavior, seeing the ways they responded to me, and reflecting on all of this. Besides the learning about philosophical issues related to childhood, I was gaining practical knowledge as well. In a small music circle, for example, when I asked a dozen pre-schoolers if we should sing another song and one of them answered with a clear "Naaaaaaw" (in that patently guttural three-year-old style), I learned not to take it personally. This was simply a child being candid, responding to my loaded question honestly.

Early on, Deb taught me that the ideal way to start interacting with a child is to accept how the child is in the moment. Since children are often not in control of their actions, it was useful to see the context first without judging it, as a starting point to directing behavior or letting it unfold. Taking the emotional temperature did help to meet a child half-way.

In the days of my child-ignorance, when I was introduced to kids, I most often spoke or acted in a dramatic way to produce a reaction, as if provoking a response showed that I was "good at meeting children." Before long, I came to understand that just as adults need room to size up a stranger on first meeting, children need the same (if not more) room to make sense of the adult and his or her intentions.

Reading the works of Eda Le Shan, Neil Postman, Marie Winn and others further opened my eyes to a compassionate view of children, one that views children to be whole people with a dignity all their own, and with unique needs as they grow, so vulnerably, towards adulthood. Of course this was what Deb, Bonnie and Bert talked of as well, and the readings helped to confirm and flesh out the anecdotal information that these teachers brought home to me.

Gradually there emerged within me a picture of the young child as a highly intelligent being who, daily, is fully absorbed in that most fascinating task of socialization. It dawned on me that children are as whole in *their* early stage of development as adults are in their current place on life's journey.

I considered the baby/infant/toddler/child in the magnificence of the young human animal: sleeper-feeder, explorer-bodybuilder, linguist and socializer—navigating the world with the compass of innocence. Naturally spontaneous, candid, self-centered, impatient, hilarious, dependent, curious, playful, reasoning, loving and creative, the child is a highly imaginative being seeking guidance. During the impressionable years of forming self-esteem and character, the child is actively learning by pretending and imitating and messing up, by trying and failing and succeeding, daring and surrendering—alive and dreaming.

I

P Y R A M I D S

Bosom born and bosom bred,
spiral galaxy nipple stars
eyes suckle in awe,
milky way
home.

PAS DE DEUX

DECEMBER 24, 1995. IN SOLITARY RETREAT ON ONE OF THE
Gulf Islands off British Columbia's coast, I am sitting in a sunlit room
in a house that friends have kindly lent me while they are away.
Spread out on the desk before me are a dozen or so black-and-white
photos of my parents and siblings, and the greater family of cousins,
aunts, uncles and grandparents. Since the unexpected death of both my
parents just two months ago, I have been overwhelmed with questions
about our family life. I pour over these precious time-piece photos as if
searching for lost memories, angling for insight in the wake of my
parents' sudden passing: Arto at eighty, Lucie at seventy-four.

Arto, suffering from Parkinson's disease for fifteen years, had
grown progressively frail in the latter part of his life, and had trouble
speaking clearly. Lucie, his indefatigable companion of five decades,
had in recent years become his full-time nurse, looking after his every
need and making sure he took the many pills he required to keep his
condition stable. She was reluctant to leave him alone for more than
a couple of hours. Several times while on his own, he had fallen
attempting to turn around or just tripping over his feet. Miraculously,
he had never once injured himself.

Frail or not, the man was strong and willful to the end. I felt his
strength when I took his hand and felt his thin but still-powerful arms.

This strength kept him going, though it challenged Lucie's patience—if not her devotion—and surely wore her out. Years of attending round-the-clock to his needs and stubbornly refusing offers of help had left her emotionally and physically spent. She put on a good show, but underneath she was a weary woman.

During my many visits to the family home just north of Toronto, I saw the fatigue in Lucie's face, the aging process, and the lines and hollows of her forehead and eyes when the show-mask was off. So I was not surprised when I heard that a prolonged loss of appetite and inability to eat required her to be hospitalized. A series of tests revealed a large tumor in her liver.

I was about to embark on a fall concert tour when the news of Lucie's condition took me to Toronto a few days earlier than intended. My sister, Ani, had just returned from a promotional tour for her just-published first book. We drove to the hospital and met with Dr. Kempston, the attending physician, who told us the prognosis was not good. He felt Lucie's time was limited. Ani was defiant and determined to see Lucie through this illness by an act of will, even as she tearfully struggled to come to terms with "prematurely" losing her beloved mother.

On my return to Toronto two weeks later, Ani and I again sat with Dr. Kempston (our brother, Onnig, having left for Armenia while Lucie was still at home). When we heard the biopsy results—abdominal cancer, inoperable—we asked all the questions we could think of. At Lucie's age, however, it seemed there was nothing we could do but ease her journey. I made room for miracles, but did not pray for them. I prayed for her.

Lucie's spirits were buoyed by visits from a steady procession of relatives and family friends who became regulars to the room now crowded with flowers. In her daily visits, Ani did her best to accommodate everyone. Lucie's only granddaughter (and my niece), Kristin, flew from the West Coast to be with her. Also present to offer comfort was Kristin's brother, Sevan (my nephew), and their mother, Kim.

It was my full acceptance of the situation that allowed me to be on the road and performing during this time, and that was what Lucie wanted as well. I called Toronto daily for updates, speaking to friends and family, doctors and nurses, and of course to Lucie, whose voice was gradually losing its luster. I sent her as much love and prayer as I could, entreating the angels to be with her. On the soul level I communed with her, holding her in my inner gaze, embracing her with light after light.

In mid-tour, I flew back to Toronto and visited my ailing father, now in a nursing home. After we talked a while, I held his hand and told him that Lucie had cancer. He bowed his head and said, "This is a great wound to me." We sat in silence.

Later that day, it fell to me to tell Lucie about her state. When I arrived to see her, the room was quiet. The window framed a bright sun over Lake Ontario. Sitting close to her on the bed, I took her hand and told her about the biopsy result. Her eyebrows raised in resignation, she asked, "Does this mean I am dying?" I answered that we couldn't say, but we also couldn't rule it out. A tear, then a swallow, and she understood. She did not complain, but she was very puzzled. "How and from where did this stupid malady come to me?" she asked. I stroked her hand and kissed it. I was thankful that Ma was not in great pain.

With Onnig's return from Armenia, we all gathered at Lucie's bedside. A few days earlier, medical complications had required my father to be admitted to the same hospital. At his doctor's suggestion that he see Lucie (now in a semi-conscious state), we wheeled Arto into the room and next to her bed. He reached out and took her hand. She awoke, their eyes met and filled with tears, and the news I had given Arto a few days ago now faced him. At Lucie's request, we called in the resident priest for a communion service. Her fate committed to God, Onnig, Ani and I encircled the bed, a shower of tears for love.

The day before I was to fly home to rest up for my next tour, I said good-bye to both my parents. I held Lucie's hand, stroked her arm, caressed her face and hair, leaned over and kissed her forehead. Downstairs, I attended to Arto's comfort, and then said good-bye to a dazed man, lost in his feelings.

I reluctantly left for Vancouver, bent on returning to Toronto the following Sunday. But on Thursday, Onnig phoned to tell me that our mother had died. He was with her at the end, and would now tell Arto the news. I took the very next flight to Toronto and went straight to my sister's place, where we consoled each other by telling many a Lucie story. Our plan was to be with Arto in the morning.

Late that night, my hotel room was unusually tranquil. Before going to bed, I sat in deep quiet and felt the most intense peace. It was tangible and unforgettable. Eyes closed, I sent prayers to guide Lucie and prayers to Arto: I am with you; in whatever you need, I send you love.

That same night, our father died. It was six o'clock in the morning when Onnig called with the astonishing news. Feeling numb, I said a prayer, and waited until eight to go and tell Ani. Now, on this stunning, tear-filled day, we were making arrangements for a double funeral. I saw it as an extraordinary chance to pay tribute to both of our parents, their life together and their final *pas de deux*.

Over a thousand people came to the funeral home to pay their respects to the couple whose lives had touched so many in the Armenian community and beyond.

Flowers filled the room. In front of the caskets sat Arto and Lucie's black-and-white engagement photo, with a large portrait of Arto on the left and his beautiful painting of Lucie on the right. My eyes took in the various family members lost in thought: Lucie's brother, Mardig, Arto's brother, Hagop, cousin Maro. For over four hours, Kristin and Sevan, their father, Onnig, Ani and I stood, legs and backs aching, accepting the countless kisses and condolences. I'll never forget the warmth of those who greeted us, and the way Sevan and Kristin stood beside me, giving me strength and receiving everyone with such poise and feeling.

Though many were in traditional mourning, I was heartened by those who saw the rare beauty of such a sudden mutual parting from this world. "How romantic," a few of them said. "Can you believe it? Inseparable. They had to be together. How exquisite."

BEGINNINGS

I WAS THE MIDDLE CHILD, BORN OF ARMENIAN PARENTS ON July 8, 1948, in a French hospital in Cairo, Egypt. It was an Armenian custom to name boys after their grandfathers. My older brother was named after our paternal grandfather, Ohannes, of which Onnig is the diminutive.

Normally, I would have been named Asadour after my maternal grandfather, but my mother had other plans. She went to her father for a heart-to-heart chat and said that much as she loved him dearly, she was not so fond of his name, and asked whether he would be hurt if her son was given another name. Asadour brushed the matter aside with a colorful Turkish expletive, saying his name was of little concern to him and she was free to choose another.

Well, with that act of generosity (thank you, Asadour), the way was clear for Lucie to name me after one of the most celebrated Armenian writers and one of her favorite authors, known by his singular *nom de plume*, Raffi. Although I've come to love the name Asadour, I'm glad my young fans had a simpler name to know me by. Somehow "A Young Children's Concert with Asadour" doesn't quite have the Raffi ring. (What luck to be so blessed at birth with a name of great heritage that also rhymes with "daffy.")

Onnig was three years old when I came along. Judging from how often we fought in the early years, I imagine he was upset at my stealing the parental limelight. Our little dog, Pomposh, was also put out— literally. His barking would so disrupt my sleep, I'm told, he was shipped off to stay with Asadour and his wife, our grandma, Peka.

When I was four, Ani was born. Ani is the name of Armenia's ancient capital and is also short for Anahid, the ancient Armenian Goddess of Purity and Light. Lucie used to tell us that one day while she was nursing Ani in the hospital and looking contemplatively at her new daughter, the chief gynecologist came along and said in French, "Lucie, are you admiring your body's work?" He then advised against eating mango: "Not good for the milk."

Onnig and I didn't fight all the time; it just seemed like it. He used his smarts to get the better of me at every turn, deflecting trouble by claiming I started it. Once he fooled my little mind into giving him the lion's share of the Middle Eastern *foole* (bean) sandwiches I loved. Being bigger, Onnig ate much faster than I did and when he got halfway through his sandwich and I still had most of mine left, he said, "Why don't we have a race to see who can finish his sandwich first!" After I agreed, he said, "Let's switch sandwiches—that way you'll have a better chance of winning." I went along with it, too young to know he'd just talked me out of a good portion of my *foole* sandwich.

* * *

Our three-bedroom apartment in Cairo holds a rich tapestry of memories:

The *salle à manger*, where the chocolates were hidden in the known place.

The living room, with the hi-fi, the sofas, the Persian rug in a pattern perfect for playing marbles. The dining table I crawled under; the irresistible smell of dozens of thin *lahmajoon* pizzas my parents bought for lunch treats after church. The toy-trunk with its treasure of wooden blocks that I turned into the architectural marvels of my mind.

The front balcony, whose railings provided me a safe place from which to watch the mysterious life of our Arab neighbors.

The kitchen, with a balcony that gave me another window to the outside world: countless birds flying in formation, turning on a breeze and leaving me wondering how they did it; white-robed laborers dismantling a multi-story building using picks and axes, hauling away the debris of stone in sun-bathed convoys of dust; glimpses of silent black-and-white movies (on a big outdoor screen) with the kissing scenes I wasn't allowed to watch. I remember, too, the ten pickling cucumbers I ate in a row one afternoon and got sick; and the door through which Ohannes Grandpa would enter with surprise gifts in his pockets, prompting Onnig and me to leave our yogurt-and-cucumber *jajek* and kiss him, leaving white marks on his cheeks.

The bathtub, where I played with a metallic boat that floated until it got a hole in it, and where I remember being small enough that I could almost swim—until the year I noticed there wasn't as much room as before. And the second washroom with the open window, where I could lock the door and be alone, with just the hot sun on my skin.

My parents' bedroom, where I slept in a crib for my first few years, where I twirled around with outstretched arms while my mother wrapped me in a blanket; the room where, first thing each morning, I reached for the bottle of *café au lait*, and where my mother would tell me a story for my afternoon nap and then tiptoe to the door, only to hear I was still awake.

The bedroom I shared with Onnig and Mayrenie Grandma (Arto's mother). My bed, with its vertically adjustable side panel, behind which I once hid to escape my father's punishment. The bed where I lay frightened, listening to my parents' frequent arguments; that bed where I first conjured up images of our solar system and thought about eternity.

And the guestroom parlor, with the fancy velvety furniture, where I would occasionally watch my mother play a ditty on the piano and then copy her. This room of mystery and awe that I would visit, often when Mayrenie Grandma entertained her religious friends (mostly women of the extended family) who would take turns in prayers of fervent emotion, tearfully invoking blessings. I watched and listened.

A FAMILY OF STORYTELLERS

IN MY FAMILY, EVERYBODY TOLD STORIES AND LOVED DOING SO. When you were telling a story, it was like being onstage. Your recollection of an event or recounting of a well-known tale became a performance of your particular version of the truth, and it usually provoked colorful disagreements among your audience.

Since I lost both grandpas before I turned seven, it is mostly the grandmas' stories I recall: Mayrenie's from the Bible, and Peka's more personal ones. They both had a lot to say about their escape from the widespread Turkish massacre of Armenians in the early 1900s.

Among the biblical lore, I was captivated by the stories of Daniel in the lions' den, Jonah and the whale, and my favorite, Jesus driving the money vendors from the temple. Mayrenie brought these tales to life so vividly that I was quite frightened at times.

Mayrenie's sole mission seemed to be to secure as many devotees to Christ as she could. She even got to work on Onnig and me at a young age. One day, after she told us about her conversion experience as a young woman, she proceeded to explain that unless we repented our sins and committed our lives to Christ, we were doomed to burn in hell forever. I was terrified. In no time I went along with her idea, and we began marking the calendar with red X's from that day on (to show my "conversion"). This exercise lasted a couple of weeks—until my mother caught on and put an end to it.

Lucie was born to storytelling. If Arto was the picturist of the family, Lucie was the storyteller. Her arms swaying and her voice nearly singing, she would weave the storyline this way and that, with dramatic facial expressions and verbal asides. Often she would pause to marvel at a certain word and share her delight in its sound or meaning, such was her love of words as living curios. When Arto interrupted, she deftly thwarted the interjection and gained a clear path to her telling.

She loved to recount the one about her uncle, the brother of Peka. According to my mother, "Uncle Minas was a teacher, very educated, and a strongman." One day, a loudmouthed Turkish wrestler was in the ring at the French Legion, daring anyone to fight him. Somehow it was Minas who was chosen to put the man in his place. But how? Minas noticed that the man was covered in animal grease, making him a formidable (and slippery) opponent. So, picture this bear of a fighter circling the ring, taunting and bellowing, and Minas pacing, pacing, thinking of a way around this unsavory predicament. Suddenly, inspiration strikes. He willfully strides over to where a huge rock sits, and takes off his shirt. With the Turk looking on, Minas flexes his imposing muscles and, with a lionous roar, swings his hammering right fist down on the rock and breaks it in two. Scared out of his wits, the Turk flees.

"How did Uncle Minas do it? Tell it again, tell it again!" we would beg. Onnig and I loved hearing this story, mostly told by Lucie in Armenian, and sometimes in Turkish by Peka Grandma or Asadour Grandpa.

Both of my parents' parents came from the part of Armenia that was under Turkish occupation at the turn of the century, part of the substantial Armenian territory that international geopolitics left within Turkish borders. Although Armenian was my mother tongue, Turkish was also spoken in my family, especially with Peka Grandma.

Like all Armenians of my generation, I was taught from a young age about the Armenian genocide, the systematic deportation and killing of a million or more Armenians by Turkish authorities. April 24, 1915, is the origin of the annual April 24th Remembrance of Armenia's greatest tragedy, a date that nationals inside the country and abroad still observe. The hope is that officials in Turkey will one day open their archives and concede the past infamy, so that reconciliation may begin the healing of this gaping wound in the Armenian community.

In the words of Lucie, from an audio-tape recording:

My father was married and had three girls; when the Turks came to take them away from their home, he put the girls on a donkey with his wife, kissed them, and said good-bye, that's all; everything was finished.

My mother was married once before, before marrying my father. When the Turks began the massacre, they took her husband to jail. Meantime she had a son. When the son was five months old, news came that they hanged her husband. On hearing this, her breast milk went bad and she had fever. The child suffered, became ill and died. When the Turks ordered the evacuation, she had to quickly gather her things; they didn't let her bury the infant.

My parents met after the war. My father was such a good storyteller, I was able to visualize everything. He was sentenced to death seven times. But each time he was interrogated, it was learned he was a building foreman, and he was set free because he could be of use. So my father would say, "Learn something that can help you someday."

There wasn't just the holocaust of the Jewish people. Armenians had their own holocaust. The Turks never acknowledged it. Even Hitler said [in 1939], "Who remembers the Armenians?"

My husband's family—just a day before they would be finished—was with the other Armenians, just like animals on the street, to be massacred. Ohannes, my father-in-law, a very religious man, very wise, said, "My God, what shall I do to save my family?" That night, as they were huddled in a room, he found a small picture of the general commanding officer in charge. His name was Jemal Pasha. Ohannes found this small picture and he said to my mother-in-law, "Give the milk to the child (my husband, Arto, then one month old) and take this candle in your hand; I'm going to draw." So he found a big piece of paper, and he drew from night to morning, a black-and-white charcoal portrait of the commanding officer—the last hope.

Somehow, Ohannes managed to get Jemal Pasha to see his portrait.

The general said, "Bring the artist." Ohannes was summoned to the general's hotel, Hotel Baron, a big hotel. "Who did this portrait?" "I did." "Go, quickly, take your family. From now on, you will be the drawing instructor of our school in Aleppo." [This was 1916. Aleppo, then among the chief cities of Asiatic Turkey, is now in Syria.] Ohannes agreed, and saved twenty-five to thirty people from the deportation caravan by saying they were family, aunts and uncles.

The family stayed a while in Aleppo, then went to Jerusalem. In the Armenian Quarter there, Ohannes prayed his gratitude to God: "You saved us from the massacre, now I'm going to do something for you." He met with the Patriarch of the Armenian convent, the St. James Convent. For nine months, on ladders, like Michelangelo, Ohannes repaired the wall paintings of the convent for no pay. The family lived in the convent, along with other refugees. And the Patriarch gave to our family a painting of the Last Supper, done on black velvet, in appreciation. [Framed, it hung in our home for as long as I can recall.]

All these stories I heard from Ohannes; they're like a cinema. After Jerusalem, the Cavoukian family [Mayrenie, Ohannes and their children] moved to Cyprus. Ohannes opened a small photo studio, with a show-window. A passerby was impressed and said Ohannes should move to Cairo. His name was Monsieur Puissant; he was a Belgian, in charge of all the streetcars in Cairo. He paid for the family's travel, then helped open the Cairo studio.

The Cavoukians' miraculous escape led Ohannes to a spiritual awakening that guided him the rest of his days. His wife, Mayrenie, had received her calling earlier by way of a vision that came as she was peeling potatoes one day. A hand appeared on the kitchen wall, writing a message telling her to repent her sins and follow God. That she did with great devotion throughout her life. Mayrenie's prayers for her husband were answered when he had a dream that compelled him to join her path. From that day forward, Ohannes devoted himself to spiritual matters, made hundreds of drawings of biblical tales, and wrote religious books that he published in Cairo and gave away for free.

In one such book, *Life or Death*, Ohannes wrote his own account of the family's liberation in a piece called "My Testimony: His Kind Hands." I translated the following excerpt:

> Tongue and pen are not adequate to illustrate our Heavenly Father's merciful blessings, which in all the days of our being are made possible by His kind hands. It was during the sad days of the Great War (1914), when, with our entire family gathered with friends, we were dragged from place to place, surrendered to the stormy winds of fortune.
>
> Despite the situation's difficult means, the Lord's kind hands directed us towards Haleb [Aleppo], where we were able to briefly catch our breath from the considerable sufferings of our deportation.
>
> From outside, news of the continual carnage of those sad days afflicted our half-worn hearts, while the claws of diverse illnesses snatched hundreds of victims from us every day.
>
> One evening when I returned home downtrodden from the day's burdens, I was given the bad news that all of our part of town had to be ready by morning to leave for Der-Zor. For a while I was speechless. It seemed to me that no human plan whatsoever would be of use. Only God could have intervened. Then, though it was totally illogical, it seemed that a Divine

impulse led me to the market. Why did I need to go to town at that hour?

The Lord sent me to the town that evening so that by running into a familiar Turkish doctor, I would find the means by which my family and relatives might for a time be spared from banishment. However, danger always hovered, like the sword of Damocles, above our heads. . . . By way of a photographer friend of mine, I obtained a photo of Jemal Pasha, the general commander of Syria and Palestine; and despite being huddled with a number of families in a corner of an underground ruin that was half-filled with cotton, after eighteen hours of laborious effort I managed to enlarge the photo successfully. In this enterprise also, it was the Lord who gave me deliberate guidance and knowledge of the task at hand.

When I expressed to the manager of the Hotel Baron—a familiar Haleb hotel—a wish to present my drawing to the Pasha personally, he told me that he had received a telegraph saying the Pasha would arrive in a few days. Then, when he saw the picture, after complimenting me greatly, he sent me home with encouragement.

God's kind hands worked in this matter also. When the Pasha's late arrival drained our patience from dread of deportation, God, on the other hand, gave the opportunity for leading government officials, who were attracted by the drawn picture, to also have similar ideas.

The next day, the head constable of Haleb suddenly called for me. After he learned that Jemal Pasha's drawing was my work, he lavished great praise on me. The question of our deportation was wholly improved. The head constable, being aware of our situation, made every effort to see to our well-being. . . .

The Pasha's timing gave me new hope and opened new doors of encouragement. Now I was able to more confidently and without hindrance approach him, picture in hand. After a most respectful greeting, I stood up and fastened the picture to the wall. After viewing it in rapture for a quarter of an hour, he gave an order that I and my family be moved to Jerusalem in order for me to render the service of teaching drawing in schools. Why was an expatriate like me deserving of such mercy?

It was a select group—not only my family, but a few other families—that arrived in Jerusalem. There as well, by God's surprising help, we settled into this gracious city. Upon seeing our group of people, the governor of Jerusalem showed me the necessary respect and help, and put us in the care of the minister of education. In this way, until the end of the war, I rendered the service of teaching drawing in a few secondary schools.

After we moved from Jerusalem to Adana and then to Cyprus, we settled in Cairo, where . . . I fervently continued my service as school trustee.

Ohannes was a learned man, born in 1886 in Mersin on the northern Mediterranean coast. He married Mayrenie Merdinian, four years his junior, whose birthplace (according to a Cyprus travel pass she once held) was Kessaria, Asia-Minor. Her occupation was listed as "Married Woman." They had three children: a daughter, Kohar, and two sons, Hagop and Harootune—my father, known as Artin or Arto.

In 1932, Arto began working in the Cairo studio, then called *Laboratoire Cavouk*. This was the same year Ohannes received a glowing letter of thanks from the Armenian Patriarch of Jerusalem, for his restoration of the many priceless paintings in the St. James Convent.

The following year, Arto graduated from Berberian College (founded in Cairo in 1876) with a secondary school diploma. Berberian was where he got the musical training that led to his impressive vocal skills and fluency on the accordion, flute, violin and balalaika.

Lucie liked to remind us that Arto played accordion at public soirées, most notably at King Farouk's wedding—but "not for money, only for honor" as she was fond of saying.

Lucie Papazian and her younger brother, Mardig, were born to Asadour and his wife, Rebecca (Peka), who were from Adana, inland and not far from Mersin. It was after the First World War that Peka and Asadour met and married; after Lucie's birth (in 1921), the family went to live in Cairo.

There, Lucie studied at a French school and received a teaching diploma. She met Arto in 1943 at a friend's wedding where she was one of six bridesmaids and Arto was playing accordion. All night long, during his breaks, Arto danced only with Lucie. At the end of the night he offered to drive all the bridesmaids home, and kept checking the rearview mirror for Lucie. Asadour gave her a hard time for her frolics with this stranger, and Arto and Lucie saw little of each other after their first meeting.

Several months later, Lucie dreamt that King Farouk's mother and father visited her family home. That very same night, Arto and his parents came to visit her. When Ohannes asked Asadour if Arto might have Lucie's hand in marriage, there was no quick reply. Lucie was all for it. Her father said he would have to think it over.

Arto and Lucie were engaged on August 14, 1943, and were married on December 26. The wedding soirée took place in the studio the following day, and then they went to Alexandria for a two-week honeymoon. They spent New Year's there, even though Ohannes had telephoned and asked that they come back so the family could all be together. Arto declined the invitation, citing a desire to spend this New Year's Eve alone with his new wife.

Back in Cairo, the newlyweds lived in the studio with Arto's parents for a while, until all of them moved into a small apartment. It was here that Onnig was born. (As Lucie recalled, it was "a very difficult birth, but natural." Peka was there to help with the delivery.)

Lucie remembered the Cairo of that time as a beautiful city and, happily for her, full of Europeans—Greeks, Italians, French and Armenians. When the Opera was newly opened, she and Arto became members. And in those early years, on moonlit Saturday nights, they often drove with their friends to the Pyramids where they would laugh and sing *avec accordéon.* "*Quel romantique,*" Lucie would sigh, eyes dancing.

The year of Ani's birth—1952—was eventful in more ways than one. While crossing the street to buy medicine for Onnig, who was sick, Ohannes Grandpa was struck by a motorcycle and fell hard on the sidewalk. He died in the same Italian hospital where Ani was born a short time later.

Onnig recalls that Arto was so stunned by his father's passing that for three days he barely spoke. He stayed in his room the whole time, coming out only to eat. Though Ohannes had been a very strict father, as an artist he had been a mentor to Arto. In recent years they had talked about the family relocating to Brazil or Australia. At thirty-seven, Arto was now left to carry on without his father's guidance.

During the post-war period, Soviet Armenia had started a repatriation campaign that prompted scores of Armenians from the Middle East to return to the homeland. Although Arto and Lucie had considered making such a move, relatives who had done so advised against it. By prior design, they were to inform my parents covertly in a letter whether or not conditions were favorable. The signal they sent clearly said "stay away."

It was also in 1952 that Cairo erupted in riots. The nationalist uprising that soon caused King Farouk to vacate the throne sent a signal to many local Europeans that life in Cairo was changing dramatically. Two family friends, Angel and Albert Noradunkian, got the message loud and clear and promptly left Egypt for Canada, much to the derision of those who stayed. However, it wasn't long before my parents, too, would heed the call to leave.

STUDIO CAVOUK

FATHER WAS THE STRONGEST MAN IN THE WORLD, I WAS SURE of that. He was also a man of great energy and initiative, a man of vision. The black-and-white photography studio that Ohannes Grandpa had started in the 1920s was transformed in Arto's hands. His mastery of light and composition, his attention to detail and his flattery of the client-subject gave his portraits an arresting quality. The bustling business that came with hard work and the studio's growing reputation allowed Arto to be adventuresome.

Like Ohannes Grandpa, my father was an accomplished artist. He loved to paint in oils, and a love of colors moved him to experiment with color portrait photography in its infancy. In the early 1950s, he established one of the first color portrait studios with full dark room facilities for printing and developing. He knew his craft thoroughly, from shooting to retouching and photofinishing, from cardboard mounting to framing. But his specialty was the art of portrait photography.

Arto worked every day, coming home around half past noon for lunch and a nap until 2:30 p.m., then heading back to the studio until after eight o'clock. That went for Saturdays as well. On Sunday afternoons, we almost always went to the Pyramids, sometimes after church. Then Arto would have sittings at the studio from five until about nine in the evening.

Sundays at Studio Cavouk, located on one of Cairo's main thoroughfares, was always a beehive of newlywed couples in wedding attire arriving for their formal portraits. "In the studio there were old salons, new salons, one with red velvet furniture, another with Venetian furniture," Lucie told me. In three or four sitting rooms, the clients would wait in turn for their call to proceed to the main salon with the ornate painted backdrop. The state-of-the-art lighting system included several tripod lamps with batteries and even electronically operated overhead lamps, as my father liked to boast. He went to great lengths to excel at his calling, taking pleasure in trying something that hadn't been done before, or modifying an existing technique.

Lucie would tell how Arto perspired so much on those busy Sundays that he went through two or three shirts before he was done. Apparently he was also the one who collected payment, so at the end of the day his pockets were full of Egyptian pounds. One Sunday night early in their marriage, as the story goes, Arto came home from the studio and emptied his pockets on the sofa. Lucie was to count the money. After she was done and told him the tally, she made the mistake of asking if he wanted to count it for himself. Arto was upset at the very idea, saying he accepted her account of the money: "You are my wife—what's mine is yours. I trust you!"

In the studio, Onnig and I would do our best to stay out of the way. I was always bugging the staff of retouchers for paper or cardboard to draw on. When I was old enough, I helped trim the black-and-white photos with the serrated edge trimmer, always careful to leave the bottom border a little wider.

For me, the fun part of the studio was the toy room. On days that weren't busy, I was allowed to take something out to play with, like the scooter with the training wheels or the metallic horse on casters that moved forward when I moved up and down in the saddle. But my favorite was a little car with push pedals (which, years later, Onnig reminded me was *his* car, when I put a photo of it on one of my album covers). That toy car made me feel very big as I maneuvered it around for what always seemed too brief a ride. Then it would be time to ask someone to please, please give me a Pepsi or a Coke. I liked the bubbly froth that formed when I shook the bottle, and I loved the sound of the cap coming off. On those hot days, more often than not, the big ice box outside the dark room would yield me my prize.

* * *

For all the tumult I remember of home life in Cairo, it is a very musical Arto that remains in my heart, the fabulous accordionist and dramatic vocalist who could charge the air at social gatherings. His emotional renditions of Armenian folksongs would instantly transport listeners to the hills of our homeland. How he played that red Paulo Soprani accordion! Emphatically, masterfully, with great flair. Lucie said that his talent was renowned in Cairo's musical circles, and orchestras would often ask him to join in when he entered the room. She'd get that certain smile telling us how beautifully—her voice rising, "how *beautifully*"—he played the tango.

More than once I was told that my father played the accordion at King Farouk's wedding reception. One day, when I was seven or eight, Arto took me to see the Royal Palace, some time after the king's exit from power. I was very nervous seeing Farouk's official receiving room, where he was said to have installed doors that opened automatically as his subjects retreated from his presence, thus avoiding turning their back to the king. I imagine a correct exit was also facilitated by the king's personal guards who, it was said, came from a regiment of Maori soldiers noted for their bravery.

Arto and Lucie also told of a chance encounter with royalty that almost turned disastrous. Arto, it seems, had heard that if King Farouk saw a woman at a soirée and took a liking to her, his bodyguards would bring her to him.

As Lucie tells it, Arto always had a car during their four-month engagement. "Of course he was Cavouk from the beginning; I was a simple teacher." One evening they went to Auberge des Pyramides, a popular cabaret with dancing. They took a table and placed their order. Suddenly, Arto warned Lucie, "Don't turn around! Don't turn around!" Farouk had just entered, dressed incognito, but still surrounded by his men. Arto said, "We have to go!" and they immediately left and went to another club.

Lucie got home very late that night. Her father greeted her saying, "Where have you been? Your mother'll kill you!" She told him Arto had taken her out to clubs. In the morning, Peka was livid, but Lucie held her ground.

* * *

What Ohannes Cavoukian had started blossomed into the magnificent studio tended by my father after Grandpa's passing in 1952. Arto was an innovator, and it showed.

The art deco studio was huge, with street frontage half a block long. As you entered the reception area, to the right sat a modern wooden desk, behind which hung a life-sized black-and-white Cavouk photograph of King Fouad (Farouk's father), flanked by other framed photos. To the left was the gallery with two spacious bays featuring rows of Cavouk portraits, notable among them a few new color works (one of Ani when she was little). From the tiled floor, the walls, clad waist-high in dark-stained wooden panels, reached up to high ceilings dotted with pot lights.

A few stairs up from reception took you inside to the waiting rooms, the main studio (with the toy room off to the side) and, farther back, the finishing room where the photos were trimmed and mounted on cardboard (and sometimes framed), and where several retouchers sat leaning over negatives, carefully at work with sharpened pencils. Beyond this area was the sunlit back room where many of my father's paintings were kept. Completing the arrangement was the technical hub of the enterprise: a well-organized darkroom laboratory where the printing and developing took place.

One day in 1956, a very special guest and his entourage made for a memorable time at Studio Cavouk. The visitor was the head of the Armenian Church, Catholicos Vazken I, and the occasion was preserved in a decorative album of photos showing a tour of the studio—

His Holiness in good cheer, my parents elated, the fond farewells. So began my parents' lifelong association with the church, during which my father photographed numerous church figures and furnished them with thousands of photos.

On another occasion a year later, Cavouk was to photograph Egyptian President Gamal Abdel Nasser. As the elaborate lighting system was being set up and the time of the sitting neared, the president's staff became paranoid about the new-fangled electronic gear and abruptly canceled the session.

This, of course, may have been a blessing in disguise for the artist who was to leave the Nile with his family in the coming year. Had Nasser taken a liking to Arto's work, it's unlikely that the president's "official photographer" would have been allowed to leave Egypt. And once Onnig reached the age of fifteen, both his name and mine would have been placed on the army reserves list, making it impossible for the family to leave.

AMBIANCE

LIFE IN OUR ARTISTIC FAMILY OF GREAT HERITAGE AND MIRACULOUS beginnings was a complicated affair for this child. In my early years in Cairo, I fell captive to the foreign culture of adults in whose midst it was hard to get my bearings.

I felt I was either in the light or in the way and, within the family's conflicting passions, as often as I was kissed and coddled, I was also cast in the role of a sinful child routinely punished for God knows what. The authoritarian upbringing of both my parents was the way they reared *their* children. Although we loved them and knew they loved us, there was more to it than that. I, for one, couldn't fathom why, given the overt declarations and expressions of love, I was treated the way I was.

At home and at school I grew up mostly in fear of adults—my parents, teachers and others. It was not unusual for me to be hit from time to time or mocked for reasons I couldn't understand. Despite the complex set of mixed signals I received at home—of loving and hitting, praise and punishment, adoration and ridicule—by some form of grace I nevertheless did feel loved. But how I felt that love was certainly colored by the duress that came with it.

I was considered a melancholy child, and said to have the oversensitivity of a poet. There was a little Armenian lament that Lucie repeatedly cast my way: "The heart of a poet is, oh, so tender!" I remember doing my best to please my parents, and hoping to avoid the trouble that inevitably found me in the form of either my brother's pounding fists on my shoulders and back or my parents' using me as a convenient scapegoat.

Interestingly enough, despite my young years, I felt undeserving of these hurts and prayed to God that one day some form of divine referee would intervene and confirm my innocence. A slap on the face was in sharp contrast to my mother's warm, perfumed embrace. The threats and tongue-lashings hurt as much as, if not more than, the smacks of my father's hands and the cane he once wielded—the same man whose legs I dutifully rubbed in the mornings and whose freshly shaven face I loved to kiss.

There is no question that my parents loved me and believed they were giving me their best. Still, I remember those early years as a great bewilderment. There was so much I was not doing right or hearing right—always something that made me wrong in my parents' view. So, for all the latest European fashions they dressed me in, the Italian ice cream and the warmed peanuts they brought home, and the many toys that surrounded me, it is turbulence that I remember as the ground of my being in those early years. I was a puzzled child, accommodating the arbitrary movements of adults, trying to make sense of unpredictable events. Directed at every turn, I felt I had little or no choice in anything.

Golden moments gave relief. I loved it when my older cousin Jano, who lived upstairs, visited Onnig and me. Jano was very moody and not always sociable, so when he came to play we felt honored. He had the gift of the gab and could tell us stories that kept us in rapture for what seemed like hours. Mostly he made them up, but it didn't matter; we just loved being with him. I thought of him as a very sensitive soul and took comfort in his presence.

The occasional family outing to the cinema was most exciting. The cartoons that ran before the feature always captivated me. Then an usherette would walk down the aisle with a tray of refreshments, and that usually meant a treat. When the theater went dark for the feature film, my initial fright would soon give way to the excitement I felt watching movies like *Quo Vadis* or *Gunfight at the OK Corral*.

The big screen made such an impression on us that Onnig and I would go home and act out much of what we'd seen. We'd make swords out of the wooden rods of local chicken cages and shields of various shapes from cardboard. I also remember having gun-and-holster sets, and one unusual toy gun with a spring-loaded shaft that could hurl a pencil clear across the room. Dangerous though it was, the thing gave me a sense of power. Another handy weapon was a simple elastic band. Sadly, the pecking order made Ani a frequent target of her brothers' pranks.

Peka Grandma and Asadour Grandpa would sometimes bring Pomposh when they came over to visit. This dog with no tail had another memorable trait. Although he was quite rambunctious, frequently barking and darting around, there was one thing that always stopped him in his tracks. Whenever we put on the record with Toscanini's version of *Ave Maria*, this dog would drop everything and be absolutely still for its duration, as though in a trance. Not even the doorbell could break his spell.

Some evenings Arto would play backgammon with his brother, Hagop, or with his dear friend Barooyr, a lawyer and writer. What fun it was to see my father in a good mood, animated by the game on his wooden backgammon board, which was beautifully adorned with mother-of-pearl patterns.

The small white dice would fly, and Arto would slam down his piece and dare his opponent to better his move, or mockingly call out a hex on the next throw of the dice. He was a masterful strategist and played with bravado. But it was all in good fun and, win or lose, Arto had pats on the head for me and jovial exchanges with Lucie. At times like these, I hovered close by and felt lucky to be watching their grown-up play.

Our family spent several summers vacationing in Alexandria. On the way there in our 1943 Studebaker, Onnig and I would be in the back seat with Mayrenie Grandma. The leather scent of that car's interior is still with me, as is the look of the broad steering wheel and the sound of its horn. Early in the drive, Arto would sing the Lord's Prayer (in the beautiful Armenian melody) for safekeeping on our journey. After a great many kilometers and several "Are we there yet?" questions, we'd finally roll into the city. That first glimpse of the sea always filled me with excitement.

Other memories aren't as sweet. Sometimes in Cairo when Dad went driving out of town to do some photography, he would take me with him. More often than not, he would leave me in the car and tell me to stay put. During the time I had to wait for him—which seemed like an eternity—he would slip out of my sight. Frustration and helplessness would reduce me to tears, and I would angrily call out to him and pound the insides of the doors.

When we had company, it seemed that I was always being made to recite a poem or sing a little ditty, often when I least felt like it. The pressure of having to perform without mistakes made it a chore at best. Having to do it on a chair in front of others made it dreadful. If I did well, I was showered with praise. If not, there was talk of doing better next time and the moment was quickly swept aside, along with my conflicted feelings and embarrassment.

My grandmas were the oases in the desert of my childhood meanderings. They, more than anyone, came closest to providing a reliable response to my being, and gave me shelter from the storms of the rest of the family.

Often my mother and I made the trip to my Peka Grandma's apartment by horse and buggy, and oh, did I love that. Street smells in the hot Cairo sun, the sharp crack of the driver's whip, the clip-clop way down crooked streets, a blur of market vendors, the worn leather of the buggy's carriage and—suddenly, we've arrived. Mama negotiates the fare. We walk up the flights of stairs and Grandma greets us with hugs and *halvah* (a Middle Eastern sweet).

The apartment would be so still you could hear the mantelpiece clock counting the time. I remember doing hand weavings there, of colored string on an empty spool with nails on the top. It was so satisfying to see the woven string coming out the bottom of the spool. The year Asadour Grandpa died, I was too young to comprehend what had happened. My mind and hands focused on the weaving.

At our place, some days I'd spend hours in the kitchen watching both grandmas make one of their special Armenian dishes, my favorite of which was *mantuh*, ground meat encased in little pasta squares, baked and pan-fried, topped with yogurt and sprinkled with hand-crushed red *sumach* spice. I watched them rolling out the dough very wide, cutting two-inch vertical strips and then the horizontal lines to make all the squares.

On occasion, my ears would catch the sound of a tambourine, then another, and a few notes of a rhythmic Arabic melody. I'd run all the way to the front balcony and look down to see a street carnival with juggling acrobats and bare-waisted women passing by—an exotic tableau right under my feet.

My mother often told of how miserable I was on my first day of school.

I was four years old, dressed in my new light-blue school uniform and carrying a big wicker lunch box, on the front of which was a brass plate with my name engraved in Armenian. When we arrived at Kalousdian School that fateful day, little Raffi was not going to go inside his classroom, no matter how hard Mama pulled and cajoled.

There I was in the hallway, unwilling to budge, while Mama conferred with Mrs. Aghavnie, the kindergarten teacher. Mrs. Aghavnie brought out a colorful toy and put it halfway between me and the classroom door, and as I slowly took a few steps towards it she drew it closer to the door. This went on until I made my way into the classroom, more focused on the toy than on the strange new world I had just entered. (Round one to them.)

Wooden desks in double rows, thirty-two obedient children, and two adults. This, too, was the world of adult rule and measure. Three years of kindergarten (each named after a flower), then a preparatory year before first grade. My memories of these school years are few: Mrs. Aghavnie pushing the outdoor swing that sat three kids at a time, the school hand bell, the drawings and paper strip weaving we did, and the Armenian alphabet (all thirty-nine letters).

As I grew older, the school tasks became more formidable, and I suspect now that we were not developmentally ready for many of them. The clearest example of this was having to use a pen-nib at the age of seven. We were supposed to dip the nibs into our ink wells and remove them with no mess, to write with no mess, and then to underline headings using a ruler—with no mess. When something did go wrong, we got trouble instead of understanding.

Kalousdian School had hundreds of students and a large inner courtyard with a spacious sand-box. After kindergarten, boys and girls were taught in separate buildings. Most of the families paid tuition fees and packed their children's lunch, but many children attended free and ate in their own part of the cafeteria where food was provided at no cost. I prayed that my mother packed food I liked; if lunch was something I detested, the teachers would still make me eat it.

Our gym teacher must have thought he was in the army and we were his recruits, the way he clicked his wooden timekeeper, pulled people by the ear into line, and barked out orders. He wasn't all that different from many of my teachers in the first and second grades. In fact, there was a distinct lack of fun in this instructional institution.

Given that my father was on the school's board of governors and my mother had been a teacher, the pressure on Onnig and me to excel was constant. To reward achievement, the school gave prizes (usually books) to those ranking in the top three of their class. But even being the best didn't merit praise. Though term after term I placed first in my class, one of my report cards from those years (which I still have) bore the identical hand-written message for both terms, saying, "We are content with the results he has brought forward; he should be less talkative in class."

The school bus that took me home amidst jeering Arab peasant children doubled the alienation I felt in those days. Some days the Arabic wailings from the minarets would combine with the drama at home to make me feel so lost that I didn't know where I belonged. It was with some relief, at age ten, that I greeted the sudden news that we were going away to Canada. All I could think of was cowboys on horseback and how, just like in my Roy Rogers comic books, I would be one.

* * *

My father had traveled to North America in late 1956 to have a good look at the move he was planning for the family. My mother, on the other hand, didn't want to leave Egypt. "We had *everything* in Cairo," she would later say, "but with Nasser things changed." Arto, however, was adamant about leaving. He couldn't forget the fiery scenes he had witnessed during the riots a few short years before. He feared for the safety of his family and the future of his art.

In Canada, he visited Ottawa, where he arranged a showing of his color photographs in the prestigious Château Laurier Hotel and, in broken English, he did interviews with the press and even on CBC TV. He knew that his special skill in color portraiture would enhance his family's chances of emigrating, and so his portraits became his calling card to the new world.

According to my father, no portrait studio was working in color in those days. People felt color was too expensive and complicated, and that it wouldn't catch on. But Arto was determined. The visit to

Ottawa also marked his first meeting with Yousuf Karsh, the Armenian photographer then based in Ottawa, who was noted for his black-and-white portraiture. So successful was my father's pioneering path with color that in subsequent years some called Cavouk "the Karsh of color."

Arto went to Montreal, Toronto and New York to see where the family might settle. "Montreal had too much snow, and New York was too big," he later remembered, "so I chose Toronto." It was a wise choice. Not only had he photographed the Canadian Ambassador (in Cairo) and had some contact with the Canadian Embassy, but he also knew the Noradunkians who had left Egypt in 1952 and settled in Toronto. They provided my father with a place to stay during his month-long visit to Toronto, introduced him to people in the United Church, and agreed to sponsor our family's bid to immigrate. These dear friends would later smooth the way for the Cavoukians and graciously open their home to us upon our arrival.

Before leaving New York, Arto couldn't resist sending Lucie a novel gift: a recording made at the Empire State Building of himself singing and saying how much he missed her.

The Big Apple dazzled him, as he wrote in a letter to Mayrenie, dated December 16, 1956. The Christmas lights in Times Square and the department store windows with their ultra-new wares made an impression he confessed was hard to convey with words. But the pragmatist in him was able to choose a smaller apple, where a chorus of angels were about to work their magic on his family's behalf.

With Toronto in his sights, Arto returned to Egypt to set things in order prior to leaving. The flight from the Nile had all the appearances of a vacation to Belgium. He convinced Lucie that we had to travel with as few personal belongings as possible so as not to be conspicuous; he was afraid the authorities might realize that our plan was to emigrate and thwart the departure at the last minute. We sold nearly all of our personal possessions, but left the studio intact, selling a half-interest in it to relatives. As Lucie would often tell it, the six of us left Cairo with just eight pieces of luggage and Mayrenie Grandma's prayers.

II

A NEW LEAF

*Be patient toward all that is unsolved in your heart . . .
try to love the questions themselves . . . and the point is
to live everything. Live the questions now.
Perhaps you will then gradually,
without noticing it, live
along some distant day
into the answers.*

Rainer Maria Rilke

NEW WORLD IMMIGRANTS

EN ROUTE TO CANADA IN SEPTEMBER OF 1958, WE STOPPED IN
Brussels where, one day, we visited the World's Fair. This giant futuris-
tic exposition was housed in large silvery spheres connected by long
metallic tubes that contained what must have then been the world's foremost escalator system. The 102-meter-high structure had the look of a
giant molecular model, dwarfing the streets like something out of a sci-
fi movie. Here were the escalators that my Dad had described as "moving stairs" when he returned from his scouting trip to North America. I
held tight to my mother's hand on the long rides up and then down.

It's hard to forget the thirteen hours crossing the Atlantic in a
Sabena World Airlines plane whose four propeller engines periodically
showed flames coming out the back. Though a stewardess assured us
in her best voice that this was normal, we got Mayrenie Grandma
praying extra hard.

When we finally arrived in Montreal (to stay the night before
continuing to Toronto), we checked into our suite at the Laurentian
Hotel and my mother began unpacking. Engrossed in this, it was a
few minutes before she realized things had got too quiet. She rushed
into the other room and there were her children lying side by side on
the floor, heads propped on hands, watching the first TV they had
ever come across—black-and-white, of course. Our transfixed gazes

must have said something to my parents because later, when we did have a TV in our first home, we were only allowed to watch it sparingly. On that, as with other things, my father was quite strict.

What a strange world was about to engulf us—a complete departure from the Nile delta. Cool and gray was how Canada appeared in my first impressions. Our multicolored life in Egypt had been narrowed to the cramped quarters of the rental bungalow on Toronto's Melrose Avenue.

The familiarity of Cairo life was replaced by a host of uncertainties in English-speaking Toronto, where I saw no horses or cowboy clothes. No more outings to the Pyramids and the Sphinx, no more surprise visits from my *hopar* (Armenian for paternal uncle) for loud backgammon games with my father.

The good news was that in school the teachers didn't hit you.

Onnig and I immediately took a liking to this new arrangement, and Lucie noticed how willingly we went to class each day. What's more, yesterday's segregated classrooms and playgrounds gave way to something quite new to us: girls! Now here was something different to think about—a welcome, if troubling, diversion. Freckle-faced Dale in my fourth grade class was the first object of my affections. Before long there would be Cathy in sixth grade, and Susan in junior high school. These adorations were strictly one-way, but they occupied a great deal of my time and energy. I was intrigued by this new world of boys kissing girls, and of boys keeping count of such kisses!

Still very new to English, in my first year at Bannockburn Public School I was set back one grade relative to my age, despite being far ahead of my classmates in arithmetic. I was the pudgy little Armenian kid with the funny name who couldn't play softball or ice-skate—and did the other guys ever make fun of me. I remember the girls being kinder.

I brought funny-looking sandwiches to school, not peanut butter and jam like the other kids. Mine were likely to contain feta cheese and sometimes pitted black olives. And if that wasn't enough, there was my unusual new lunch box. Lucie was so pleased when she came home one day having bought a lovely turquoise metal box topped with a thin aluminum handle. "See," she said, "there's even a tray inside." She'd bought me a fishing tackle box, not the Roy Rogers lunch box I wanted.

This new life affected each of us kids a little differently.

Little Ani had a rough time in the early going. For some reason, she was not sent to kindergarten in the same school I went to, and so she was on her own. Lucie told us that Ani didn't complain, but for the first six months she was numb, hardly speaking. I guess it was all she could do to take in the big changes and learn a new language at the same time.

Onnig was pretty upset at not getting the horse that Arto had promised him before leaving Cairo. Besides that, he too had a very unusual name and spoke English with a slight accent, neither of which helped him fit in at school. He soon changed his name to John. It's a move I often wished *I'd* made. There were days when I truly wanted to be anything but Raffi—Ralph, Ray, anything.

I really missed Peka Grandma. The few months we had to wait for her and Uncle Mardig to join us seemed like forever. (They were supposed to be bringing our backgammon games with them, and I prayed they'd hurry up and get here.) Eventually the Papazians did arrive, and came to live in the basement of our little rented house.

It was amazing how well the two grandmas fared in this new world, with their dark dresses and handy "no English" answer to phone calls or people knocking at the front door. Over the years, Mayrenie's figure had assumed a short and portly shape, and she had considerable difficulty moving around. Peka's posture, however, remained tall and trim, and conveyed a certain village dignity. And even though they were from such different social backgrounds (my mother's family having been rather poor), I imagine that being of the same generation and having survived similar trials allowed them to bring some comfort to each other.

Uncle Mardig was trained in tool-and-die skills, and he went out every day looking for work, soon landing a job at a local aeronautics company as a machinist. In winter, even when the snows came and

1 My father Arto, with his parents Mayrenie and Ohannes Cavoukian, early 1920s.

2 The Papazians in Cairo: my mother Lucie, with her parents Peka and Asadour, and brother Mardig, mid-1920s.

3, 4, 5 Arto in youth and adolescence; Peka and Lucie.

6 One of 250 drawings done
   by Ohannes Grandpa, later
   donated by my father to the
   Armenian Church in
   Echmiadzin.

7 My namesake, the writer Raffi
   (1835-1888).

8, 9, 10
   Cairo: the newlyweds;
the three kids with mom in
Studio Cavouk; Arto.

12 ABOVE: My kindergarten class at Kalousdian School in 1953, Mrs. Aghavnie standing at the back on the right. (I'm in the middle group, second seat from the front on the left.)

13 BELOW: Ani and the boys.

11 PREVIOUS PAGE: Arto at the studio with a portrait of King Fouad (Farouk's father), painted by Ohannes Grandpa.

14 Ani, age two (giving her first speech).

15 My first day of school.

16 Me and Onnig with Ohannes Grandpa.

17 Lucie in a pose for Arto at Studio Cavouk in Cairo.

18 The Cavouk exhibit at
    the Canadian National
    Exhibition (1960).
    Subjects include Toronto
    mayor Nathan Phillips
    (left of Arto), the Earl and
    Countess Mountbatten
    (below), and Ani with a
    pony tail (on the desk).

19 This was taken at the
    studio on my winning
    a poster contest when
    I was 13. The desk photo
    is of Ruth Kilgour.

20 Our first winter in Canada
   on Melrose Avenue, with
   the '58 Chevrolet.

21 *Les danceurs* . . .

22 In the living room of our rented
   house (TV shows a church service).

23 Ahhh, the '60s—I went to see a Jefferson Airplane–Grateful Dead double bill in that outfit: corduroy jacket, suede tie and all.

24 With sideburns and guitar at the Mackay residence, playing what looks like a C chord.

25 Deb and me at a high school prom.

26 Carefree in London, England (1970).

27 The young Cavoukians in Moscow with Anastas Mikoyan (1972).

28 With Deb in 1973.

29 On signing myself to
Troubadour, outside
our garage (1975).

30 The family at Ani's graduation from Toronto's Glendon College (1976).

31 Fred Penner (seated), with me, Mike Mulholland and Glenn Sernyk at Fred's signing with Troubadour (1978).

32, 33 Ken Whiteley (left) showing how to play the jug; and brother Chris Whiteley blowing his horn.

34 Bonnie, me, Deb and Bert in New York (1983).

35 The album that started it all in 1976.

piled a foot-and-a-half high in our driveway, he would stoically leave the house without a scarf or gloves, much to our amazement and concern. It's a wonder his ears didn't fall off from frostbite. He kept warm by cursing Christopher Columbus for his role in all this. On the mornings Mardig's '54 Dodge wouldn't start, he'd undo some part of the engine and bring it into the kitchen to warm on the stove, biting his lip, shaking his head and cursing all the while.

Oh, the COLD! That did take some getting used to.

The dark brown ear muffs I wore to prevent the dreaded frostbite would hurt when I took them off—the metal rivets holding the muffs to the head band always pulled my hair. Why didn't anyone else complain? I even had to learn how to walk in snow; I kept slipping on hidden icy patches and falling down hard. At school there was a paved incline that turned into a hill of ice and my class-mates loved to take a run at the top and whoosh down like ski jumpers. I, on the other hand, after my first tumble or two, saw it as yet another trial to endure.

On Sundays we went to the Armenian Apostolic Church, where later I sang in the choir. It wasn't exactly a child-friendly environ-ment. Armenian Holy Fathers often wore a black hood, and our own priest cast an ominous aura in his formal attire, rhythmically spreading thick clouds of incense from an ornate brass dispenser.

For a long time I wondered about the whole notion of God's representative being up on this high altar, in the flesh. I found this hint of the Divine somehow unsettling. The music of the weekly liturgy, though very soulful, was mostly in the sad minor keys, with a heavy, depressing feeling about it. And while I did like the sound of the organ and the glow of the candles, I couldn't relate to much of the service, whose words and ideas sounded foreign to my young mind.

Our first TV was a fine piece of wooden furniture, with brass-handled doors that would slide back along both sides of the cabinet to reveal a black-and-white world-in-a-box. A magic box.

I came to love the Toronto Maple Leafs hockey team. I even loved Foster Hewitt, the voice of *Hockey Night in Canada.* Every Saturday night at nine o'clock (after *Leave It to Beaver* and *The Donna Reed Show*), we'd get up and turn the channel selector to the CBC to watch this fast ice show of men on skates carrying wooden sticks and chasing a small rubber puck. Onnig and I took to hockey right away. Ani couldn't stand it. Lucie watched her sons in fascination. Arto sort of followed the action, but never really caught on to the game. Nevertheless, every Saturday he'd buy us a big pie—blueberry, cherry or lemon meringue—and at a crucial point in the game when the Leafs scored, we'd celebrate with a piece of pie. Luckily, the Leafs scored often in those days.

There was sort of a myth and mystery to these live TV broadcasts from Maple Leaf Gardens that apparently all Canadians were simultaneously tuned into. While the stirring yet comforting music of the Esso gasoline jingle played "There's something you're aware of, your car's been taken care of . . . ," the neon Esso sign would give way to a view of the hockey emporium itself and we'd hear the excitable Voice of Hockey welcoming fans from coast to coast. Because the night game actually started an hour before it came on TV, we never knew how much of the second period had been played. (I used to cross my fingers hoping there was still more than half the game remaining.) These telecasts were a big part of my Canadianization. If I couldn't skate like the other kids, at least I could have my skating heroes.

The first English composition I ever wrote was about the Toronto Maple Leafs. I pretended to be Foster Hewitt and made up a play-by-play segment of a game between the Leafs and the Montreal Canadiens, their arch rivals. I still remember how exciting it was to write this, almost like it was *me* on the ice, gliding with the big guys.

My favorite by far was number 27, Frank Mahovlich, with his free-wheeling skating and stick-handling style. The Big M, as he was known, thrilled the crowd with his end-to-end rushes and his booming slap shot. Lucie would say his name slowly, Ma-*haaav*-lich.

"If they can say *that* name," she'd huff, "why not Cavoukian? *Mon Dieu*, it's easier than Diefenbaker!"

The grandmas had their TV favorites, too. Peka took to Perry Como. She loved watching him sing and referred to him as her son. Mayrenie's pick was evangelist Billy Graham, whom she had heard about in Cairo. (Any PR person for Jesus definitely made her day.) And, of course, we all watched Ed Sullivan on Sunday night.

Besides the *Lone Ranger* and other cowboy fare, what also caught my fancy was *The Three Stooges*. I loved Curly; he was so sweet and innocent. The rough stuff aside, he was a comic genius who more than made up for the predictable scripts. Nobody ever replaced him, as far as I was concerned. One year the Stooges made an appearance at the Canadian National Exhibition in Toronto, but my enthusiasm waned when I found out Curly wasn't there.

If I was at home Saturday afternoons in the summer, I'd watch major-league baseball or the *Polka Hour* on WGR, the NBC station in Buffalo, New York. Television in Toronto carried all three major U.S. networks and I did watch a lot of American programming.

The Milwaukee Braves caught my attention long before I even knew where Milwaukee was. I can't explain why I liked them, or why the Saturday afternoon *Game of the Week* on NBC would excite me if it had the Braves. Whether it was the uniforms with the red trim or the team's baseball cards I liked, I don't know. However, I do recall the Braves had many stars, including Eddie Matthews, Lew Burdett and Warren Spahn. My favorite was right-fielder Henry Aaron—incidentally, the first black person I ever took notice of. (It seemed there were few blacks in Toronto in the late 1950s and I certainly didn't know any.) Again, I can't explain it, but I just loved everything about "Hank" Aaron, from his outstanding play to his gentle demeanor.

Once, I got to see the Braves in action when they came to town to play the International League all-stars. I can't tell you who won, but I sure remember my hero Hank beltin' one out of Maple Leaf Stadium that night, probably clear out to Lake Ontario.

GUARDIAN ANGELS

Lucie was counting every penny while Arto got the studio up and running. Our limited financial resources and our parents' patience were stretched thin in those early months when nobody came in to be photographed. The early going was a test of faith for Arto and his vision for color portraiture in our new country.

The second-floor studio at 95 Bloor Street West had only a tiny show window at street level. Concerned that this wasn't enough to attract clientele, Arto rented another show window nearby at the Park Plaza Hotel, a prestigious Toronto landmark. In this space he displayed a color portrait of Arthur Kilgour, the Secretary to the Canadian Ambassador to Egypt, whom he had photographed in Cairo before our departure.

One day, Lucie was alone in the studio—"like a wild animal, very sad but unable to speak what I am feeling." There was a knock on the door. "I was afraid, I have to speak English. A very *chic* lady came in and said, 'Today I saw my son in the show window of the Park Plaza Hotel.'" The lady was Ruth Kilgour, the first Canadian to befriend us. Lucie called Arto to come to the studio, and they learned that Arthur, Ruth's son, had sent a copy of that photo to his mother in Toronto. Mrs. Kilgour was very impressed with the quality of the portrait and now, having met the Cavouks and sensing that they were struggling, asked if she could help. We were sure an angel had been sent to us.

My mother remembered that time clearly.

Mrs. Kilgour said she was a friend of the newly appointed Lieutenant-Governor of Ontario, Keiller Mackay, the Queen's representative for the province, and offered to make introductions for us.

Arto did a portrait of Mrs. Kilgour, and it so pleased her that she showed it to Mackay, explaining Cavouk's situation. The Lieutenant-Governor liked what he saw and agreed to a sitting.

At 10 a.m. on a Wednesday, a black limousine pulled up in front of 95 Bloor Street West and out stepped Keiller Mackay and his wife, Kay. The lack of fanfare—no soldiers in the streets, no stoppage of traffic—amazed my parents. Over Armenian coffee (Lucie wouldn't call it Turkish coffee), they were impressed to hear that Mackay had read about Armenians to familiarize himself with our family's culture. All was going well until, right in the middle of my father's photographing Mrs. Mackay, there was a power blackout. Fortunately, Kay was most gracious and the sitting turned out to be a great success.

Two 16 by 20 inch color portraits of the Lieutenant-Governor and his wife graced the first Cavouk show window on 95 Bloor in December of 1958, just five months after our family's arrival in Toronto.

The Mackays invited the Cavoukians to all the social functions at Queen's Park, the site of the Ontario legislature. Lucie fondly remembered one occasion, in March 1959, when Mrs. Kilgour took down the paintings in her home, replaced them with a number of Cavouk portraits and held a cocktail party for the elite of Toronto, the so-called "carriage trade."

Among the guests that evening was Lieutenant-Governor Mackay, attired in the family tartan, kilt and all, right down to the dagger in the knee-high socks. Mrs. Kilgour put a corsage on Lucie's navy-blue dress, and I can just imagine the Cavouks flitting among the guests, playing the part of charming artist and wife, overwhelmed by such a heady dose of Toronto *chic*. By nightfall Lucie needed two aspirins. The party kept on going, with midnight heralding a buffet for thirty people. When Arto and Lucie finally left, a light snow was falling— the finishing touch to a magical evening.

Mrs. Kilgour was also a friend of Roland Michener, then Speaker of the House of Commons in Ottawa. She wrote to Roland and his wife, Nora, asking if they too would help the Cavoukians.

Before long, Arto and Lucie were invited to Ottawa to photograph the Micheners, who subsequently introduced them to various ambassadors. Soon Cavouk photographed Governor-General Georges Vanier, in full regalia, and his wife, Pauline, at their Rideau Hall residence. The imposing portraits, in the large 30 by 40 inch format, were highly praised, and the Governor-General's photo became his "official" portrait. We Cavoukians felt very proud.

Our family was astounded at the extraordinary events that met our arrival in Toronto. The kindness that Canadians showed us was something my parents often talked about.

In the years to come, invitations to have Christmas dinners with the Mackays delighted us. Although we three kids felt awkward and nervous on these outings, there was no mistaking the honor of being included in the warm hospitality of Keiller and Kay, whose spacious house was the first "mansion" we'd ever seen. With a roaring blaze in the fireplace, dinner served by a maid, and carolers singing outside the front door, it all seemed like something out of a movie. You couldn't get more Canadian than this, we thought.

KEEP IT PEACEFUL

ONE DAY WHEN I WAS IN SIXTH GRADE, I WAS UNEXPECTEDLY called into the principal's office. Mr. Norman informed me that I was to receive free art classes at the Ontario College of Art once a week. Although the news was puzzling to me at that moment, I gradually realized that I had received some sort of scholarship. My parents confirmed this when I got home, though they were short on details as to how it had come about.

In any case, I was soon spending my Saturday mornings downtown at the art college. In class with about twenty other students, I received instruction in drawing and painting, though I never really felt like I fit in and don't recall much improvement in my skills. What I do remember is the life drawing class that took me by surprise one morning. A woman in a bathrobe came in, was introduced to us, and then promptly disrobed and struck a pose. She was naked! I held my breath and angled for a better view. I could hardly wait to tell my brother.

For three summers in a row, Studio Cavouk exhibited dozens of framed color portraits at the CNE, the long-standing Canadian National Exhibition held annually in Toronto at the end of the summer. The year Lieutenant-Governor Mackay opened our exhibit was a particular thrill for our family, and it was the first time I met him. During the three weeks of the CNE, I used to go there with my parents almost every day.

In the center of the Cavouk exhibit area was a desk with a catalogue of the portraits displayed. Though not yet into my teens, I was fast learning English and, at my parents' encouragement (though I didn't have much choice in the matter), I eventually was able to sit behind the desk by myself and answer people's basic questions. I would also hand out Cavouk business cards to as many visitors as wanted them.

My father didn't like to advertise, preferring word of mouth to do the selling for him. Handing out the cards was therefore important and I was glad to be useful. Still, I got antsy sitting at the desk and looked forward to venturing off to see the sights.

Money being tight during that time, I didn't have a weekly allowance. I was given essentials like busfare, but I was always having to ask "the minister of finance" (as I called my mother; Arto was "governor-general") for spending money to have some fun on the midway. Not that I was into the roller coaster or the ferris wheel; they made my stomach churn. It was more for the Cokes and soft vanilla ice cream cones that I needed an extra 50 cents here, and 50 cents there. That is, until I discovered the Food Building with its free samples and treats.

Of course there were a number of other free events to take in all over the exhibition grounds. During my breaks away from the Cavouk desk, I would watch Little League baseball teams playing or marching bands rehearsing, and take in the floral displays at the Horticultural Building.

What I also enjoyed were the free music programs at the bandshell, especially the variety of American symphonic bands which played fabulous marches like *The Battle Hymn of the Republic* and others. I found the rhythms, melodies and brassy sounds exhilarating.

On one occasion during my strolls around the CNE grounds, I noticed a Smokey the Bear fire prevention poster contest. It was free to enter. You just had to sit in front of one of four easels and, using the paper and crayons provided, draw a poster that promoted fire prevention. So I did, and feeling all excited about winning the $100 first prize, I ran to tell my mother. She was all for it, and nudged me more than once to return and draw some more. The next time, I took my Laurentian colored pencils. I did a couple of drawings that day. One was of a forest coming out of a box, with the title "A Gift of Nature: Handle with Care." The other one also showed a forest scene, with a "No Hunting" sign fixed to a tree. A bird perched on the sign and the poster's title read "Keep It Peaceful."

One morning, four months later, I was puzzled when my mother insisted I wear my good sweater to school. I couldn't get an answer from her as to why *this* morning should be different from any other, but I went along with it. That same day, our grade seven class got a sudden call to join the ninth grade assembly in the gymnasium. Something was up. We filed in and saw they had saved the first two rows for us, right in front of the school band. The principal welcomed us and then introduced a special guest, Ontario's Minister of Lands and Forests. The reason I was wearing my good sweater became clear. Apparently, Lucie had received a call telling her that, out of the 5,000 entries to the poster contest, mine had won first prize and the presentation would be made at school. And now here was the minister to present me with a check!

I was in a daze when my name was called. The lights went bright, a TV camera came on and somehow I sauntered up onto the stage to shake a hand and receive my prize. And there for all to see was the poster I had drawn: Keep It Peaceful. The minister said he liked the title and thought the poster should be displayed in all the schools. I was dumbfounded.

But there was more—I also learned I was going to be on TV.

It was an after-school children's show called *The Professor's Hide-away*—not exactly my favorite. I vaguely remember meeting "the Professor," but the rest of the show is a blur. What I couldn't forget, though, was that very special feeling I had at the school skating rink over Christmas break. Everybody had seen me on TV, and that was almost as good as skating with Susan Berry.

Many Saturdays, my parents took me to the studio (partly so Onnig and I wouldn't fight). Often I'd be in the darkroom with my father while he printed and developed his portraits. I was amazed how he could find things in the dark, with just the dials on the timer of the printer giving off a faint glow. The printing and developing were demanding tasks. To get the colors just right often required several "proofs" before the final print was achieved.

Some days, if my parents were busy with clients, I'd answer the phone in the small reception area. If things were slow, I'd busy myself with drawing anything that caught my fancy, like the brass Middle Eastern coffee tray and cups that sat atop the carved wooden base, or my father's modern teak desk that held dozens of art books.

While my father did his retouching, we would often listen to the radio. It was usually the middle-of-the-road CFRB on AM or the classical CBC station on the FM band.

On *The Earl Warren Show* I heard all sorts of crooners: Andy Williams, Peggy Lee, Frank Sinatra and so on. I recall a lot of instrumentals, like Earl Grant playing *Ebb Tide* on the Hammond organ, or some orchestral arrangement of *Moon River*. With a cardboard box and a few elastic bands I fashioned a home-made guitar that gave me hours of pleasure playing along to the radio (mostly when my parents were out). Earl Warren used to close his afternoon show with good-byes and his trademark "and you there in the kitchen, mother." We listened to the CBC because my father insisted that an appreciation of classical music was very important in life. As for the FM popular music stations, I mostly noticed that their commercials (compared to those on AM) were much more genteel—soothing soft sells of jewelry and other well-heeled items.

Occasionally, I sneaked a peek inside Arto's photography books, the ones with the dreamy black-and-white photos of women in various forms of undress. How I loved to see the beauty of the feminine form. Even though my father never talked of this stuff, let alone showed me these books, it was both exciting and somehow comforting to have them there in the studio.

I still remember the day I figured out that all the love songs on the radio were about men and women getting together, getting married and such. It was like being let in on a big secret, but one that wasn't a secret at all. I felt slightly dizzy when it sunk in that this love stuff was mostly what grown-ups were up to.

Not only were there no cowboys on horseback in Canada, there were none of the mules and donkey-carts that were so much a part of street life in Cairo. But there were lots of cars. When we were newly arrived in Toronto, Onnig and I spent hours, from the second-floor window of the studio, counting the cars that went by. He was thirteen, I was ten. He'd count Chevrolets, I'd count Fords. There was a simple thrill in seeing another one of "my team" and spotting it from a distance. To say we were into cars is an understatement: we were mesmerized by the chrome and colored shapes of the various makes and models. (And for once we weren't fighting.)

I still remember the excitement I felt seeing the faces and tails of these late '50s and early '60s cars: their eyes and eyebrows, their body curves. Even the names were marvelous: Impala, Thunderbird—I didn't know what they meant, but they sounded great. Naturally, I fantasized about someday driving one of these.

I'll never forget when Dad traded in the turquoise '58 Chevy Del Ray for an ivy green '63 Buick Le Sabre, a car with power steering (you could turn the wheel with your pinkie), power brakes and a flat front floor where the transmission hump used to be. Well, you'd think we'd just been granted immortality or an invitation to Frank Mahovlich's house, the way we went on about that car. The power steering, which I'd first seen demonstrated at the CNE's Automotive Building, was now ours to play with and, more importantly, to show off to everyone.

The Buick gave way to a stately 1966 Lincoln Continental. Black outside, burgundy leather seats inside—now this was an automobile. Power this, power that, it just oozed class. And, like the '43 Studebaker in Cairo, its rear-hinged rear doors were unusual, opening from the center of the car—*très élégante.*

Then there was the '76 Oldsmobile Toronado, with its two big doors half the length of the driveway. The really neat feature of this model was its power eye lids: the headlights actually had a cover that electronically flipped up or down at the flick of a switch. Unfortunately, being a two-door car, it just didn't suit our family. At least it had fit nicely into our renovated garage, unlike its successor, an '82 Lincoln that was a tad too long.

Lucie howled with indignation when the descending garage door came to rest on the trunk of the new car whose rear end stuck out half a foot for all the neighbors to see.

CANADIAN CITIZEN

IN 1963, AFTER FIVE YEARS IN THE NEW COUNTRY, OUR FAMILY was about to face a judge's questions in order to qualify for Canadian citizenship.

I was nervous, scared that I'd answer a question incorrectly or forget to name all the provinces. (The joke going around Toronto's Armenian community was, "Can you name two famous Canadian generals?" "Sure—General Electric and General Motors!") In the end I passed the test, and felt proud to be in the multicultural group of faces given the good news that they were now citizens of Canada.

There was something about this country that staggered my young mind. At first, I saw it as the big pink country I drew from my geography books. Drawing maps was something I was good at. At Kalousdian School in Cairo, Onnig and I had traced elaborate maps and colored them. (With a razor blade or small knife, we would scrape a fine powder off a colored pencil, and with a piece of cotton we'd smudge the powder on the page. It made for beautiful maps.) I would render shorelines in dark blue and the surrounding coastal waters gradually lighter out to sea. I loved how atlases showed countries in different colors, though I wondered who decided what country got what color.

Canada sure looked huge on paper (bigger than America), and I'd heard much of it was colder than Toronto. Both were hard to imagine. For some time, my sense of the country's geography seemed to come more from the Canadian Football League than anything else. The first time I waited for the start of a televised CFL game involving the Edmonton Eskimos, I half expected to see the team in sealskin parkas and snowshoes. (Funny how things are named, I said to myself, seeing the Eskimos outfitted much like their opponents.)

I spent a good deal of the sixth grade making murals of the Vikings' arrival on Canada's eastern shores, and then learning about the French explorers Cartier and Champlain sailing up the St. Lawrence River, and about the *coureurs de bois*, French fur trappers and traders.

With my class I visited the Huron Village north of Toronto, where we learned about the Native people who once lived there. What with all the stories I read about the Hudson's Bay Company and the building of the railroad, and all the cowboys-and-Indians movies I watched on TV, I sure got a limited and distorted picture of the original settlers of my new home. And although schoolbooks taught that Canada was formed from two cultures, I found it curious that the names Toronto, Ottawa and Ontario were neither English nor French.

I finally got it straight that Ontario was once called Upper Canada and Lower Canada had become Quebec (formerly New France). When I learned that this upstart "Team Canada" won its one-and-only war against the Americans (in 1812), I felt the first rustlings of patriotism for this new country. I even liked the quirky Prime Minister, John Diefenbaker, whom my father photographed, and was tickled by his distinctively warbling speeches. I used to imitate him, much to my family's delight: "Ah . . . *one* nation . . . ah . . . *one* Canada," I'd say, shaking my head a little for the right sound.

For that matter, I used to imitate President John F. Kennedy as well, inspired by hearing impersonator Rich Little on the radio. As Rich's JFK used to say, "Who says Canadians don't have a sense of humor? Why, just look at their defense policy!"

Gradually, I got introduced to the great outdoors.

My first memory of an outing was the family piling into the '58 Chevy to see the fall colors at Belfountain, a wooded area not far from Toronto. My father was amazed at the blazing autumn foliage before our eyes. He took many photos, one of which he turned into a painting. I, too, loved what I saw, yet there was such a wide open feeling that I found it a little frightening to be out in the country.

In seventh grade, my class took a winter trip to the Albion Hills Conservation Area, where we stayed for a whole week. It was my first time away from home and I was very nervous about sharing a four-bunk room with guys I didn't know that well. While I was tickled to think that field trips counted as school work, outside the familiar confines of home and school I felt uneasy, as if I didn't belong. I did come to love the experience—tuna casseroles and all—and I made drawings of the stone and glass main building and its surroundings.

The thing I remember most vividly, however, was the campfire singalong the night before our return to the city. That night, when I heard the song *Jamaica Farewell* for the first time, its words and melody swept through my heart. Joining in brought tears to my eyes, and I realized I didn't want to go home. On the bus into town the next morning, I cried most of the way as we sang that song over and over again.

Back to the cold of Toronto and the snow-covered streets, back to the sound of shovels scraping snow; Onnig and I clearing our endless driveway for hours, our parents' eyes inspecting from the window for any spots we missed or some stretch that could be improved. Finally, into the house through the back porch and off with the galoshes. The comfort of Grandma's roast-and-noodle dinner, which I shoveled down in heaps. The muted sounds of our neighbors (the Kutcy boys) playing road hockey in their driveway, tennis balls hitting the garage door now and then.

ADOLESCENT TWISTS

BY 1961, ARTO AND LUCIE HAD SAVED ENOUGH TO PUT A $3,000 deposit on a brick one-and-a-half story house at 394 Melrose Avenue, only a couple of blocks from number 554, the rental bungalow where Peka and Mardig continued to stay. We three kids were glad for the move: we got some needed breathing room and Peka Grandma was still just down the street. During school, I'd occasionally have lunch at her place, feasting on flank steak and her home-made french fries and baklava.

My parents' restrictions on just about everything that might be fun put a dent in my social activities. For one thing, I wasn't allowed my own bike. (While I could occasionally borrow one from a school-mate, I wanted one of my own.) And I wasn't allowed to try out for the softball teams in my neighborhood, the ones sponsored by local businesses. So I spent many an evening going to the park and just watching the games from the triple-row stands behind the wire fence.

All this meant I had little in common with many of the neigh-borhood kids, which made it difficult to develop close friendships. As for those awkward dances in junior high, having to be home earlier than everybody else made them trickier than they already were.

Evenings at home, to get away from various family arguments, I would head to my room. Though I shared it with Onnig, sometimes I could be there alone, and I used to love listening to the radio while I did my homework. The two AM rock stations fought for your allegiance, playing the Top 30 countdown of love songs—the Beach Boys, Neil Sedaka and some Motown as well. Listening to the call-in "dedication" programs, I got to feel the emotions of sender and receiver as I let my sub-urban imagination go. Since I wasn't allowed to date, this was one way I could keep in touch with the socializing my schoolmates were doing.

My parents were always after Onnig and me to go to the church hall for the youth nights (Ani was too young), but these Armenian socials didn't interest me. Having to go down there and hang around, I felt out of place. For one thing, Onnig hardly wanted his younger brother close by, cramping his style. For another, I didn't have any friends in that circle, at least no one that I saw outside of church.

Singing in the Armenian Church choir with my father came as something of an unexpected pleasure. When he first announced the idea, I don't even remember protesting that much. From the basic music reading I had learned while playing the violin in grades seven and eight, I could follow the melodies in our choir books, and I found that I actually enjoyed the singing. I was surprised to discover that my first experience singing in public pleased others as well.

In 1963, my father suffered a heart attack and was hospitalized. The news alarmed all of us, but we were relieved to learn that he was expected to make a full recovery, as long as he didn't rush things. He would need a long convalescence. But as it happened, Arto wasn't the only one in pain.

Much to my father's annoyance, Onnig had started playing football at Bathurst Heights Secondary School, and when he broke his nose, Arto forbade further play. Nevertheless, Onnig continued anyway without Arto's knowledge, only then to suffer a leg injury. It was very painful, but Onnig didn't want the family to know he was hurting—and certainly didn't want to incur his father's wrath. So, for an entire year, he secretly took six aspirins a day to get by. One day in school, his football coach saw him limping and, upon learning of the nature and duration of the condition, sent Onnig to have his leg X-rayed. The X-rays of the thigh bone showed a tumor that needed immediate attention.

Poor Mom. In the middle of caring for Dad, she now had to contend with Onnig's pain and the impending surgery. But where would we find the money to pay for it?

Luckily, one of the last people Dad had photographed before he had his heart attack was Dr. Paul McGoey, an orthopedic surgeon and chief of staff at a nearby hospital. When Dr. McGoey came to the studio to pick up his portrait, he saw Lucie in tears and heard of the family's predicament. The next day he examined Onnig's X-rays and immediately scheduled surgery, saying that if it had been a couple of months later, the leg might have had to be amputated. Fortunately, the tumor was successfully removed and Onnig was back on his feet before long. This kind man didn't charge us a penny for the surgery, and he looked after the hospital bills as well.

Meanwhile, the studio was about to move.

The Colonnade, a new building at 131 Bloor Street West, just two blocks down from number 95, was one of the first mixed residential-and-boutique buildings in North America—boutiques on the first two floors and apartments on the next dozen or so above. The landlords had been wooing Cavouk to sign a lease and, when a special price was secured, Arto had agreed. Now it fell to Lucie to organize the move.

She was already feeling the pinch: "No money, my husband ill, Onnig on crutches." Between packing boxes for the move and riding buses and streetcars for hours each day to visit the two hospitals where Arto and Onnig convalesced, the strain on her was tremendous. One night at home she even collapsed, but she was back in action the very next day. She showed the strength of her Uncle Minas stock, and somehow, with the rest of the family helping in whatever ways we could, by summer the move was complete.

Arto was never quite the same after the heart attack. He must have been so afraid of a recurrence that he took the doctors' advice for recovery and multiplied it ten-fold. He moved so very slowly (especially going up and down the stairs), had everyone do this and that for him (way more than before), and just got downright fussy. It drove us crazy. "Put the window up a little. No, not that much, down a bit; up a little again." This is where Lucie's nursing of Arto began, and continued until the end. But at least she now had a new tactic to get us kids to do what she wanted: "Your father can have another heart attack!"

Out of all this, an enduring burden also fell on Onnig. With September approaching—and just after he had got his driver's license so he could drive his father to work during his recovery—Arto and Lucie asked him to quit school to join the studio. When he refused, Arto told him he had no choice but to do this for the next six months; there was no other way to look after the family.

So as not to lose ground in his studies, Onnig enrolled in night school to get his grade twelve. And, as if this weren't enough, Arto didn't let him attend his high school football games as he had promised, but instead insisted he take art classes two nights a week in order to become a better photographer. Onnig did not want to be a photographer, let alone work for Cavouk. But what was he to do? He felt trapped. From the back windows of the Colonnade studio, he would watch the University of Toronto footballers on the practice field of Victoria College down below.

Over the next few years, Onnig worked in the close confines of that tiny studio one flight up from street level, just to the right of the escalators. It took him two years to complete grade twelve at night school. He might have got his grade thirteen (as was needed in Ontario for university entrance) if he hadn't fallen in love with Kim Soth, a student nurse he had met through a high school friend. Between taking more night school classes or being with Kim, it was no contest. Their love sustained heavy pressure by my parents, relatives and others to break up the relationship (the issue being that Kim was an *odar*, meaning "outsider" in Armenian). Within a year they were married and had an apartment of their own. But amidst the fear, guilt and the survival needs of the day, Onnig stayed on at the studio, unable to make a path for himself. Although he is now able to look back philosophically at all this, it pained his life and relations between us for a long time.

At the studio, where I worked during my early teens on Saturdays and often in the summer, it seemed as if life were wholly about appearances. There I learned about the art of retouching, the skillful alteration of a photograph to flatter a face and make it look years younger.

Retouching was a two-step process.

First, my father would work with the negative. A metallic box on a desk would hold the film, behind which shone a bright light. A magnifying glass above made the image easier to see. The idea was to reduce the lines, wrinkles and imperfections that photographic lights had accentuated on the subject's face. In the case of a wrinkle, Dad would apply a very sharp pencil to the light-colored line on the negative, filling it in and neutralizing it.

Then, on the positive image of the printed and developed photograph, where the pencil's gray-black now showed in a whitish tone compared to the surrounding skin, he'd mix flesh-tone watercolor and, with the tip of a soft brush, apply it to fill in and smooth the area.

If you did too much retouching, you robbed the face of its character and flattened it. If you had too much pigment on the brush, you made too dark a mark. It took a great deal of care and hands-on experience to get the right balance.

It was this second half of the process that Arto taught me and which, for the most part, I mastered. I worked only on the positive image, and even that was very time-consuming. Doing the face of one medium-size portrait often took an hour or more, and then there were all the little dust spots in the rest of the photo to take care of.

Dad was a master retoucher because of his painter's knowledge of facial anatomy. But, despite his respect for facial contours, many times I was appalled by how far he would go in rendering a face more attractive, less fat, less wrinkled. It seemed to me that we were doing too much retouching and, when I said so, his answer surprised me. He said that if we didn't, clients would not accept the photo likeness of themselves. Apparently the need for self-delusion was such that, even with the level of retouching we did, there were still some people who asked to be more blemish-free.

This photographic play of light and shadow furthered what I was already learning: that things were often not as they seemed. Gradually, I was connecting the dots between my experience of family life, school, the business world inside and outside the studio, and the preachings of society.

By the time high school came along, I was ready for the relative independence of my first private locker. At last, a few cubic feet of my own. Sir Sandford Fleming Secondary School was named after the Canadian who (among other things) invented the concept of global time zones. The spanking new brick building may have looked like a prison, but at least it had a central courtyard and modern science labs. I felt some excitement in being among the inaugural class of students.

The mile-long walk to Fleming from my home was usually with Ron Hustwitt, my good friend who lived nearby. Ron had been my first friend in Toronto and, though at times we were in different classes as we grew up, his friendship was a comfort to me. In grade eleven, he went with me to a downtown pawn shop where I bought my first guitar, a used nylon-string model that cost $24.

It was in Ron's basement rec room where we spun the latest singles, shaking our heads at Dylan and wondering what "everybody must get stoned" meant. This was where we talked about girls and hatched strategies to meet them, and where I could let off steam with a sympathetic soul.

In the social mix at Fleming, it was hard to know where I fit in. More than three-quarters of the 1,200 kids were Jewish. On Jewish holidays, the place was almost empty, and there was so much talk of things Jewish that I often felt left out. And because I elected to take art instead of music in grade nine (you had to choose one), I wasn't in the school band or orchestra. I wasn't a jock, a brainer or a hood either. As a result of all this, I mostly felt my connection with people on an individual basis, not in groups.

Like most teenagers, I worked a great deal on my looks. Going through department store catalogues to check out the Perma-prest pants and the increasingly mod shoes became very important. Clothing was one thing, but my hair, now that was *really* important. It took a lot of time and effort getting the hair to part just right, and combing it back sideways from my forehead.

In my aim to please, you might say I was square, except that I did get on well with girls, even if I wasn't dating them. In the court of social standing, I might have pleaded "square—with an explanation." I fluttered around the fringes of various cliques and got to know a lot of people.

One who stood out was a great guy named Morris Frimerman. Here was someone who cared so much about people, it was infectious. Morris taught me to empathize, to really go outside myself and care about others. He had a way of reaching out to people he knew were struggling and he very simply—with a few kind words or an arm around a shoulder—lifted them up.

Sitting beside Morris at lunch you'd get at least a bite of Mrs. Frimerman's giant bagel delights or, on a lucky day, a whole quarter of the sandwich, which, along with the double fries with gravy, was to die for. A strong antidote to the Maudlin Math or Lethal Latin classes coming up.

Morris was also a very good singer. Along with our friends Judy and Greg, we would work out three-part harmonies to *Four Strong Winds* and other folk songs that were popular. We often lit up a pizzeria or a bagel joint with our peppy version of *Yellow Bird*, with or without guitar. It wasn't long before Morris got elected school president, and even led the carol singing at Christmas. We became best friends.

If I felt at home anywhere in school, it was in Mr. Lindsay's art classes. His great sense of humor humanized art history and enlivened our work. I felt somewhat comfortable in his class, often cracking a few jokes of my own. And I gladly volunteered to paint sets for school plays. It was wonderful to be trusted after school with a task that involved the responsibility of handling supplies from the stockroom. It was also good fun working side by side with other kids in a cooperative effort.

When Uncle Mardig got me a summer job at an arts supply warehouse in downtown Toronto, I was a naive and earnest fifteen-year-old, glad for the chance to make some money and get out of the house. For the first while, I spent days assembling, by hand, hundreds of wooden painter's easels that came in three parts and needed to be bolted together.

To make the mind-numbing work bearable in the grungy ware-house setting, I listened to the radio—the Beatles, Van Morrison, Donovan, the Supremes—counting the minutes until coffee break, lunch and, finally, quitting time.

The warehouse foreman took some getting used to. He was a big, burly guy with such a foul mouth that I found it a challenge just to talk to him. The vivid monotony of his obscenity was clearly the outward expression of a seething and out-of-place man who appeared to be angry at everything—even at corrugated cardboard. Only when the supervisor walked in did he ease off, performing an instant verbal ballet of deference around her. I was shocked as much by the man as by his language, and yet I had to work with him.

It struck me how arbitrary things were in the world: who you happened to get for a boss or a teacher could ruin your summer or your whole year. You were just supposed to chalk it up to experience and somehow find a way to cope in the meantime.

The foreman's crude sexual allusions, coupled with the nude pin-up calendar in the back room of the warehouse, were part of my shadow introduction to sexuality—typical for kids growing up in sexually repressed families like mine. Sex was never discussed at home, and scenes of sexual attraction on TV (even kissing) met the clear disapproval of my parents, who obviously were uncomfortable with public displays of affection and gave me the sense that physical attraction itself was not right.

I managed to stay with the job for the whole summer, punching my timecard when I got to work in the morning, devouring huge toasted cinnamon buns on coffee breaks, and making friends with one fellow who at least appeared to be from the same planet as I was. And so it passed, my first exposure to the adult world of working for money.

* * *

As much as any influence I can remember, it was the music of the Beatles and Bob Dylan that swept across my adolescence. The song *She Loves You* had a powerful energy that touched me like a surrogate love. So many of the Lennon-McCartney songs seemed to speak to my inner world. They stirred my imagination as much as the personal odysseys and oddities of the Fab Four did.

And what can I say about Bob Dylan? To me, his *Mr. Tambourine Man* was poetry in motion, and it even became the subject of discussion in an English class of my most eccentric teacher, Leonard McGravey. When the lengthy *Like a Rolling Stone* was on the charts and the radio blared the organ intro to the opening nasal vocals, my mood shifted profoundly. I didn't always understand Dylan, but I sensed an unfettered and explosive genius there, working beneath the veneer of society I was only beginning to understand.

For me, the appeal of what we called folk songs lay in their lyrical idealism, something that I saw not as some dreamy utopian quality, but as a potent force for good as demonstrated, for example, in the civil rights movement in the U.S.

Pete Seeger and others were singing a number of "Negro spirituals" that called for liberation, and Peter, Paul and Mary's songs were also full of the social justice spirit—a feeling I came to know and value. Those days it was called "universal love." I remember how moved I was to read a book of quotes from Bobby Kennedy's writings, mostly about equality and racial tolerance.

In retrospect, I'd have to say that the Beatles, Dylan and folk music put vibrational fault lines under me. When the '60s shook society with "flower power" and anti-war sentiment, I felt its rumblings. Still, I couldn't know to what extent the "respectable" world of power and authority was about to be exposed, and how, along the way, I too would come undone.

FIRST LOVE AT LAST

WITH FLOWING BROWN HAIR AND WARM BROWN EYES, DEBORAH Joan Pike was my first love, my high school sweetheart and the first person who loved me for who I was. Our romance caused a bit of a stir initially, as she was a cheerleader at a rival high school, a point my friends liked to razz me about.

I met Deb through a United Church youth group that used to gather on Sundays and some weeknights. A friend of mine invited me to the meetings and I found them fun. (Most importantly, they gave me a legitimate reason to get out of the house, since my parents didn't see anything wrong with my spending time in a church youth group, even if it wasn't Armenian.) One day I walked into the meeting room and there she was, Debi Pike, radiant in a short turquoise dress. I was breathless, thinking that if I could date her I'd be the luckiest guy in the world. In a few short weeks that dream came true.

She won my heart, but I couldn't believe that she would have me. What did she see in me? I wrote her poems, bought her flowers, took her to the prom. We went on hay rides, we went skating and bowling.

Occasionally my brother even lent us his car. First it was the 1965 red Corvair with the white leather bucket seats, and later his 1967 burgundy Cougar with the V-8 engine, white vinyl top and eight-track tape player belting out Herb Alpert's *Tijuana Brass*. Pure sex, as Onnig used to say.

There was only one problem: I couldn't tell my parents about Deb. My father was of such an old-world mind and so strict about my comings and goings that I wasn't actually allowed to date anyone for all the time I lived at home. Arto was the patriarch engaged in a losing battle: fighting to keep the old ways with tight reins, struggling to preserve the Armenian roots in a new society of TV and pop music. Lucie was his partner in this venture and deferred to his style of control and manipulation. Culturally raised to support the husband's position even if she disagreed, she had little room to maneuver with him, given that she had her own battles to fight.

I had to get special permission to go to high school dances, and there were times that this was denied for no apparent reason. Dad was just like that and Mom took her cues from him. To give one example: even though he had been a Boy Scout, he wouldn't let me be one. I was in Cubs for a while and really wanted to go on into Scouts, but he put an end to it: no reasons, no discussion.

This confined home life made it very difficult for my brother and sister too. When Onnig decided to marry Kim, he had to wrestle with my parents' adamant opposition and withstand a lot of heat to go through with it. His marrying this *odar* instead of an Armenian made them very unhappy and their feelings only changed after the marriage. (It helped that the Mackays came to Onnig and Kim's aid, hosting the wedding reception and bringing my parents around to the whole idea.) As for Ani, she was coping with the social restrictions as best she could, though I remember her getting very depressed, her only salvation being her studies.

I was hard pressed to have a functioning social life. At school I was too embarrassed to say why I couldn't always join in or why I had to be home so early. To be eighteen and not allowed to date was just unbearable. Often I ended up lying to get out of the house, especially to see Deb. At least I could say I was going to group meetings, even if they were in very small numbers and of a very private nature.

Deb's and her parents' love for me saved my life. It was a whole new world—my first intimate contact with a Canadian family. Deb's brother, Tim, had a rock band that practiced in the basement, and his dad drove him to the hockey rink in the early mornings. Now this was a normal family, the closest thing I'd seen to *Father Knows Best* and *Leave It to Beaver*. In the Pike household, I felt so loved and accepted that it was hard to believe at first. They trusted their daughter to keep her agreements with them, and they trusted me too. I didn't let them down.

On Saturday nights in winter, I'd brave icy winds waiting nearly half an hour for the bus to take me to my oasis. And if Deb just wanted to stay home, that was fine; I'd watch some of the hockey game on TV with her father, Stan. Some Sundays her mother, Daphne, would invite me for roast beef dinner, an invitation I gladly accepted (even if I could never quite understand the fuss over Yorkshire pudding). In the warm months, Daphne would make strawberry shortcake when I was coming for dinner; she knew I loved it. You can bet that I helped with washing the dishes. It was another way I felt part of what was, in my mind, my surrogate family.

Stan was very kind to me. He was working at Simpson-Sears and got me a summer job there, in the production department of the store's merchandise catalogues. I was thrilled to be making $75 a week, and got my first glimpse of production schedules and the precision teamwork it took to design, put together and turn out a complicated piece of work. Fortunately, this job experience was very pleasant compared to my previous working stint. Although the affable regulars didn't take this seasonal employee too seriously, they didn't mind my good-natured prodding if they got behind in their work.

Many times when Deb and I went out, Stan let us use the family car (a Plymouth Fury), and some nights after our return he would give me a ride home, dropping me off a couple of blocks away so that my parents wouldn't see. I hated the deception, but I didn't know what else to do.

Deb and I were in love, and although she was only sixteen and I was nineteen, we dreamed of someday being together in our own house. But after we had dated for a year and a half, all that came to a halt.

As I was about to enter the University of Toronto (the same year as Deb's last year of high school), it occurred to me that this was the first real love either of us had known. I also knew that I was about to meet a lot of new co-eds, a prospect that I looked forward to, though with some feelings of guilt. So, I thought I would suggest to Deb that instead of "going steady" for four more years and getting married, perhaps we ought to ease things a little—still stay together, but maybe for a while date other people too, so as not to have regrets later on. When I broke the idea to her, it went over like a lead balloon. I didn't realize how much I had hurt her. She stopped seeing me and wouldn't return my calls, and her family closed ranks in support. In no time at all I was shut out. The pain of suddenly losing Deb (and her family) was excruciating, and I don't know how I got through it. Over the following weeks, many mornings I just didn't want to wake up.

III

NOT KNOWING

Nothing in the world is as soft and yielding as water. Yet for dissolving the hard and inflexible, nothing can surpass it.

Lao Tzu

PARADOX

ATTENDING THE UNIVERSITY OF TORONTO FOR A BRIEF TIME was an exciting and broadening experience for me. University, I used to say, opened my mind enough to see that I could leave. I came across a wide range of people and heard very different ideas than I had before. This new landscape also helped me come to terms with losing Deb.

Like most of the other guys I met, I joined the beer drinking and girl-chasing frolics. The seemingly wild abandon at the frat parties I sneaked into and the frequent campus dances were like nothing I'd ever experienced before.

A few months into the school year, I made a bold move. After playing guitar and singing with friends all through high school, I finally got enough nerve to perform in front of an audience. My friend Tim Wynne-Jones and I formed a duo—I added guitar music to poems he had written—and we sang in dimly lit rooms here and there for a few dollars. Then I did some solo gigs at a couple of coffee houses and handled these just fine. I was playing a nylon-stringed guitar and my repertoire included songs by Dylan, Joni Mitchell, Gord Lightfoot, Leonard Cohen and others. My Johnny Cash imitation was a hit, and so were the other comedy bits I did. That boosted my confidence and made me want to perform even more.

As to my studies, sociology and philosophy caught my attention, along with Religious Knowledge, a course that touched on comparative religions. Oddly enough, Economics 101 was also among the subjects I took. I still remember not being entirely satisfied with the idea of "maximizing profit" or with the explanations given about "profit and loss," and wondering if, in a finite system, one person's profit wouldn't be another's loss.

It took me a while to get the hang of this new life: the campus, the expectations of me as a student, and the laissez-faire ambiance—not to mention comprehending the subjects I was studying. What I really wanted was to be in residence so that I could really feel I belonged, that I was a "man about campus." I wanted to complain about the cafeteria food like the other residence kids and be part of their world.

In my second year of studies, the writings of Lao Tzu that first introduced me to paradox were a timely gift in my young adult life. Lao Tzu was a Chinese sage who lived about the same time as Confucius, and his *Tao Te Ching* is a classic of ageless wisdom. For me, his strange-sounding ideas had a ring of truth like riddles do.

One day in the library, I happened on the passage of his that said water was the strongest substance because it could take the shape of any container and so not be broken, and in time it could erode mountains. I kept on reading, amazed by Lao Tzu's ancient insights and profoundly moved. Something in me changed that afternoon, and when I walked out onto Bloor Street my familiar world looked very different. Though the campus carousing didn't stop, at a deeper level some new enlightenment started to take hold in me.

Embracing paradox was pivotal in my life, the thing that most helped me get outside the narrow either/or world that I knew in my early years. In time I came to value what Taoists refer to as the yin/yang complementarity in Creation, the balance of opposite elements in a harmonious universe. Paradox helped me understand the spiritual idea of unity/diversity, in which the many religious paths are but manifestations of one divine source; the feminine/masculine qualities in every person; and birth, death and rebirth as part of the same eternal dance.

LEAVING HOME

It's all right Ma, I can make it.
                              Bob Dylan

THE BUSINESS OF LEAVING HOME NEED NOT HAVE BEEN SO DIFFICULT, but my parents hardly eased the way. Against their stated will, my hopes and dreams simply didn't count.

I remember a turning point—I was seventeen or so—when Arto and Lucie were about to visit friends and wanted me to go with them. After years of having no choice in these matters, I suddenly knew that this time they simply could not drag me along. I wasn't going to visit people of no interest to me, whether they had kids my age or not. My mind was made up. After a few rounds of "You're going!" and "I am not!", my father thundered his final command to "Hurry up, we're going!" Frightened but strangely sure of myself, I stated firmly, "No, I won't go with you." Maybe there was something in my voice that made him drop the matter; I'm not sure. Whatever it was, that act of standing my ground paved the way for my later flight to freedom.

In 1969, on a sunny day in late spring, my sister and I left home together, as though we needed our combined strength of purpose to pass through that door. I was twenty-one, Ani was just seventeen.

When Ani and I had both been attending Fleming, we'd shared the basic predicament of home and school, comforting each other when we could. Occasionally we'd go down to the Riverboat, Toronto's premiere coffee house, and catch some music. One song that I found particularly poignant at that time was Murray McLauchlan's *Child's Song* which began, "Good-bye mama, good-bye to you too, pa." Another was the Beatles' *She's Leaving Home.*

After completing grade twelve, Ani couldn't stand the thought of one more year at home. With the help of a family friend, she got a full-time job at an insurance company and announced her decision to leave both home and school. Being a girl and the youngest child made her act of rebellion in this family all the more daring.

Mayrenie Grandma didn't know what to say to the two of us. She was a very loving presence and we respected her. But she hardly knew what advice to give us, other than saying we shouldn't upset our parents. After Peka's death two years before, Mayrenie was left to watch our changing behavior with some concern and exasperation. Most days she'd sit by the front window, reading the great many religious brochures she kept, praying to the heavens and watching the proceedings on the street.

Arto and Lucie were saddened beyond belief to see us go. We had no desire to hurt them and told them repeatedly that our moving out was not about them, but something we had chosen to do for ourselves. They simply would not understand. Lucie kept asking what they had done to us that we would want to leave.

Several weeks earlier, I had left university just six weeks short of completing my second year, to become a singer-songwriter full-time. It was a decision that was several months in the making. All during that year, I had spent more time and energy playing guitar and singing in coffee houses than studying my major—Chinese and Japanese history.

The Vietnam war was raging, society was in upheaval. America's treatment of war protestors had taken the lives of four college kids, shot dead by the National Guard at Ohio's Kent State University, and resulted in the arrest of the Chicago Seven. Crosby, Stills & Nash sang the '60s generation sentiment, "We are leaving, you don't need us." For me, it was a profoundly disorienting time. I was trying to make sense of the great array of campus influences—from the frat parties to the coffee houses, from the rhetoric in the *Varsity* newspaper to the anti-war postures of the left. It soon turned into a cyclone of questions about who I was and what I thought and valued, as distinct from what my parents and society had to say.

A sociology class I took in first year had shed new light on my understanding of interpersonal life, in which our persona plays in two different worlds, "onstage" and "backstage" (or offstage). The prof had just put words to what I had long observed in my parents and other adults: how they behaved in public was very different to how they were in private. This, I learned, applied to both family and individual behavior.

I realized that the wide discrepancy between these domains can be very confusing for children. When I was young, I found it hard to reconcile the little lies my parents told (the phone rings, my mother answers, it's for my father: "Tell them I'm not in!" he yells) with their insistence that I should always tell the truth ("Don't you lie to me!"). Like many children, I had lived with repeated and routine lies like this, and many others directed to me. One Cairo example, from when I was a little boy: my parents were all dressed up to go out for the evening and, when I cried and begged my mother to stay, she said they were going to the doctor, an answer which only hurt my feelings more because it was obviously not true. With so many instances like that, I felt I couldn't trust my parents to tell me the truth.

I had seen this dynamic not just in my family, but even in TV families: the two parents acting one way with people outside the home, a different way between themselves, and another way towards the children. The emphasis was on appearances meant to impress people, to make them think you were somebody to be envied and respected.

It was really "keeping up with the Joneses." I later realized that it was a display of living for outside approval, as if constantly needing to prove one's worth.

The sociology class description of onstage and backstage captured my family experience precisely. I couldn't stand it when my parents showed off, and I hated the dishonesty of facts being stretched and distorted for self-glorification.

The sad thing was, although my parents tried to instill certain values in me, the gap between what they said and what they did really confused me. Adults do as they please, but it's different for us kids, I said to myself. I was forever made to say I'm sorry and ask forgiveness for all manner of things, with only a faint idea of the issues involved. What's more, when Dad made a mistake, it was no big deal. I sure didn't hear *him* apologize. When Onnig and I would fight, Dad would tell me that I should be big about it and let it go. That didn't help me at all. Nor did it do anything to alleviate the constant aggravation that came from being a convenient (and weaker) scapegoat for my bigger brother in his own battles with the family authorities. And on top of all this, the argumentative relations between my parents didn't exactly provide a useful model of behavior.

My father wanted and expected me to follow in his footsteps, just as Onnig had done. But I knew the turmoil in this family's working life and wanted none of it. That's why I had chosen to go to university in the first place, with the intention of getting a degree and then teaching high school. Not that I was interested in teaching as a vocation; it was more that I really couldn't think of what else I would do, and I vaguely thought that maybe I could provide for students the understanding that was in such short supply for me.

And now this, too, was on hold. Seeing the film *Woodstock* confirmed my growing sense that I was no longer a part of the mainstream. I didn't know what to believe in, though I knew I didn't identify with the facade of society and wasn't interested in its superficial goals of accumulated prestige. (As I learned later, I was part of the first generation to openly talk about the hypocrisy of their parents' lives. The '60s phrases "generation gap," "sexual revolution" and "counter-culture" were born, and public analysis of society's ills began.) The hypocrisy I saw in my parents' lives I now saw all around me. That realization was deeply upsetting.

Through events in the Vietnam war, I had caught a glimpse of American foreign policy and its ties to the pervasive "military-industrial complex" about which U.S. President Eisenhower first warned his country in the 1950s. By now it was clear that I couldn't trust authority figures in suits, and I didn't care about being a high school teacher anymore.

My friend Boris was the first to hear that I had decided to withdraw from university (I didn't like to say "drop out"). We both felt the quiet exhilaration of my decision. I went to inform the college dean and told him, in an air of rare assurance, "I have confidence in myself and in life, and if I want to pursue teaching again at some point, I'll do whatever it takes to make that happen." He huffed and said that I just had "exam time panic," that there were pills that could help me stay up and cram for the exams—"Why waste your year?" My answer went something like this: "Look, I don't feel this year is wasted; I just turned my attention to other things. And even if I crammed and got my year, it would mean little to me, because I haven't learned much, and I haven't been in class enough, and my head's really been turning, and I want to leave. If I change my mind later, I'll come back."

What I really wanted to do was get a place of my own, play guitar all day and write songs that would change the world. It was practical naiveté. I had read somewhere that if you didn't follow what was in your heart, you might regret it for the rest of your life. I wanted to play music.

Out of school and out of the family nest, I savored my first feelings of freedom. By selling newspapers on the street, I scraped together first and last month's rent for a room in a communal house downtown, near Chinatown.

That's how my search for identity began.

I didn't know who I was. I stopped shaving, let my hair grow really long and played at being a hippie, with my embroidered headband and beaded necklace. My friends were musicians, writers and artists also trying to figure out where they fit in. We were smoking pot to take the edge off things, drinking Oo Loong tea, and listening to the Beatles, the Stones, Simon and Garfunkel, Joni, Bob, Joan, Gordie, Neil, and Crosby, Stills & Nash.

In the summer of 1970, I went to Boston and hung out for a week with a drummer I knew from high school. Hirsh was studying jazz at the Berklee College of Music and spoke a cool new language (like "I'm hip to the cat," which meant "I know the guy"). Walking the Boston Common with James Taylor's *Fire and Rain* in my head, I wanted very much to write and sing like that. I set off to England with my backpack and guitar, planning on staying there for a while until I saw "what was happening," as I explained to the customs agent at Heathrow airport. He abruptly stamped my passport and said, "You've got six weeks maximum. Good day. Next!"

Got a flat in north London, drank Guinness, burned incense, listened to Bruce Cockburn LPs, saw Pink Floyd in Hyde Park (couldn't relate), sang a few songs in Bunjie's coffee house downtown, and hung out at Trafalgar Square. Took off with a long-haired woman to hitchhike the Continent, but soon figured she wasn't "my kind of scene." Continued to Amsterdam, toured the Heineken brewery and drank free beer. Thumbed through the German countryside, went to a rock festival in Frankfurt and paid a brief visit to Munich. Got homesick for my mother's Armenian coffee and baklava. To Paris and sleeping in a park, at dawn watching the city sweep itself awake; lazy afternoons *en soleil*. Within a couple of weeks I was back in England for the long flight home.

WANDERING MINSTREL

I'm goin' to the country, sunshine smile on me.
                                    Bruce Cockburn

I SOON GOT THE ITCH TO TRAVEL ACROSS CANADA AND GET TO know this vast territory I had heard so much about. So I headed out west, particularly keen to see the Rockies. Prime Minister Trudeau's Liberals were hip enough to accommodate the growing number of transients who were hitchhiking along the Trans-Canada Highway in those days: they kindly provided a network of information kiosks and youth shelters for us young idealists. Cool. With my backpack and my new $300 custom-made guitar, I set off in the late spring of 1971 to see what I could see.

Hot sun on pavement, side of the road, my thumb asking each car to take me, please, farther down the highway. I felt like I was enrolled in Life 101. I got a taste of the small towns and truck stops, romanticizing as much of it as I needed to get by. Feeling very unsure of myself, I played with it all, toasting my success at mimicking what others were doing, imitating enough so I could "rough in" a new personal style, assessing the pros and cons of this new-found freedom, and trying to cut through the hippie shit to figure out who was for real.

Golden prairie. Flatlands. Not a care in the world. Rode into Winnipeg, the city just springing up before I knew it. Did a guest set at a coffee house and got a paying gig for later that month. Took the train to Regina and played the Folk Festival; downed beer and pizza with wonderful people—good guitar players and fine women. On to pretty Saskatoon and another gig, then back to Winnipeg before heading out to Alberta.

It was dark when the bus rolled into Banff and I made my way to the "people's park" where camping was free. In the distance was a big bonfire, the sound of guitars and singing. I happily walked my tired body over there, found a place to set up my tent, crawled into my sleeping bag and crashed. The next morning, Whoa, what a sight! My first taste of the Rocky Mountains, ice-gray slabs on blue sky. I was in wordless awe, feeling *yes!*, a resounding yes. Busking on the main drag in Banff, I got enough money for a good meal, folks checking out my beautiful hand-made "ax" (though the neck was starting to warp a little). I was meeting friendly people and sleeping in their homes.

Vancouver-bound on the trans-Canada train: catching mountain views from the club car, through clickety stretches of spruce and rock into British Columbia's stunning beauty, with the curves of the Fraser Valley winding the river's way on out to the coast. A rainy Vancouver welcome opened an enchanting two-day visit to the Dewdney Trunk Road Pleasure Fair out in the country, and a surprise appearance by Joni Mitchell, whose acoustic songs in a big warm barn cast a spell over the cozy gathering. In Vancouver's Gastown Saloon did a guest set during the gig of an excellent singer-songwriter named Bim (Roy Forbes, as he's now known, and still a good friend).

Back in Toronto, I stayed at a rooming house midtown, within walking distance of my father's studio as it turned out, and a few blocks from where Ani was staying. My room cost $12 a week. For another $13 a week I could feed myself and hang out in a number of coffee houses that the early '70s offered. Though I occasionally visited the family home and came away with food that Lucie provided, I was basically fending for myself. And that was fine by me.

Wanting to be known for who I was, I never used my father's name to open doors for me. And, from the start of my folksinging, I used the single name Raffi.

I remember very well my voluntary poverty. Some weeks the gig money wasn't quite enough to make ends meet, so I'd do things like selling the alternative newspaper *Guerilla* on the street (you bought copies for a dime and sold them for a quarter). When Lucie's friends told her, she was mortified. "Wearing a headband—*mon Dieu!*" Once I even did a two-week stint of guard duty at the university art gallery. As luck would have it, I was staring at large gray paintings of what looked like creased bedsheets. God, it was hard to stay awake. At two bucks an hour, though, the extra money helped.

There were days when I really craved a cheeseburger but didn't have enough change in my pockets to get one. Sometimes a balanced meal was a hot dog with ketchup, relish and fries. Amongst my friends, the social gig of those times was to scope out the neighborhood joints where you could get a jug of beer half-price between 5 and 7 p.m. and cheap food. Somehow we got by and ate well enough. The state of having very little produced in me a mixture of feelings: on the one hand I fell into the trap of feeling morally superior to those who had money, and on the other hand I wanted some too, so I could buy better quality guitar strings, a good stereo system and maybe a car.

In the fall of 1971, I almost managed to bus it all the way from Regina to Arkansas. On my return trip out west, I met up with a pretty good American show band playing in the dining room of the Regina Inn, and we hung around together for a while. They asked me if I wanted to go down to an Arkansas hotel and sing in the lounge (next to the dining room where they'd be playing), for good cash and all the food I could eat. It was an offer too good to pass up. Within a couple of days, I borrowed enough money to fly to St. Louis, and then took the bus through the Ozarks to my destination of Fairfield Bay, Arkansas.

For six weeks in the lounge of a posh American resort, I sang weekdays from five to eight in the evening in exchange for all the food I could eat and $300 cash. This was excellent pay at the time, and certainly the most I had ever earned singing. And I made the deal work for me. The restaurant being a steak house, I ate sirloins, New Yorkers and T-bones enough for several lifetimes, washed down with lots of beer.

There was something slightly odd about this Armenian-Canadian man Raffi, with the long hair and bushy beard, pink T-shirt, beaded necklace and army pants, entertaining the "happy hour" crowd—but the clientele and the bar staff didn't seem to mind. I drank bourbon and sang a variety of contemporary folk and country songs, including my own tunes, some Canadian content and a send-up of Merle Haggard's *Okie from Muskogee*. What a weird gig it was.

When I made it back home, I rented the second-floor room of a music store and honed my guitar playing and songwriting. Through my musical friends, I got to hear the recorded works of a variety of musicians in bluegrass, country, folk and jazz, including Hank Williams, violinist Stephane Grappelli, and gypsy jazz guitarist Django Reinhardt and his Hot Club of France. I kept busy with gigs at the Oxford Inn folk lounge and the venerable coffee house Fiddler's Green, and occasionally took part in the merriment of university orientation week for new students.

Many an evening I spent at the Riverboat seeing the likes of Neil Young, Joni Mitchell, and Seals and Crofts. I was making progress with my music and learned a lot of my craft by watching these and other performers, and then going home inspired to improve my skills. Flashy guitarist David Rea, who had worked with Ian and Sylvia, was a regular at the Riverboat. I didn't mind paying the $4 cover charge, plus 75 cents for cappuccino and 50 cents for strudel, to see David's mesmerizing playing. I picked up so much from him about flat-picking and finger-picking guitar styles and, for a while, I sang a number of his songs on the way to finding a style of my own.

CAVOUK IN THE COLONNADE

ALTHOUGH I KEPT IN FREQUENT TOUCH WITH THE FAMILY, relations were a bit strained in the years after my leaving the nest. Ani and I were doing all right, and living on our own brought us much closer. It was different when I dropped in to the studio, where I was met with a very mixed reaction: Arto and Lucie appeared glad to see me, but they made sure my long hair and beard got a pointed (and hurt) look of disapproval. This conditional welcome was not the best incentive for visiting. I knew it couldn't have been easy for Onnig either, seeing the brother who got away.

Since Dad's recovery, the family business had pulled together and turned the new space of about 900 square feet into a functioning enterprise. Favorably situated on the second floor of the Colonnade, just to the right at the top of the escalator, the studio had full glass frontage revealing an inviting gallery. Immediately inside the front door and to the left was the small reception area with Danish furniture and a Middle Eastern coffee table. Farther along, behind a teak desk and chair, hung a large painting of Ohannes Grandpa done by Arto some years ago.

The gallery, with the Persian rug in warm reds and blues and walls displaying dozens of framed color portraits, doubled as the sitting room. Towards the rear was a passageway to the darkroom and a retouching-finishing room, and a curtained-off dressing area that also housed the lighting gear on movable tripods. Whenever there was a sitting, the full-length curtain at the front of the studio (just behind reception) would be drawn, making the gallery a private space. Then the lights would be rolled out onto the carpet and positioned around any one of a number of antique chairs in which the client would sit. And to complete the preparations, one of four weighted paper backdrops mounted on the ceiling would be rolled down. The all-important camera—a Linhof—always stood on its own tripod, under a cloth cover in the middle of the room, ready for action.

Although the studio attracted a great number of dignitaries, the portraiture was open to anyone who could afford it. Lucie and Onnig each played their roles in aid of the master photographer. Lucie would warmly welcome clients and see to their comfort. While they shared conversation over coffee, Arto would study his subject and gain an impression of how to proceed with the sitting. Onnig would set up the lights and lower the backdrop into place, and soon the client would move to the dressing room for last-minute touch-ups. When all was in order, Arto would work his magic, with Lucie attending to details of the client's attire and Onnig providing technical and artistic support. Sometimes the sitting would involve more than one pose, another chair or a change of clothes. Still, in most cases, my father took only a dozen shots.

Six to eight weeks after a sitting, the portrait would be ready. As a rule, my father did not show proofs, preferring to make the final selection himself. On the rare occasion that the client did not approve, Arto would do everything possible to guarantee satisfaction. Judging from the results of his work, the quality of his clientele and the acclaim he received, his artistry was outstanding.

Throughout his career, my father had given exhibits of his portraits in a number of cities including Ottawa, New York, Toronto, London, Paris, Moscow and Yerevan, the Armenian capital.

Visitors to the studio were greeted by portraits of a veritable "Who's Who" of society: Indira Gandhi of India, Israel's David Ben-Gurion, Charles de Gaulle, Harold Macmillan of Britain, the Earl and Countess Mountbatten, Queen Elizabeth II and Prince Philip, the Queen Mother, U.S. Vice-President Hubert Humphrey, Canadian Prime Ministers Diefenbaker, Pearson and Trudeau, and several mayors, lieutenant-governors and governors-general. Artists, dancers, singers and composers were also well represented: Charles Aznavour, Maureen Forrester, Vladimir Ashkenazy, Aram Khachaturian, Yehudi Menuhin, Celia Franca, Zoltán Kodály, Oscar Peterson, Anne Murray, Patrick MacNee, Gordon Pinsent, Lois Smith, Simon Samsonian, Ervant Kochar and many others.

When the Queen Mother visited Toronto's Queen's Park (seat of Ontario's legislature) in 1965, I was there when my father took her portrait. After setting up the lights in the room designated for this occasion, Arto was notified he was allowed just two minutes with his royal subject. As Her Majesty entered and the introductions were made, he noticed that she liked to raise her right hand to her pearls. Arto quickly moved her into position and asked if she would repeat the hand gesture. She obliged, and that glittering moment was such a success that the Cavouk portrait adorned the Queen Mother's personal Christmas cards that year. Her smile also attracted many passersby to the impressive image that graced the front window of the studio for some time.

Lucie loved her life at the Colonnade: the fashionable boutiques, the camaraderie with other merchants, her role as gracious hostess at the studio, sharing her *joie de vivre* with visitors. She was a full partner to her artist husband, even though—as she herself said—he was a very demanding boss. As Arto put it, "There can only be one captain on the boat: I am the captain."

PORTRAIT OF CONFUSED YOUTH

IN 1972, MY FATHER TOOK A PICTURE OF ME WITH MY SHOULDER-length hair and bushy beard. I was wearing a blue shirt and a tan wool vest, and looked quite serene in the photo that I saw. But apparently it was incomplete. Over my image, Arto superimposed a colorful abstract oil painting, and the result was both a captivating portrait and an artistic statement open to interpretation. He was boastfully proud of this double exposure and included it in his photo exhibits with the title "The Indecision of Youth."

With my friends, I jokingly referred to it as "Portrait of Confused Youth," and it's curious, as I reflect back, that I don't remember being upset about it at the time. I was just pleased to have been made an artistic fuss of. And at least indecision could imply that I was considering something important.

Eventually I came to see the picture differently. Arto took this portrait of composure and covered it with paint, not accepting what his lens had captured that day. In lieu of seeing his son in the moment, he had produced an artistic cover-up. An honest name for this portrait might have been "The Son Who Won't Do What I Say," or "How Dare He Look So Well in a Life of His Choosing."

Gradually I understood that my parents were culturally and personally incapable of seeing me as a legitimate "other," someone with my own life to live. In later years, so that I might be a more frequent presence in their lives, my mother would increasingly say, "We take our life from you"—a phrase her parents used to say to her. I knew that, on the one hand, this spoke of the joys a parent derives from seeing her children. But she said it over and over, with great emotional force, as if she were imploring me not to deny her my life-energy. And when I *did* phone her, she'd begin the conversation by saying that I never called her. I'd say, "Ma, I *am* calling you now, let's talk." In the same way, when she really wanted something from me she'd say, with great emphasis, "Won't you do this *one* thing for your mother?" as though nothing else I had ever done for her counted. The manipulation did not let up, her need was so great.

Given the almost total lack of boundaries in my family, Lucie's statement "we take our life from you" confirmed what I had felt growing up—namely, that I didn't exist other than as a part of my parents.

I came to see that my experience of self was of something missing rather than of what was there. Most of the time my glass felt quite empty.

I remember that even after we moved to Canada, I dreaded bringing home report cards from school. I usually did quite well in seven out of eight subjects, but my father's first words always pointed to what was lacking. In a demanding voice he'd say, "What happened here?" Of course I felt crushed. All the good grades were not enough. Any shortcoming was unacceptable.

In 1990, during a long conversation with a dear friend, I discovered that I had no "middle." In childhood, caught between praise or censure, indulgence or punishment, I had lacked the experience of a middle state of being. Amazingly, that core deficiency was still with me. This was a profound revelation. I wrote about it in my journals and set out to understand what having a middle might feel like and how one might get there or have one. Only after three or four years of deep questioning, did I find myself walking in the answers. I noticed that I was no longer postponing joy, but making room for it in every single day, knowing that each day was all I really had, and that peace and joy *were* available in any moment to the extent that it wasn't filled with dread from current or old fears. I learned that anxiety crowds the heart in the moment, and having a middle is the ability to simply be, without applause or critique, just glad to be alive, pleased with this peace, this moment.

Arto's "confused" portrait reminds me of how tough my path of individuation was. I left home a disillusioned young man in search of my own identity, distinct from the one my parents would sculpt for me and the one society offered.

My quest became a search for the "holy grail"—my true voice. I was on a path of self-determination so that I might know what was in my heart, what I longed for in this life. The years ahead would bring me face to face with many dragons on a road full of trials, exhilarations and only occasional feelings of serenity.

EAST TO ARMENIA

WHILE I LIVED AT HOME, MY PARENTS PRAISED ALL THINGS Armenian. They needed to instill in their children a pride for their illustrious heritage and, in this way, preserve Armenian culture in a new land. Unfortunately, their relentless efforts had the opposite effect on me. It might have been different if our overall relationship had been better, but either way, my reaction was to reject what sounded like propaganda. This wasn't simply an act of rebellion; it was a position I came to after a good deal of thought, and it even prompted me in high school to write an essay about the folly of ethnic superiority.

The way I saw it, the world had many cultures whose people had good reason to feel proud of their heritage. Greece had its heroes, India and Egypt had theirs. What culture couldn't boast of greatness? And for that matter, what culture was without failures and short-comings? Why did my birth into an Armenian family confer superi-ority? It made no sense to me—no more sense than if I'd been born into a different group and told the same thing.

I had no quarrel with the greatness of Armenian culture. What bothered me was the superiority that my parents went on about. In my heart and in my experience, being Armenian did not make me better than anyone else and, from my perspective, I could have given you reasons for thinking it wasn't exactly desirable. As for the repeated stories of Armenian glory, of its writers and artists, architecture and music . . . oh, I'd get so fed up with it, I just couldn't stand it. (Much later in my life I realized that my parents were given to the over-compensation of a people who, for centuries, have known persecution and vowed never to forget or crumble.) But there was more to it than that.

Over and over I was being told to remember and value a heritage by elders who had not even acknowledged my own sense of self. I began to see what I now understand more fully: you cannot command someone to feel a certain way. Love and cultural identity cannot be forced upon or willed inside another person.

Having said all that, when the chance came for a three-week expense-paid trip to Armenia courtesy of the Armenian government, I did—with mixed feelings—accept the invitation. Besides my misgivings, there was curiosity. I did want this opportunity for whatever insights it might yield, and (there was no denying it) I wanted to see the land of my origins, even as it lay in the shadow of the Soviet dictatorship of the times.

In 1970, Arto and Lucie visited Armenia, where Cavouk photographed a number of dignitaries, government officials and artists, among them his old acquaintance Catholicos Vazken I, and Anastas Mikoyan, president of the Soviet Politbureau.

Sittings were also arranged for Aleksey Kosygin in Toronto and Leonid Brezhnev in Moscow. This last occasion had yielded a small but unusual prize besides the new formal portraits that were now included in Cavouk exhibits. At the end of the amiable session with Brezhnev, the Soviet President agreed to have an informal shot with my parents on either side of him. This little photo, tucked inside both Arto's and Lucie's passports, caused quite a stir when they showed it at the Moscow airport and certainly eased the arduous entry-and-exit process. (Lucie used to love telling this story, complete with dramatic portrayal of the excited customs inspectors saluting the photo and exhorting their comrades to gather round for a closer look.) When my parents made a second visit to Armenia in 1971, Ani went with them.

By this time, Cavouk had made a name for himself internationally and his portraits were the talk of Yerevan. One way or another, this is what led to Onnig, Ani and I becoming guests of the Armenian Soviet Socialist Republic in the summer of 1972.

The three of us were excited, not to mention relieved, when the Russian-built Aeroflot plane we boarded in Moscow finally rumbled into Yerevan's airport. I remember a rather dark roadway leading us to the Hotel Armenia where, after getting settled into our rooms and whispering a few jokes about how they were probably bugged, we went to the only place open in the hotel at that time—the art deco bar. It was a scene right out of a Bogart film, complete with cigarette smoke. We had drinks and toasted our good fortune, and yet it felt odd to have people address us in Armenian.

I gained twelve pounds in three weeks of Armenian hospitality. Everybody loved to feed us and we just couldn't say no—either to the delicious food or to the emphatic manner of the offering. "These aren't just any tomatoes," our hostess would say, giving us a knowing look, "these are *Armenian tomatoes*." A vast array of foods, often served in an unknown number of courses, left us no way to pace ourselves.

One particular dinner at the apartment home of family friends still stands out. No sooner had we eaten a copious amount of the first course of cheeses, breads and garnishes than a second course of chicken arrived in such huge helpings that we were sure there couldn't be more to the meal. We dug in, aided by generous rounds of brandy and vodka, which both whetted our appetite and loosened our judgment. We were near bursting when the next course came (whatever it was, I've blocked it from memory) and we were told in no uncertain terms that this was it, the main course: "Now we eat!" (I considered a quick plunge off the balcony to a sure and long sleep.) How we managed the rest of the meal, I'll never know.

It seemed that the natural impulse of Armenian hospitality was augmented by a need for people to let us tourists know that the nationals were doing well. Also, for a culture that had known much persecution and suffering, food was a sacred offering. This constantly made it a challenge to decline the hospitality of our hosts.

Such was the case when we visited a remote mountain village. The car moved slowly, winding uphill along a bumpy road, and by the time we arrived, we were very late and worried about a timely return to the hotel which our driver said was imperative. The problem was that the villagers had slaughtered a sheep in our honor and planned a full meal for us. The most delicate and long-winded negotiations ensued and luckily produced the reasonable (if begrudged) compromise that we would eat a little bit, have a quick look around and then be on our way.

One day we took a trip out of town to Echmiadzin, Armenia's beautiful mother church, built in the 4th century. In 301 AD, Armenia became the first nation to adopt Christianity as its religion, and today the entire countryside is still dotted with churches in the distinctive architecture of domes and crosses. The one recurring motif is the ornamental cross on stone (*khachkar*), bas-relief sculptural rendering reminiscent of Celtic design, outstanding in its intricate detail and beauty of form.

Through our parents' connections we were introduced to a diverse and stimulating group of people: intellectuals, artists, actors, musicians, dancers and poets (like the famed Sylva Gaboudigian). Our days were filled with sights and sounds of Yerevan: the museums, the busy central marketplace, the impressive quarters of the Main Library, and the tranquil parks. I remember the absence of billboard advertisements and thinking how lovely it was that this ancient city of green and pink—green leaves and pink building stone—was free of the commercial clutter of other cities I knew. Whatever the political reality of daily life, there was a calm about the city, an understated quality I appreciated.

The people we met while strolling the city streets were very friendly. Several people we didn't know invited us to come for coffee and share our stories with them. Whether it was curiosity or a feeling of familiarity, the overt friendliness had another side to it. In the elevator in our hotel, a cleaning lady with a wrinkled smile asked why it was that I didn't shave. Another time in the city's concert hall, prior to the start of the evening program, a woman in the row behind me tapped me on the shoulder and asked if I was from abroad and why I had a beard.

We came to learn that some questions were better not asked at all. The confining reality of life under Soviet socialism was most easily discernible in conversations with our relatives and with the new friends we made. These residents of Yerevan would often say to us, in response to a question we might ask about some aspect of their lives, "Don't ask, just don't ask." A couple of times, an innocent question about a certain building or a government policy would elicit the same response: "Friend, please, don't ask why. It's better not to ask." This sad resignation revealed a closed and unchangeable social system that unnerved one's senses and assaulted the spirit. I was amazed at the people's ability to function day to day, at the inner accommodations that allowed them to stay vital and creative inside their invisible cage.

It was also shocking for us to discover aspects of privilege that the ordinary citizen knew nothing about. Our government friends invited us to stay at a resort in the mountains for a few days. In the remote location, we arrived at a very long and palatial building surrounded by well-kept grounds. Sprinklers watered the gardens and four meals a day fed the elite members of government, their families and friends. Was this the communism that Lenin intended? I thought that privilege had no place in an egalitarian society and that elitism could not exist. These lavish surroundings jangled my innards as I pondered the reality gap between dogma and human frailty. When we told people back in Yerevan about where we had been, our description amazed them. They simply couldn't imagine it.

Towards the end of our visit to the homeland, I was saddened to think that the three of us were free to come and go, whereas our compatriots were frozen in place, denied the basic right to travel. On the day that we were to leave Yerevan, friends and relatives were at the airport to say good-bye. It's a picture hard to forget: their hands clutching the restraining chain-link fence, their tears flowing as we walked away to board the airplane.

In Moscow, where we stopped for our last two days, we had a memorable encounter. We were invited to the home of Anastas Mikoyan, the famous Armenian whom my father had photographed two years before. A long-standing member of the Politbureau of the Supreme Soviet, Mikoyan was among the highest ranking officials of the Brezhnev-Kosygin presidency. (It's worth mentioning that my father was not at all political; he was simply interested in the *people* he photographed.)

A chauffeured car with a little Soviet flag on the front drove us through the gray streets of Moscow. From the back seat, Ani, Onnig and I noticed that policemen saluted as the car went by. Soon we were out of the city and in the Russian countryside, eventually arriving at what appeared to be a private villa. This beautiful *dacha* by the Moscow River was Mikoyan's home.

Inside, my eyes were drawn to the many black-and-white framed photos gracing the walls, momentos of Mikoyan's meetings with various world figures including Ernest Hemingway and Fidel Castro. No sooner had I taken a breath to contemplate where I was than our host himself appeared, a robust man with a short mustache and imposing eyes. I was glad I had worn my dark-blue suit, white shirt and red tie, somehow fitting to the occasion.

During dinner Mikoyan told stories and asked about our parents. Onnig did most of the talking for us, being the one most agile in the tricky eastern vernacular of the Armenian language. At one point, Mikoyan stood up and proposed a toast to the Soviet Union. It was one of those moments when one's philosophical hands are tied. We drank five-star Armenian brandy.

As we were leaving, Mikoyan said he wanted to give us a gift for our father. Looking up to the paintings on his wall, he selected a beautifully framed rendering of a falcon with wings fully extended, soaring in flight. With a grin, he assured us his aide would help us carry it to the plane at the time of our departure. He was as good as his word.

The next day, we were chauffeured to the airport and the aide, carrying the well-wrapped gift, walked ahead of us and took care of our bags, breezing us past saluting airport officials and right onto the plane. We took our seats, with the painting placed directly in front of us. No one was allowed to take art out of the Soviet Union in those days. I was learning that life had its ways.

IV

A SONG IN MY HEART

Baby beluga in the deep blue sea,
Swim so wild and you swim so free.

"Baby Beluga"

LOVE RETURNS, I SING FOR CHILDREN

AFTER RETURNING FROM ARMENIA, I REMEMBER BEING IN THE din of downtown Toronto in the middle of summer and longing for the billboard-free look of Yerevan. In this more familiar reality, I was light-years away from the communist pretense. Now I was back in the capitalist pretense where the systems of privilege—run by the bankers, lawyers and accountants and supposedly open to everyone—worked best to keep the system humming for the rich and powerful.

Again living in the noisy room of the second-floor music store, I continued with my guitar playing and songwriting. My friend John helped me with my flat-picking technique and taught me fiddle tunes that we played on our guitars. Our friend and landlord, Drago, covered our frequent cash shortages.

I took to playing as many clubs as the city had to offer. To make ends meet, I had a few guitar students and occasionally took the odd bar gig, although I hated singing to inebriated audiences who couldn't care less if I was there or not. (The good thing was that I managed to write a song or two about the experience.) At times it was lean, but at least I was making a living. My noisy living space started to get to me, though, and I soon moved into a communally rented house in a quieter but still colorful neighborhood, at the time a poor part of the city called Cabbagetown.

Then, out of the blue, the gods smiled on me: Deb came back into my life. During the four years we were apart, I had never stopped thinking of her. A few years earlier I had even written a song about her called *Thinking Only of You*. Finally I got up the courage to call her and ask if she would come and see me at a downtown club where I was performing. It just so happened that she had recently broken off an engagement. She sounded genuinely delighted by my call and, yes, she would see me.

That evening at the Oxford Inn, I included her song in my performance and it worked wonders. We spent time catching up on our lives, and I learned that Deb was about to begin teaching. In fact, things went so well between us that we spent the next three days together and, within a few months, we moved into our first rented house. Deb's parents, Stan and Daphne, accepted the news calmly and welcomed me back into the fold. Arto and Lucie were shocked.

It required some give-and-take for our different worlds—Deb's structured professional life and my loosely defined artist's existence— to accommodate each other. Yet, miraculously, in a roundabout way, the dream we once shared came to life.

Our two-bedroom house in the Beaches part of town was close to the lake but far from everything else. The cozy place had wooden floors and a large kitchen, although, as we found out in winter, the exterior walls had no insulation whatsoever. At $42 a week, we weren't complaining.

Though I was working hard on the music side, Deb was to be the primary wage earner thanks to the regular income from teaching. What little we had in the way of furnishings was also mostly Deb's, up until we got a used sofa and armchair courtesy of the Mackays. While Deb was at work, I was the house body, playing my guitar, writing songs, and doing domestic chores like checking the newspaper for supermarket specials.

Around that time, my father had an exhibit of his portraits at the Royal Ontario Museum in midtown Toronto. I, the confused youth, was invited and, when I accepted the invitation, I told my mother I would be bringing Deb. After the opening ceremonies, presided over by Ontario Premier Bill Davis, I waited for an opportunity to introduce her to my parents. (They had never known of our prior dating.) When the moment arrived, it certainly didn't go the way I had hoped. Arto and Lucie politely shook her hand, but said not a word. It was as if Deb didn't exist. And except for Ani and Onnig and one family friend who embraced us both, the Armenians in attendance greeted me warmly but went cold when meeting Deb. I was furious. We left immediately.

Who did they think they were to ignore the love of my life? Did they think that I was still under their thumb? I promised Deb that if my parents expected to keep seeing me, they would have to accept her as well.

For the next month or so, whenever Lucie phoned, I was calm but immovable. I answered her chit-chat with silence or yes-no answers. She knew I was upset. When she would invite me for Sunday lunch, I'd say no, that Deb and I had other plans. One day, after a few of these strained conversations, she invited me over again, this time asking if Deb would like to come too. We accepted and lunch went . . . well, all things considered. It wasn't long before my parents came to love Deb as I knew they would. (I was more relieved that she liked them.) They were pleased she was a teacher, and clearly regarded her as someone who would rescue their wayward son.

Little did they know that the one who changed my life once would do it again.

And little did *I* know that the love Deb and I now shared would produce something so unexpected. Our offspring was to be a new direction in my music, one in which Deb would play a huge part. The catalyst was Deb's mother, Daphne, the director of a nursery school in a north Toronto suburb, who asked me to come and sing for the preschool children there. When I said yes, I knew I needed Deb's help.

I hadn't grown up in an English-speaking home, so I didn't know the complete words to even the best-known songs like *Baa Baa Black Sheep, Mary Had a Little Lamb* or *Workin' on the Railroad*. Deb became my coach, suggesting what songs I might sing, teaching me the words, and advising me to take it easy, be gentle and enjoy the children for who they were.

My first day in nursery school I felt a bit lost, although I did my best not to show it. There I was, sitting on a small rug on the floor, tuning my guitar, when in came a dozen or so little ones and two or three grown-ups. Everyone sat down and we began.

It was all new to me, from the children's welcome song and Mrs. Pike leading us in *What Shall We Do with the Drunken Sailor?* (while I accompanied her on guitar), to my first rendition of *Eensy Weensy Spider*. The children sang with me and giggled at my antics when I relied on my make-them-laugh strategy to cover the awkward moments. In this first sitting, I learned that the children's participation itself was as important as the content of what they offered. All in all, I had a good time and it seemed the staff and kids did too.

Over the next little while, Daphne asked me back a few times. And, as my repertoire grew, I found myself singing now and then in elementary school classrooms through the MITS program, "Mariposa in the Schools," an offshoot of the Mariposa Folk Festival. Singing in the morning, no booze, no cigarette smoke—these gigs were definitely different. Though I did wonder whether I really had something of value to offer my young audience, this new line of work certainly supplemented my meager folksinging income. I was still firmly dedicated to my folksinging career, however, and adult gigs were very much my main concern.

By this time, Mayrenie Grandma was confined to a wheelchair and staying at a nursing home. When I went to see her (most weekends), Deb often came with me. Grandma welcomed her and, even though they couldn't share conversation, there was genuine affection between them. Usually we would enter her room to find her peering through thick eyeglasses, intently reading the religious pamphlets she always kept nearby. Many of these were tattered and torn, so I would take her rolls of tape and shore up the broken pages as best I could. Although Mayrenie was in considerable physical pain in those last years of her life, her religious fervor did not fade. Neither did the warm glow of her kind face.

The summer of 1974 was eventful on a number of counts.

The *Ottawa Citizen* ran a color photo of Queen Elizabeth, one taken by Cavouk during the Royal visit to Canada the year before. According to the accompanying article, the Canadian government deemed this an official portrait and distributed copies all across the country. (For many years to come, I would see my father's portraits of the Queen and of Prince Philip on display throughout my travels.)

South of the border, there was the Watergate scandal. I followed the whole ordeal and was shocked by this revelation of corruption in high places and the flagrant violation of public trust. Wounded idealist that I was, I was still trying hard to find something in society to respect, something I could hang my hat on. Watergate and Richard Nixon didn't help.

On a brighter note, I got a call to sing at the Winnipeg Folk Festival in August. I was thrilled. It was my first invitation to a major folk music festival. Deb and I drove out to Manitoba in our Fiat station wagon, camping along the way with our newly acquired retriever-spaniel named Bundles. Performing in front of thousands as the sun set, I was extremely nervous, but I got through it.

This nervousness was not new to me. In fact, most of the time I sang for adults I was so uptight that it took me at least a couple of beers to settle my nerves so that I could play. I'm not sure it did a lot for my delivery, but I was so lacking in confidence that the booze at least let me get up and do whatever I could. While this proved to be good enough to get me work, I was all too aware that my best and most relaxed performances happened on nights when there were very few people in attendance. Those nights were charmers.

FORMING TROUBADOUR

SEEING THAT THE BETTER PAYING GIGS WENT TO THOSE WHO had a recording contract, I set out to do the next best thing. Taking the example of other Canadian folksingers, I formed my own record label in 1975. I called it Troubadour.

The name came from the image of the minstrels of old who went town to town singing love songs and the news of the day. My family had known an elderly Armenian who was such a singer, and to us he was known as the *ashoogh*, or troubadour. He played the *kemantche*, a vertically held stringed instrument that he bowed horizontally, and my father had once taken a very soulful photo of him. Thus the name Troubadour. It had meaning. It had a nice ring.

A friendly bank manager was taken by my effusive pitch about making a folk music record and self-promoting it with a view to breaking even. So, with a small loan and the capable help of several talented Toronto musicians, my first album of contemporary folk songs was born. I named it *Good Luck Boy*. Its cover showed a black-and-white picture of me holding Bundles whose tongue hung down over the photo's bottom line. As the album cover's designer (and I use the term loosely), I did the entire layout with Letraset and handwriting. My first "press kit" (and I use that term loosely) sported a glossy photo of me in front of the garage shaking hands with myself. The caption read something like: "Troubadour Records President R. Cavoukian welcomes singer-songwriter Raffi to the label."

The recording featured fine local players such as harmonica whiz Lance Bennett, with whom I'd done a number of gigs around town, piano great Pat Godfrey, and violinist Ben Mink, who went on to make music with Canadian diva k.d. lang. Produced by my CBC Radio friend Paul Mills, the album was well received in folk music circles and got good reviews in the independent label category. It also helped me land an appearance at the Riverboat. In time, I was able to sell enough copies at my gigs and through a few local retail outlets to pay off the bank loan.

What didn't change was the fact that my career was mostly frustrating and that the music biz and I didn't seem to get along too well. I never wanted to be a big star. My modest goal was simply to have a respected career—like that of James Taylor or Bruce Cockburn—and to play concerts in medium-sized halls. Unfortunately, it just wasn't coming together.

Once again, the gods came to the rescue. Just when I was seriously thinking about hanging up the guitar and taking up carpentry, along came an idea that Deb and I both said yes to. Early in 1976, after one of my visits to the nursery school, Daphne said to me, "You know, you should really consider making an album of songs for young children. There are very few good albums for children to listen to, especially the very young."

I shared the idea with Deb and, out of respect for Daphne, we gave it serious consideration. Visits to record stores and purchases of several titles revealed that there were indeed few children's recordings that kids might enjoy and that we could stand to listen to. There was either the Disney bin of cartoon and family movie soundtracks, or the so-called educational records that were either dry and instructional or syrupy sweet and condescending. We talked it over with our good friends Bonnie and Bert Simpson (also primary teachers) and they confirmed our sense that Daphne was onto something here.

By June, Debi and I had made a decision—well, two decisions. We invited Stan and Daphne over for a drink and told them we'd decided to get married. This was met with happy faces, albeit held in customary English restraint. We opened champagne and they gave us their best wishes. But when we told them our second decision—that we had decided to record a children's album—Daphne let out a joyful whoop and nearly jumped off the couch, she was so excited.

Getting married was more important for Deb than it was for me. We had been living together for three years and I would have been happy to continue the way we were. (I simply wasn't big on formalities to speak of, and weddings weren't really my cup of tea.) However, among her teaching colleagues, Deb had felt more than uneasy about our cohabitation outside of marriage. When she raised the subject again, I felt moved to say yes.

The day of our wedding it rained and the dog ran away. We drove all over the neighborhood yelling "Bundles!" before we found him at last, and then set off for the informal ceremony which was being held at Onnig and Kim's place.

Our handwritten invitations had encouraged guests to dress for comfort. As it turned out, the ceremony and the reception that followed had to be indoors because of the weather. Deb looked beautiful in an off-white summer dress, and I wore a cotton outfit of similar shade. Although Lucie and Arto might have wished for more on this occasion, they were pleased to see us legal, *enfin*. Stan and Daphne were delighted, and Stan and I were already calling each other Dad and Son. Our friends and relatives showered us with love, buoyant on our behalf.

SINGABLE SONGS—THE BASEMENT TAPES

AFTER THE FRIENDLY BANK MANAGER GAVE ME ANOTHER LOAN, my first children's recording was conceived in a group effort involving Deb, Bonnie and Bert. We called the three of them "the Committee."

The first time we met to choose the songs I would sing, the selection process revealed our need to state what the idea of this recording was—what we called BAP, the "basic album philosophy." We wanted an album of songs that would be fun for kids to sing, sung with respect for the young listener, and musically pleasant to the adult ear as well. We decided to offer a variety of songs that children could make their own, and that's where the word "singable" popped up. These would be singable songs for the very young.

As a newcomer to this task, I relied heavily on the Committee. They knew children and worked with them daily, and Bonnie and Bert had two of their own. So, with all this experience, they not only helped me with song selection, they also helped shape the tone of my singing.

As for a producer, I asked Paul Mills and he declined, saying I could probably do it myself. I wasn't too sure about that, so I looked around for someone else to help me.

Soon after the first few album planning meetings, I enlisted the aid of Ken Whiteley, one of Toronto's foremost folk musicians and one who could play a dozen instruments. I knew Ken from coffee houses and from catching his performances as a member of the Original Sloth Band, a trio that played a relaxed blend of crazy tunes from the '30s and '40s. Ken would often delight audiences with his command of the jug, a homemade instrument fashioned from an empty plastic or glass container. His diverse musical skills, together with his experience in performing for children (through MITS), made Ken the perfect choice to help me produce this album.

Now all we needed was a recording studio. Enter the Lanois brothers, Bob and Dan, who, in the basement of their mother's house (an hour's drive from Toronto), had an eight-track studio. Besides being equipped with excellent microphones, this place also had the advantage of being very affordable. And so off we went, Ken and I, to the Lanois house in the small town of Ancaster.

At first I had thoughts of keeping the musical arrangements sparse, with little ornamentation, but as the project unfolded I got excited by what I was hearing and went for a little more gusto. After each day at the studio, I'd drive home eager to play the rough mixes for Deb, and then we'd drive to Bonnie and Bert's for listenings over pizza and beer. They were free to "yea it or nay it," but they loved what they heard and offered just the right questions and guidance.

There was a fresh beginner's quality about the music. It sounded natural and not overdone, similar to what we appreciated on a record by the Babysitters, a group featuring the actor Alan Arkin, the late Lee Hays (of the Weavers) and Doris Kaplan. With the Lanois's recording skills, Ken's musicianship and the Committee's sound educational advice, I had all the support I needed.

Boy, did I work hard. Apart from having a good time, there were countless details to attend to. On the legal side of things, there were tasks such as tracking down song origins, arranging for royalty payments, and ensuring proper credits for lyric adaptations. In all of this, I was helped by an excellent entertainment lawyer, William Hinkson. I learned all about the legal end of the music business (albeit at $125 an hour), like how to protect my artistic freedom, give others credit and thus ensure a good night's sleep.

Then there was the album cover design. It felt right to have a children's drawing and rendering of my name, and I had obtained these very elements during a visit to a school in rural Manitoba the previous year. I took out my crayons and Letraset and had a ball, trying out various colors for the title, before settling on the right typeface: Century Schoolbook, lowercase. Because I was a novice at all this, there were few rules to follow and much fun to be had, designing by feel. The result was as fresh as the music inside which, like the front cover said, was "great with a peanut butter sandwich."

The repertoire was a blend of traditional children's songs, along with a few "third-party compositions" (songs written by others) and three originals that I made up with the help of the Committee.

In the studio I would usually sing and play the guitar at the same time, with Ken playing along and sometimes singing live as well.

If anything, our performances were a tad under-rehearsed, and that kept us and bass player Bob Doidge alert and spontaneous. An early defining moment in these sessions was the decision to have Bob play the bass (instead of Ken). That allowed Ken to be in the control room and think about the actual sound quality, after Dan Lanois first turned to him and asked, "How do you like the bass sound?"

After a good performance of a song was recorded, it was time for "overdubs," the addition of musical tones and colors as needed: a wooden flute solo here, a trumpet arrangement there, and sometimes vocal harmonies. And, to round it off nicely, the voices of children (including Bonnie and Bert's young sons, Justin and Joel) singing naturally—not always in pitch, but perfectly delightful. Among Ken's many unique contributions to the music were the jug and harmonica on *Little Red Wagon*, giving it that jug-band feel, and a surprising "Hawaiian guitar" on *Must Be Santa*.

By the sounds of it, we had an irresistible children's recording on our hands, and Daphne shared the excitement that Deb and I felt. I put together a new press kit, complete with quotes from educators saying wonderful things about the music. We had a thousand albums pressed, housed in double covers that opened like a book to reveal song lyrics and incidental notes.

The strongly positive reaction of friends and educators who heard it bore out our feeling that we had an important album here, and we were keen to let everyone know about it. Towards that end, I had a full-color promotional poster made.

On the birth of *Singable Songs for the Very Young* in November 1976, a whirlwind of activity ensued. I took the album around to Sam "The Record Man" Sniderman, owner of Toronto's biggest record outlet. Sam did not let me down. That first purchase order for fifty albums from his influential store helped get things rolling. Then, on the advice of MITS colleague, Lois Lilienstein, I went straight over to the Children's Book Store, a children's literature mecca that also carried a few records. Proprietors Judy and Hy Sarick welcomed my offer to leave a few albums on consignment with the understanding that, if these were sold, for the next order I would be paid in full upon my delivery of the new batch.

Deb, Bonnie and Bert were also busy talking it up and placing copies for consignment sale in small bookstores here and there. I was making the rounds in my station wagon to as many shops as I could find—when I wasn't doing a coffee house or MITS gig or teaching guitar lessons at home.

There just weren't enough hours in the day for all that was going on. I spent many evenings exhausted, watching hockey on TV while I stamped envelopes for mail orders or autographed the bottom right-hand corner of album covers.

The record was an instant hit. People loved it and, as word got around, they started buying three or four copies to give as gifts. Although I convinced retailers to carry it at the full suggested list price, cash sales through me were a clean $5, "priced to sell." Every store where we had left copies to sell on consignment called to say it had sold out right away and wanted more. To avoid bookkeeping hassles, I let stores know that I required full payment in cash or cheque when I delivered the next batch. Even though this was a departure from the customary net thirty or net sixty days delayed payment, the proprietors agreed.

But the best was yet to come.

We had hired our friend Rob Williams to contact the Toronto media to generate some press and radio interviews, and he did very well. When I was featured on Touch the Earth, Sylvia Tyson's radio program on CBC, her interview and playing a couple of album cuts immediately generated thirty mail-order requests from across the country. And just before Christmas, *Singable Songs for the Very Young* got rave reviews in all three Toronto newspapers. (I still can't get over that.)

The hot little album was about to take off. With 2,000 copies sold in the first four months, a regional record distributor took notice and agreed to carry the album. Sales went through the roof.

FROM FOLKSINGER TO CHILDREN'S ENTERTAINER

WHAT A WONDERFUL, CRAZY, CHAOTIC TIME IT WAS. THE BUZZ OF success was an entirely new experience for me, and what had eluded me in folksinging was about to be mine by way of a path I had entered through the side door.

On a snowy spring day in 1977, when I appeared at the Children's Book Store to sing and sign autographs, I was amazed at the number of people lined up to see me. The place was so crowded that we had to have three sessions to accommodate everyone. I was inundated with requests to perform at schools and libraries, a result of both my MITS experience and librarians hearing the news. All this led to my first public children's concerts in small theaters, often presented by an early childhood education organization. Deb cried when she first heard a large audience sing *The More We Get Together* with me.

But I wasn't going to leave my adult folksinging behind. The years spent writing and singing meant too much to me and formed a large part of my identity. It wasn't something that I could just let go in favor of a new and growing source of income, as real as that was. So my university friend and manager, Doug Powers, was still booking adult gigs for me, and I was keeping up with playing my guitar and rehearsing love songs, even while I sang *Peanut Butter Sandwich* and *Baa Baa Black Sheep* in schools. I thought of myself as a folksinger who also sang for children, yet more and more people came to know me—and refer to me as—a children's singer. In a short time, I felt an unsettling identity conflict growing within me.

I ignored the advice of friends to just drop the past and embrace this new musical field, partly because I was committed to the adult music and partly because I lacked confidence in what I had to offer as a children's performer. I didn't yet know what it was, this gentle call to children. Then, just when people were asking when I was going to record another children's album, I had a bigger idea. I would make two albums: one for adults, one for children. And I would promote the two of them at the same time, doing afternoon concerts for kids and evening shows for grown-ups. Oblivious to how much energy all this would require from me, I figured that the parents of the kids who loved my children's music might come to see my evening shows. I was ready to give it all I had.

A wonderful musician named Don Potter, whom I had first seen performing at the Riverboat, agreed to produce my adult album. The repertoire included a new love song I had written for Deb called *Lovelight*, one about Bundles (*Out in the Yard*) and another, *Little Kristin January 28*, to mark the birth of my niece—Onnig and Kim's first child—the previous year.

The Lanois brothers were out of the basement and we were to record in their new Grant Avenue Studio in Hamilton, less than an hour's drive from Toronto. These were exciting sessions, and I learned a lot about recording from Don and the other talented musicians I was working with. By the end of August, the record was done. It was well produced and, I felt, did my new songs justice. *Adult Entertainment* I called it. My friend and accountant, Mike Mulholland, dubbed it *Tax Loss*.

After a tour of the Yukon, where I sang both children's and adult songs, planning began for the new children's album. Again the Committee and I met to look at songs and ideas and again I turned to Ken Whiteley for musical and production help. He and I had done very well on our first try and, besides, the guy had a way with a kazoo and could quack like a duck. Indispensable.

I was a bit nervous this second time around. Would our beginner's luck hold? How could we top what we'd done the first time?

What if people didn't like this one as much? But, with such a supportive team, I needn't have worried. Working with the Committee and Ken gave me my first taste of the concept of synergy—the total energy being greater than the sum of the individual parts—and yielded unusual results.

When I returned to Grant Avenue Studio in November to record *More Singable Songs*, I was warmly welcomed by Bob and Dan, who went to great lengths to make me comfortable and aid the project's success. The thing I liked about making a children's record was that I could do what I wanted without thinking about radio airplay. Unlike adult recordings that had to be in a certain style—say, country, pop or rock—to fit the music formats of radio stations, children's recordings could offer up a variety of styles on one album.

Once more, the spirit of the project kept us all in good humor. We even got an unexpected contribution from Stan Rogers, the great singer-songwriter I knew from the folk music circuit. Stan, along with his brother, Garnet, who had recorded with me previously, paid a surprise visit to the studio, and Ken and I invited them to sing with us. It made for a spirited *a capella* version of *Workin' on the Railroad*. The rough mixes I took home got rave reviews from the Committee. When all was said and done, I felt we had a sequel that was both like the original and unique.

I had done two albums in the span of four months (a feat I am unlikely to repeat), and I designed a new poster that said "Raffi: Both Sides Now." With this and a new round of press and radio promotion, I set out to win some of my children's music fans over to the adult music. The new press kit had two biographies—"Raffi for Grown-ups" and "Raffi for Children." There was just one problem: the plan didn't work. Hundreds of children and families would come to sing with me at an afternoon performance, but an evening show in the same hall would draw only fifty people. After this happened a couple of times, I wondered if life was trying to tell me something.

Sales of my children's albums kept right on climbing. *Singable Songs* was approaching gold (50,000 copies) and fans were hungry for *More Singable Songs*, gobbling up great numbers in a hurry. The adult album, over time, sold a respectable number, but nothing like the other two.

By now the success of my independent record label allowed me to rent an office not far from home. Troubadour had expanded to a staff of three to manage the rapid growth of my musical career. Joining Doug Powers was Joyce Yamamoto, whom I knew from the folk music scene. Joyce became our office manager, and besides her attention to administrative details, her artistic talents came in handy in album and poster design. Mike Mulholland became head of "business affairs."

In every stage of the production process I was quality-minded. I learned about "lacquering," chose superior vinyl at extra cost, attended "test pressings" and listened closely before I approved the mastering process and production runs. When Columbia Special Products (Troubadour's supplier) pressed the initial 10,000-album run of *More Singable Songs* without first getting my test pressing approval, I didn't accept the order. The pressing was faulty (with inner groove distortion and unacceptable "tics" and "pops") and I refused to pay. At my insistence, and with the support of my lawyer, the company scrapped the defectives and redid the entire order. Troubadour was selling a top-quality product for an important audience, and I was determined to give it our very best.

Early in 1979, I made a key decision. I would no longer pursue my adult music, but would instead devote all my time to writing, performing and recording for children. Throughout my struggle to hold onto my folksinging, Deb had been gentle and supportive. When she tried to get me to face reality and I wasn't ready to hear her, she let it go; she knew it required an inner change in me. Having tried everything I could to play "both sides" and seeing that it was my children's music that clearly stood out, I needed help to resolve the mixed feelings I had. Together, Deb, Bonnie, Bert and Glenn Sernyk (who had joined Troubadour to be my new manager) enabled me to view things in a new way.

Deb helped me to see that music was an important part of a growing child's life, and that songs were a lovely way for children to explore the world around them as well as the inner world of emotions. Talks with Bonnie and Bert bore out this concept and underlined the fact that singing is a natural play activity for children.

Understanding this—the importance of child play—was key to my valuing this new music. I realized that play was the way young children learned, and that songs offered a wonderfully playful learning experience that could be both individual and shared.

Glenn pointed out that I had a gift for singing to family audiences that few entertainers had. It certainly was true that many entertainers were downright frightened by the notion of singing in front of children. What he said helped me get over the notion that this musical path represented a lesser road. I realized that, if anything, there was something rare about devoting oneself to making music for children.

Hearing all this was what I needed, because it countered the music industry's notion that children's music was second rate. In record stores, I had seen the signs myself: the small children's record bin contained cut-priced stock that looked like cheap plastic toys. It hardly inspired one to pursue a career in such a seemingly unglamorous field. What I came to understand was that the industry reflected society's view that children weren't important and therefore neither was their music. At the center of it, the child was not seen to be a whole person, with important feelings and perceptions at a vitally formative stage of life.

How ironic that *I* should become a channel to shine a musical beacon on this issue of the child as a whole person, not having had that experience myself. Nevertheless, here I had produced and independently released a children's album that reached "gold record" levels. And what's more, the album was selling at full list price, outside the industry norm.

As for my adult music not working out, fortunately I was able to offset my regrets by realizing that my musical gifts were meant to succeed in a way I had never imagined. It took the sting out of failure, seeing that some doors close so others might open. My inner voice now understood the difficult transitional process that led me to this unique opportunity, and I was grateful for the patience and gentle handling of those who cared about me. Two years after the birth of *Singable Songs*, I had come to fully value my new calling.

YOGA AND CONSCIOUSNESS

IT WAS IN 1974 THAT I WAS FIRST ATTRACTED TO YOGA THROUGH my readings of spiritual books on esoteric wisdom. For me there was a mystique about yoga and a feeling that the postures and meditations put one in touch with the divine. My first few classes with a slim young Hindu teacher allowed me to leave the everyday world behind the moment I walked through his door. In that calm oasis in mid-Toronto, a block away from the chaos of Yonge Street, the incense welcomed me into an expanded state of mind.

I enjoyed doing the postures, even though the lotus position looked at first to be utterly undoable. It amazed me to see how, when given the chance, the body gave and stretched. Practicing the postures, along with reading *Autobiography of a Yogi*, offered me a new way of contemplating the world. According to the wisdom of this ancient tradition, to know the workings of one cell of the body was to know the universe. At the time, I had little understanding of that pearl of wisdom.

Deb was also coming to classes and we were soon introduced to meditation. This clearing of the mind was not as easy as it sounded, but the very effort showed me how the mind's incessant chatter claims one's attention. Progress was slow, but I was glad to be meditating, however well I was doing it.

We also got to do some chanting. In one session a dozen of us, led by our teacher, chanted *Aum* for about twenty minutes and then followed this with a period of silence. The chanting itself was a powerful experience and a bit dizzying. In the emerging unity with others in the room, I felt a loss of individual identity. I had a slight fear of falling apart or vanishing, and yet at the same time I sensed the sweetness of expansion. The silence that followed was glorious—very full, utterly peaceful.

When our first teacher left town we found another, an older woman whose classes took place in her apartment living room in a high-rise building. Observing the differences in her approach, I realized that the ancient postures were subject to individual interpretation. With a move to the suburbs, we met Axel, our third teacher, a follower of the venerated and now-departed Yogi Sivananda of India. Until 1981, whenever possible, I attended two ninety-minute classes a week, often with Deb, who worked them in around her teaching. While we all did the postures, Axel spoke about various issues in our lives, inviting us to share stories and ask questions and responding from a yogic perspective. He stressed awareness of the body and its wondrous workings, and the need for healthy nourishment. He also spoke of reincarnation and the law of karma, as well as the benefits of meditation.

At times these classes seemed like group sessions of spiritual psychology. Although I had mixed feelings about this, I found it mind-expanding to look at aspects of living—from personal relationships to food choices—with a spiritual perspective. Soon meditation became more or less a daily practice for me, a cherished time to clear the mind of the day's demands.

It wasn't long before Deb and I began to reduce our meat intake, and, after a while, we stopped eating any meat or fowl altogether. I still remember the shocked look on my mother's face when she learned the news. The fact that I would no longer eat her *koefteh* (a type of ground meat) was hard for her to fathom. Lucie was almost speechless, a rarity for her. For the first few months, she sometimes looked at me in disbelief, shaking her head. I simply reminded her of what her eyes could readily see if she would let them—that I was in excellent health and not wasting away. To her credit, after she accepted the situation she went out of her way to accommodate us, always including vegetarian dishes at family meals. (Besides, I could still feast on her home-made *bâton salé*, a salted-stick snack I'd always loved.)

One teaching that brought me surprising insights in later years was the cultivation of "detachment." Detachment has to do with taking a step back and seeing the entire drama of human life: the ego-play of personality amidst the timeless principles of the soul and the universe. As one develops an ability to view events, good or bad, with detachment, there is no lessening of love and compassion. One simply gains a sense of how attachment to temporal desires affects daily life, and gradually learns to make wiser choices. Detachment activates in a person the "witness," a part of the self that has a simultaneous, slightly removed (and often different) perspective of a given situation. In this way, detachment can alleviate emotional pain and enrich experience.

Another benefit of yoga came through the recommended books I read—Swami Sivananda's and others'—on the power of positive thinking and its influence on daily life. I learned that negative thoughts (and projections) have the power to attract and thereby increase negativity, while positive thoughts can accentuate and increase the positives in life. This simple truism played on my mind and in meditations, and its practical effect turned up in my song-writing. I doubt that my best-known song, *Baby Beluga*, would have made the splash it did had it been a mournful anti-whaling song. But, as a celebratory love song, it made waves.

BABY BELUGA

EARLY IN 1980, AT THE AGE OF THIRTY-ONE, AT THE HEIGHT OF my yoga and meditation, I paused to review Troubadour's success.

My first two children's albums had received gold record awards, and the subsequent release of *The Corner Grocery Store* had attracted national distribution by way of A&M Records. For some time, Mike Mulholland had been talking to the top brass of A&M Canada, President Gerry Lacoursiere and Vice-President Joe Summers. Mike's number-crunching work paid off. The talks yielded a multi-year agreement whereby A&M would distribute any Troubadour release, in cassette as well as vinyl.

Thanks to A&M, my music was now in stores all across Canada, and sales were about to increase dramatically. With three albums that won rave reviews from teachers, parents and children alike, I was performing sold-out concerts across the country, sharing singalong joy with thousands. Deb and I had bought a modest suburban home: a small, two-story brick house with a big back yard for Bundles.

One day when I sat down to meditate, my thoughts turned to this moment in my life. It appeared that everything I had ever wanted when I was younger was now mine. I was with my high school sweetheart, living in our own house, and enjoying a respected musical career of concerts and recordings. And yet, right in the middle of this fullness, something was troubling me. It was a disquieting feeling, as if I had reached a fork in the road, an impasse that was hard to name. I felt humbled that I had been given so much so soon. However, I was uninterested in simply more—more money, sales or possessions—for the sake of more. What did I want to do now?

The meditation turned to prayer. I thanked the Creator for all my blessings and, now that my needs had been fully met, I prayed that I might come to know what I could do to give back, to serve a greater need. What would You like of me? How may I serve? Those words became my mantra that day, and a guiding prayer in the years ahead.

During the weeks and months that followed, I moved increasingly into the idea of service. I was working on a new album and decided to include a number of songs of spirit, like the gentle *Thanks a Lot.* In recording these newly expressive songs I felt quite vulnerable. But my courage was rewarded when people singled out the Raffi songs (written with Deb, Bonnie and Bert) for praise.

Baby Beluga itself was a love song. In 1979, Kavna, a beluga whale at the Vancouver Public Aquarium, stole my heart and I set out to write a song about this beautiful creature. I asked Deb for advice and she said to make it about a *baby* whale because young children love babies and it would further endear the song to them. Right she was! *Baby Beluga* became an instant hit and caught the fancy of listeners young and old. The positive focus produced a song of far greater power than a "save-the-whale" lament, for to care and protect something or someone, you've got to love it first. And for three-year-olds, loving the beluga was the key as far as I was concerned; a seed that could grow with time.

In a similar style I wrote *All I Really Need*, in commemoration of 1979's "International Year of the Child." I carried the basic words and melody of the chorus in my head for about six months before finishing it. I wanted a strong "protest" song on behalf of every child everywhere, written in the first person so that any child could sing it with truth, regardless of personal circumstance. And, by singing about the basics of life—song, food, love, clean air and water—I was emphatically excluding the trappings of consumer society (without naming them), using the most positive imagery I could find. The song went on to become a big hit with my fans.

The *Baby Beluga* album was many times blessed. The combination of musicians, recording studio and repertoire had a synergy all its own. This was the fourth recording at Grant Avenue Studio in Hamilton, where Bob and Danny Lanois amiably hosted and provided expert technical assistance for the most demanding of my productions to date. (Dan has since gone on to make his own music, and was the producer of notable albums for the likes of U-2, the Neville Brothers and Bob Dylan.)

The close rapport with my friend and co-producer Ken Whiteley was by now bringing new musicians and new colors to my recorded work.

A trio of Toronto singers known as the Honolulu Heartbreakers supplied great harmony vocals on *Baby Beluga, All I Really Need* and my bluesy version of *This Old Man* (on which Ken played an inspired ukulele solo). The tasteful contributions of drummer Bucky Berger and bassist Dennis Pendrith kept us musically "in the groove" (as we used to say in the vinyl days). In fact, Bucky and Dennis really brought the *All I Really Need* track to life. I also scored a guest appearance by Bruce Cockburn, one of my early faves among songwriters and guitarists. I was thrilled to hear his inventive guitar licks on *Water Dance*, a guitar instrumental I wrote and played in a style similar to his. Bruce's playing also graced the song *Thanks a Lot*.

One gutsy call on this album was the inclusion of the six-minute *Joshua Giraffe* (edited down from the original twenty-two-minute version), about the liberation of a little giraffe who was "stuck in a zoo, with buffalo poo." Co-written by Dennis Pendrith and Len Udow, this song was often requested by my fans. Because of its length and complexity, I only performed it on one occasion.

The more I learned to trust my ears and take chances with each album, the better I liked the surprising results. And, with *Baby Beluga*, I again relied on Deb's advice and that of Bert and Bonnie to keep me on course—as well as the counsel of the one who got me started in all this, Daphne.

ENTERTAINING CANADA

By 1981, MINE WAS A CELEBRATED NAME IN CANADA—A HOUSEHOLD name in households with kids. Since devoting myself to my new pursuit, I had toured the country a number of times, singing my singable songs, either solo or with Ken as a duo.

Flush with early sales success, we in the Troubadour office decided back in 1978 to become an active independent record label. Our thoughts turned to releasing the works of other artists.

First we issued *Junior Jug Band,* an excellent children's album by Ken and his brother Chris Whiteley. Then came a swinging album by the Original Sloth Band. After that we released a couple of albums by Chris and his partner, Caitlin Hanford. Chris and Caitlin wrote the most wonderful country songs and sang in sweet harmony. We had fun doing these releases and gave them our best, though they didn't carry huge sales expectations. We just really loved the music and wanted to support it.

At the Winnipeg Folk Festival that summer, I noticed the talents of a big man with a big voice (and size 13 feet). His name was Fred Penner and his signature tune was *The Cat Came Back,* the title song of his first independent children's recording. A fine singer with a strong theatrical background, Fred delighted his hometown audience with an engaging performance. Following the show, I introduced myself to him and we got talking. Not long after, Fred signed a recording contract with Troubadour and we reissued his charming first album, with a plug from me on the back cover. We went on to do three more releases of Fred's music.

That year also brought a surprise. It was a new children's album from three veteran MITS performers, Sharon Hampson, Lois Lilienstein and Bram Morrison, who started a musical trio called Sharon, Lois and Bram. Along with percussionist Bill Usher, they formed their own independent label called Elephant Records and, backed by a group of investors and with great fanfare, released their first kids' album, *One Elephant Deux Elephants*. (Bill was the drummer on my first folk album in 1975.)

Bram had made a name for himself with his instrumental work backing vocalist Alan Mills. Lois was well known in early childhood education circles in Toronto, and Sharon had been folksinging for a number of years. I had credited Sharon and Lois in the liner notes of *Singable Songs* for the advice they had given me on various songs, and Lois wrote a glowing review of *Singable Songs* that I included in my first press kit.

So, at a MITS party in mid-1978, when they broke the news of their just-completed debut album, I was stunned. They hadn't said a word about it to me. Certainly, all three were good musicians and their album (as it turned out) was full of fine singing and playing. I wished them well, but I must admit the situation really challenged my cooperative spirit. It felt like colleagues and friends were now competitors. In the coming weeks and months, the debut album sold very briskly and their concerts were a big hit.

The formidable success that greeted *One Elephant Deux Elephants*, as well as the albums to follow it, showed that the trail blazed by *Singable Songs for the Very Young* and *More Singable Songs* was here to stay. Interestingly, sales of my albums were not affected. If anything, there was a perception of a burgeoning children's recording field in which a number of Canadians, including Fred Penner and Chris and Ken Whiteley, were making their mark—and a living, to boot.

MITS did release its children's album, too, featuring a diverse cast of talented performers. Many of them previously held a mild contempt for singers who had recorded works, which they considered music gone "too commercial." Those same performers now found it exciting to promote their new record, and sold it enthusiastically both at concerts and through the MITS office.

The year 1979 was notable for a number of reasons. Not only did we have the signing with A&M Records and the release of *The Corner Grocery Store*, but it also marked my debut at the Vancouver Children's Festival.

My first sight of the red-and-white-striped tents on the grass of Vanier Park, with its backdrop of water, city and mountains, was a jaw dropper. I couldn't get over the beauty of it, and singing in those tents was fun, like being in a big tent party. Even from the stage I could see the healthy faces of the West Coast crowd—the kids, parents and teachers who came to sing with me.

Artistic Director Ernie Fladell, a retired advertising executive from New York, just loved to extol the virtues of the festival, showing Glenn and me around the tents where various acts from around the world would perform. We met a theater troupe from California called Magic Carpet, who did a great show called Kids' Writes, acting out vignettes of short pieces kids had written about whatever tickled their fancy. And Kaze Noko, a Japanese theater company, entranced everyone with a playful rendering of children's games from their culture, performed with a low-key charm. Clowns and mime artists, jugglers and storytellers—this festival for kids (and the young at heart) had it all. My first visit marked the beginning of a long love affair with this unique performing arts event, and with Vancouver's stunning natural setting.

It was a concert-filled year for me, criss-crossing the country. More and more I was accompanied by Ken on piano, guitar, jug, banjo, mandolin and what-have-you; and at times, we were joined by Chris on trumpet, guitar and harmonica. In the summer, Ken and I had the pleasure of giving a number of performances in Newfoundland, our first visit to the province.

An educators' conference in Lethbridge, Alberta, allowed me the rare pleasure of having Deb come with me. In addition to my evening concert, the organizers had arranged for us to do a morning session about music for children. It was great for me to hear Deb laud the value of singing for young children, and her words were well received by her colleagues in the teaching profession. I was delighted that the one who had given me so much was receiving her own applause that day.

Back home, Ken and I did our first two shows at the University of Toronto's 1,600-seat Convocation Hall, an appearance that for years became an annual Christmas event in the city, much like Gordon Lightfoot's springtime concerts at Massey Hall.

The following year, I stretched musically during the *Baby Beluga* recording sessions and, with Glenn's nudging, grew to include Dennis and Bucky with Ken and me in our live performances. With four of us on stage, I now had to learn the crucial bandleader skill of "counting in" the songs. The guys all coached me in this, but it took a long time to get it right. It wasn't just a matter of counting a-one and a-two, and so on. During the brief few seconds of applause for the song just ended, you had to conjure up both the rhythm and the tempo of the song you were about to sing, and vocalize or signal these so the band could start the song together and in time. Quite a trick but, as with all things, it's easy once you know how.

My first public appearance with the band was a personal thrill. The aisles of Convocation Hall were full of dancing kids, grooving to the bouncy beat the guys laid down. Parents roared their approval. Glenn dug it. And my concern about kids losing their Raffi focus was for naught. For Deb, Bonnie and Bert, the band show was definitely a thumbs-up.

When I wasn't doing concerts, I was kept hopping at the office. There was a lot of business to attend to at Troubadour, including ongoing career planning and financial management. For one reason or another, the monthly overhead for an office and full-time staff often required the bank's help. Mike and I would occasionally have meetings with the bank manager and, though I brushed up on sales figures beforehand, I was still learning the "cash flow" and "credit line" etiquette.

To round out the year, Ken and I did four shows out West in the Vancouver East Cultural Centre, this time sharing the stage with special guest Fred Penner. His rousing rendition of *It Ain't Gonna Rain No More* was a big hit and well timed for the wet season on the coast.

Home again, I had great fun singing at Firgrove Public School, an inner-city school where Deb was teaching. Meanwhile, she and I gave the go-ahead for renovations on our house, work that kept us busy with dust and details. And at Christmas that year, the gathering on Melrose Avenue included a beautiful new face: my nephew, Sevan, born in September, Onnig and Kim's second child.

*　*　*

In 1981, television came knocking in the form of a CBC special named "Raffi, Belugas and Friends." Producer Cathy Chilco shot scenes of me exploring the Vancouver Aquarium with a group of kids and singing *Baby Beluga* to the whales in the beluga pool. I was thrilled to see Kavna and the other two belugas again. I really got the feeling they enjoyed hearing me and the children singing their praises. During the shoot, a little boy wandered into our chosen group of singers just as we started *All I Really Need*. We kept on going and he smiled and sang along with us.

Back then, saving the whales from slaughter and extinction was far more the issue than the later controversy over releasing whales from captivity. My meeting Kavna at the aquarium inspired the song I wrote and recorded, complete with beluga sounds mixed in. While I am not in favor of taking whales from the wild and keeping them for show, I was amazed at how my own love of belugas, kindled by seeing the captive Kavna up close, had turned into such a well-known song. I trusted that the bond with whales, felt by anyone who heard *Baby Beluga*, would go deeper than a trip to the aquarium. I prayed it would. In the song the whale swims wild and free.

As for being a TV star, I had mixed feelings. Shooting a scene over and over to get it right, waiting for airplane noise to pass by, waiting while the crew set up another site for shooting, making wardrobe decisions—I just wasn't sure about all this. It certainly didn't make me want to do more TV. The thing I disliked most was the lip-synching that was required.

The music performed on TV is not usually played and sung live-to-tape. Sometimes you sing "dummy vocals," your mouth moving in sync to the prerecorded instruments and vocals. But if you complain enough, as I did, the instruments are recorded without the vocals, leaving room to sing actual vocals live-to-tape. Not understanding the needs of TV logistics and budgets, I kicked up a big fuss about lip-synching. It felt so fake.

In doing the special, I learned a lot about the nature of TV production, its biases, and its demands on-camera. I learned about the need to shoot the same thing from a number of different angles; for TV, the greater the variety of shots, the better. True, you also do repeated takes in a recording studio, but there you're only concerned with audio. For TV, visuals are most important, and thus it's quite an adjustment for a singer to have the musical performance be so affected by video considerations. My grumps aside, Cathy went a long way to accommodate my needs. We became good friends and went on to do more TV in the years that followed.

By now I was a regular at the Vancouver Children's Festival. There was such a demand for tickets to my shows that the tent where I performed kept getting bigger from year to year. We easily sold out eight shows in a 1,000-seat tent. At each performance, when I walked on stage dressed in my Hawaiian shirt and Arctic moccasins, it seemed that every available square inch held an eager face. The only trouble was that my popularity made it hard for me to get around the festival grounds. From the moment I arrived on site, the cry of "there's Raffi!" would follow me everywhere I went. Festival organizers gave me a two-piece yellow rain suit for camouflage.

Yes, all that attention did go to my head, and I reckon I was a little full of myself in those days. I would hang out at the performer's lounge, trading laughs and drinking beer in the sunshine with the likes of vaude-villian performer Al Simmons, mime artists The Potato People, and many other entertainers. It was both a carefree time and a heady experience.

Glenn was getting all kinds of requests for concerts. One invitation put me on an outdoor revolving stage at Ontario Place, a Toronto lakefront attraction frequented by families in the summer. The band and I played a Canada Day concert to some 7,000 people who not only loved it, but wanted an encore. Whatever trepidations I had about the size of this unusual venue and the lack of control I felt were somehow offset by the holiday atmosphere. The crowd had waited a couple of hours for showtime, and we walked on stage to a huge welcome. They sang *Day O* like there was no tomorrow.

Among the Troubadour entourage backstage there was a new face. Tina Hann, who had just been hired, was at her first Raffi gig—quite the introduction to my career. Tina was to be my able assistant for a good many years.

In the fall of 1981, Ken and I did an extensive tour in Western Canada, with Fred Penner taking center stage in the middle of the show, singing a couple of his own songs, and returning to join us for the encore—an *a capella* version of *If I Knew You Were Comin' I'd Have Baked a Cake* in three-part harmony.

Back home, there was a special weekend at Convocation Hall. Including Chris Whiteley, we were now five on stage. On Saturday we did two shows that featured Chris and Ken as guests, and on Sunday I made way for Fred to sing a few. Quite the gang of troubadours we were.

In December, we threw a big party to commemorate the half-million mark in sales of Troubadour's catalogue. Selling 500,000 albums was a tremendous feat for an independent record label, especially in children's entertainment. By this time, Sharon, Lois and Bram had become very popular, with a couple of Juno awards to their credit and a CBC TV series. Now team Troubadour felt it was time to trumpet *our* unprecedented achievement.

At Toronto's Sutton Place hotel, Mike Mulholland was our hilarious master of ceremonies, handing out gold and platinum awards and presenting plaques to thank those who had worked so hard on our behalf. In addition to many friends and family members who came, the whole gang from A&M was there, from execs to sales people, including top brass Gerry Lacoursiere and Joe Summers and Sales Manager Bill Ott. At one point, to my surprise I saw Gerry, Joe and Bill coming my way carrying something huge above their heads. It was a six-foot-long representation of the number 500,000—and the zeros were gold albums!

Congratulations also came from the beaming parents, Lucie and Arto and Daphne and Stan. It was quite the party, and Deb and I were elated. To top it all off, a friend gave us a very tasteful gift: an LP-sized replica of a vinyl record, complete with grooves and center label—in chocolate.

The success of *Baby Beluga* gave me confidence in my own songwriting abilities. In 1982, when I next felt the urge to record, I decided to focus on self-esteem, the all-important childhood theme. With that in mind, I wrote *Rise and Shine*, an up-tempo tune of encouragement and awakening to love. The album (of the same name) was the first of two that Ken and I made at Inception Sound, the suburban Toronto studio of Chad Irschick, a gifted engineer and producer.

This album was also strong on performances. Virtuoso harpist Erica Goodman graced the title track and also played a medley of two nursery rhyme instrumentals with a Mozart-like intro. A rendition of *Daniel in the Lion's Den* featured Ken on slide guitar and Chris on harmonica. Jazz flautist Kathryn Moses and accordionist Tom Szczesniak also contributed to the blend of sounds that mark this album. *The Wheels on the Bus*, a traditional children's favorite, was sung by the primary choir of Firgrove Public School. (I was at the school to drive Deb home one day and, on our way out, the sound of the singing children was so captivating that we stopped to listen; I knew I just had to record them.) They also gave life to a rousing accordion rendition of *Thumbellina*.

That year saw the opening of a new concert venue in downtown Toronto. Roy Thomson Hall, named after a publishing magnate (whom my father had photographed), was the glittering new showcase for the Toronto Symphony. To mark the opening, a week of gala concerts by Canadian artists was arranged. I was amongst those invited to perform. We were thrilled, the band and all of us at Troubadour, to have two sold-out shows (an amazing 5,000 fans) at this prestigious new facility.

My second CBC TV show was aired in the fall. This time it was an hour-long network special called "Raffi's Really Big Show." Shot at the Vancouver Children's Festival a few months earlier, it featured performances from several artists, with me as host and also singing a few songs with Chris and Ken. Though it made for an extra-busy festival week, I had a lot of fun doing it and met some wonderful performers.

The only concert I have ever done with an orchestra was also the only one I've shared with another Raffi. He is Raffi Armenian (pronounced Ar-men-yun), a conductor who, at the time, was with the symphony orchestra in Kitchener-Waterloo, an hour's drive west of Toronto. I accepted the invitation to do the "Raffi Meets Raffi" show, provided that Ken accompany me on piano. Excited and nervous about singing in front of an orchestra, I needed him to help me make this artistic stretch.

Ken and I gathered a list of songs that would lend themselves to orchestral enhancement and also engage the audience. Raffi sent us his musical arrangements and we went over them, suggesting changes here and there. This was not a simple matter of showing up and singing with a different band. I knew I had to put together a new show, one that acknowledged both the extraordinary situation and Maestro Armenian. We accordingly decided to include a brief demonstration of sections of the orchestra in the program.

Before the big day, there were a couple of "note rehearsals," where we went through the whole repertoire to make sure what was on paper was accurate, note for note. Just as important, the rehearsals were essential for my own comfort level and to help me commit my part to memory.

At showtime, the orchestra gasped and chuckled when Raffi and I made our entrance similarly attired. Like me, he was wearing a Hawaiian shirt and moccasins that I had lent him. The lively afternoon began with an unusual version of *The More We Get Together*, "for my name is *your* name, and *your* name is *my* name!"

In 1983, Christmas came in May and June. That's when I was recording my Christmas album at Inception Sound, once again with Ken's help. Given the warm weather, we brought in a string of colored lights to put us in a snowy mood.

In the planning sessions, the Committee and I consciously stayed away from an overtly religious repertoire, opting for a blend of festive favorites. However, there was one well-known song we discarded, the one advising children not to shout, pout or cry. The idea of kids being "bad or good" and only getting presents for the latter was contrary to our vision of the child as a whole person. After all, what adult can be said to be simply bad or good? The repertoire did include an accordion-laden *Petit Papa Noël* and the country-flavored *Christmas Time's A-comin'*. Among the other musical delights was a studio appearance by the Canadian Brass, a renowned quintet (now disbanded), who added to the album's festive ring.

The really big news that year came from Ottawa: I had been included in the annual selection of Canadians for investiture into the Order of Canada.

I was totally taken aback by this honor. My first reaction was to wonder why my father hadn't received the award after all he had done for government figures with his pioneering art in color portraiture. But then, as Deb and I let the news soak in, I was very happy about it, for me, for Deb and for our work together. I felt I was receiving this recognition on behalf of the work itself—that of promoting the dignity of children and their shining light. Deb and I were off to Ottawa for the ceremony.

Inside Rideau Hall, while a string quartet played, I thought about the number of times my parents and Onnig had been welcomed in this place by governors-general when Cavouk had taken their official photographs. Curiously, on this auspicious occasion, I also began to think of the original dwellers of this land in their native home, long before the Europeans arrived. Pondering the name Canada—derived from the Iroquoian word *kanata*, meaning village or meeting place—I found my mind wandering to the sixth-grade murals of a Huron village, and "native" names like Toronto and Ottawa.

Before I knew it, my name was called. Governor-General Ed Schreyer presented me with my medal and a personal greeting for Arto and Lucie. It was a proud moment. I was exhilarated by the occasion and the wonderful evening Deb and I shared.

In the morning, I phoned my very excited parents and told them all about it. Arto invited us to the studio for a sitting, before I had to return my rented tuxedo. The result was wonderful, and the portrait still hangs in my office.

By late fall, *Raffi's Christmas Album* was everywhere and I embarked on a Canadian tour—my first-ever with the band. Audiences loved the show and belted out their Christmas favorites, especially *Must Be Santa*. For an encore, we slipped on our red tour toques and tip-toed onto the stage to wild applause. Booked by Toronto promoter Rob Bennett (a friend from my university days and a big fan), the tour was very successful and the publicity it generated sold lots of "product." So much so that at the tour's end in Convocation Hall, I could hardly believe my eyes: the A&M brass walked into my dressing room with a platinum award for 100,000 sales of the Christmas album.

* * *

All this success didn't make for the easiest family gatherings on Melrose Avenue. When Deb and I went over for birthday or holiday dinners,

Arto and Lucie were so delighted with news about concerts and music sales that, if unrestrained, my career stories could dominate the table talk. I know it wasn't easy for Onnig and Ani at times to hear it all. Not that they weren't happy for us—far from it. It's just that sibling rivalry has a way of persisting far longer than useful, especially in a family with very critical parents. And naturally I was excited to share the latest developments. Try as I might to be sensitive, I know I went overboard sometimes without even being aware of it. At least talk of my career was a diversion from the many tensions that were an intractable part of these occasions.

Oddly enough, over time I came to play the role of mediator in many Cavoukian family squabbles, but mostly between Onnig and our parents. Lucie called me the Kissinger of the family.

There were aspects of mediating that I enjoyed. It taught me a lot about how truth has many faces and about how old emotional wounds often make common ground hard to find. I came to see that people don't hear each other when emotions rule and dramatics are involved. It calls for every ounce of ingenuity to create a mood or space that conflicting parties may share, however briefly, before retreating to entrenched positions.

In 1982, it was Cavouk Week at the Colonnade, in honor of my father's fifty years in portraiture. One evening on the mezzanine, in front of the studio, a glittering party took place attended by more than one hundred invited guests. I arranged for a harpist to provide live music and Ani acted as emcee for the evening. She introduced Lucie and Onnig, who spoke for the studio because my father's speech had been adversely affected by Parkinson's disease. Among the assembled dignitaries who paid tribute to Arto, Lucie and Onnig was former Governor-General Roland Michener.

If ever there was a time when Arto could have handed over the reigns of the studio to Onnig, this might have been it. His son had dutifully stood behind him for almost twenty years, most of the time working at the back, doing the bulk of the printing and developing. While Onnig also assisted during sittings, Arto was the sole photographer for many years, except occasionally when he was out of town.

Onnig had been vitally important to the success of the business, but his contribution wasn't clearly visible. I tried unsuccessfully to get through to Arto and Lucie on this matter a number of times. But the decades-long power struggles in the family made for frustrations all around. Arto seemed to want something that he wasn't likely to get: an overt display of passion for photography from the son who had not chosen this work. Lucie wasn't about to let go her position at the studio. So even if Arto did step back to let Onnig assume the helm, Onnig would have to share the confines of that small space with Lucie—an arrangement that wasn't going to work either. Realistically, Onnig would need new help to manage the studio and attract clientele.

When the conflict finally came to a head, a difficult and uneasy transition was negotiated. Arto and Lucie would stay home and, with the understanding that Arto would still take the occasional sitting, they agreed to let Onnig run the business. I helped put an ad in the paper, interview applicants and hire someone to assist Onnig in his new position. In many ways, the change was hardest for Lucie, whose whole life revolved around her friends at the Colonnade and the artistry she and her husband had shared for so long.

Ani's professional career was on a different track entirely. After receiving her PhD in Psychology from the University of Toronto, she got a job in 1980 as a senior researcher in the Ministry of the Attorney General for Ontario. A year later, she was appointed Chief of Research Services. After six years there, she moved on to the Information and Privacy Commission.

Ani actually had a second full-time job: fending off Lucie's constant nagging to find someone to marry. Between that and the frequent distress calls from various family members, life was hopping. She and I often put our heads together to see if we could sort out one family matter or another. Not working in the family business allowed us a clearer view of the dynamics that greatly challenged relations inside the studio, contrary to all outward appearances.

Lucie's wish for more grandchildren just wasn't getting the cooperation of her younger son and daughter. Ani wasn't likely to have any kids outside marriage. As for me and Deb, much as we loved children, neither one of us had felt the urge to have kids of our own. We had talked about it, of course, on a number of occasions, always coming around to the same conclusion: that we might adopt a child some day.

Deb and I felt the world was already overcrowded and so many children needed good homes. But it was more than that. Without a strong desire to produce our own offspring, we didn't see the point in having kids just because people wanted us to. "Maybe that's not what we're meant to do in this life," we'd say, noting that parenting wasn't a fulfillment issue for either one of us. Besides, there was no shortage of children in our lives.

SINGING IN AMERICA

Sold-out concerts in Carnegie Hall, success in Peoria, Wolf Trap, Tanglewood, Nashville and Broadway: how was I to know in 1980 that all this lay ahead of me, and that America would go for my music in such a big way?

It all started with a plant-the-seeds campaign that Troubadour did in 1979. Things were humming along very well in Canada, and we were getting mail from people in the U.S. who had got hold of my records (through friends or relatives) and were writing to say how much they enjoyed the music. This gave me the idea of sending a free copy of

Singable Songs for the Very Young to more than 200 nursery school associations in the U.S. with an introductory covering letter and an order form to allow group mail order purchases.

The response was terrific. In addition to lots of individual replies, there were a couple of big orders. We were excited to learn that our American neighbors reacted as we hoped they would: children and parents alike found the songs irresistible.

Around this time, Mike Mulholland had found a small distributor to act as an outlet for our music in the "educational" market. It was also arranged that I would give my first workshop to American teachers, in Biloxi, Mississippi. Glenn and I flew down with a sense of excitement, but there were more than a few butterflies in my stomach. I needn't have worried. Not only did my presentation go well, but all the teachers wanted to buy *Singable Songs* for their classrooms. Excitedly, I phoned home to tell Deb the news. From this one session, I knew our records would be a big hit across the U.S.

Success south of the border didn't come overnight; it grew gradually but steadily through a lot of hard work by the Troubadour staff. A key factor was that the music found its way to children's toy and book stores—the specialty shops. Once available in these outlets, our records quickly became their best-selling children's recordings. Soon people began to ask if I would be available for concerts.

This was the case in Portland, Oregon, the site of my first public concert in the U.S. For some time, my music had been sold by A Children's Place, a lovely little bookstore catering to a clientele that cared about quality books for children. Proprietors Jan Bruton and Lynn Kelly gave the kind of personal service that helped the records sell, and soon this created demand for a live performance. "A Young Children's Concert with Raffi" the posters said, and the fans bought lots of tickets—so many that we needed two separate shows in the 500-seat theater to accommodate the 950 people who came to listen and sing. And sing they did, young and old. They stomped their feet, clapped their hands, bumped up and down in their little red wagons, and shook their sillies out. Jan and Lynn were delighted, made lots more sales on the spot, and sent their customers home happy. I was thrilled: my American debut had been a great success.

After the show, I sat in the lobby and greeted my smiling young fans and their parents. There were so many people that signing autographs took as long as the show itself. It was a happy fatigue that carried me back to the hotel for a rest and a dinner to celebrate and review the day.

The success of this appearance gave us the confidence to book concerts with other proprietors of specialty shops. Nancy O'Conner of the Rutabaga Bookery in Dallas was a big early booster, and I still have the huge stuffed polar bear she gave me after one of our sold-out concerts in the Lone Star State. (The bear's name is Ursula, and she sits in my living room, giving much enjoyment to children who come to visit.)

California also welcomed Raffi from the start. First it was Laurie Sale at the Children's Book and Music Center in Santa Monica, where sales were brisk; then teacher Bev Bos in Sacramento, teacher and consultant Shirley Handy, and Linda and Dennis Ronberg of West Coast distributor Linden Tree. They all went out of their way to sing the music's praises and keep the sales moving.

Minneapolis rolled out the concert welcome mat, big time. Cynthia Gerdes, owner of Creative Kidstuff, really got into it, selling countless concert tickets—and product to boot. Her enthusiasm was contagious, and it spread from her equally excited staff to the grown-up fans, the kids, and Glenn and me. The shows got rave reviews in the papers, and we sensed the beginnings of American Raffimania.

The coming months and years came to show that my U.S. experience was not a regional success but a national phenomenon. I learned that when Americans like something, they let you know, and that when they are moved by a loving musical presentation that touches their kids and enriches family life, they are very vocal in their praise. This increased the demand for personal appearances, and soon Glenn was putting together small U.S. tours like the ones we enjoyed in Canada.

Glenn worked hard to help bookstore owners and educators new to concert presentation do both the big and little things needed to ensure a pleasurable experience for all. For example, he'd suggest that organizers rent extra lamps to augment the limited lighting facilities of a high school auditorium. (Glenn stressed that sound and light "production values" were important to the optimum musical performance that artist and audience both wanted.) Or he'd suggest that the concert presenter put only a work phone number on the poster, to avoid getting hundreds of calls at home.

We cared about what we were doing: we cared for the children, the parents who brought them and the growing number of people who organized the shows.

What a way to see the USA—in a rented car, taking in the scenery and being greeted warmly and applauded wherever I went. We made wonderful friends in college towns like Columbia, Missouri, and Madison, Wisconsin, traveling through cornfields of the heartland, crossing the desert lights of the southwest. From Spokane to Boston, in small towns and in the big cities, people loved the concerts for my gentle approach and humor as much as the songs themselves. Our "amateur" concert promoters brought in special catered foods and also welcomed us in their homes for dinners, after which we often talked about children and learning long into the night.

Even my New York debut was a hit. Sponsored by Hunter College, two complete sell-outs preceded my concerts in the big city. At dinner our hosts said how pleased they were to find in my music the values that they loved in the popular folk music of the '60s and '70s. The next day at Symphony Space, I sang with gusto and the audience was in fine form. After the show, when Deb and I arrived at a reception thrown for us by one of the organizers, we entered the apartment to prolonged applause. It was something out of a movie, this being treated like Pavarotti.

By 1983, Troubadour reached the one million mark in overall unit sales. This called for another celebration, so Deb and I invited Bonnie and Bert to join us for a weekend in New York. We stayed at the Plaza

Hotel and kicked up our heels. And there was more celebrating ahead: we soon got word from A&M Records in Canada that the parent company in Los Angeles had requested a meeting to discuss U.S. distribution. Not only had we racked up impressive tallies at home, but the U.S. numbers, thanks to a New Jersey educational distributor named Kimbo, had also been very respectable.

For any Canadian artist to have a U.S. record contract was a big deal. For an independent Canadian label to gain national distribution south of the border was a major coup.

But that's exactly what landed in our laps in 1984 when Troubadour signed a six-year distribution agreement with A&M U.S., a significant contract for a number of reasons. All six of my recordings were included, as were three of Fred Penner's, with no proviso for new product (new recordings) within a specified time. Though this last point was unusual in the record industry, we argued successfully that, since the existing titles were perennial sellers (with a new audience for them every three years), A&M was already getting six "new" albums within the term of the agreement.

As was the case in Canada, this was a "clean license" deal, whereby Troubadour retained full ownership of its music, only leasing the rights for sale in America. Once again, I had secured my artistic freedom and the right to approve how my music was sold. This latter point was especially important to me, because children's products in the U.S. were usually marketed on Saturday morning TV shows using cartoon characters, and through commercial endorsements with breakfast cereal or toy companies. We had been up front with A&M as to our reservations about children and television, and made clear our refusal to cash in on our success by "going commercial." Whatever our sales indicated, the integrity of our work and its child-centered focus spoke clearly of our true mission.

In the mid-1980s, a number of celebrities and their kids came to my concerts and visited me backstage. Among these were some comedians

I was very fond of: in San Francisco, the one-and-only Robin Williams, and in L.A., the Second City (SCTV) gang of Dave Thomas, Rick Moranis and John Candy. I was beside myself and literally on the floor laughing when John and I did a few lines of his "Schmenge Brothers" routine. "Oh yeeess," we joked, "the coffee is hot and delicious, just like Mrs. Viviatchke's cabbage rolls!" I was in heaven.

An unusual meeting during this time occurred in 1986 when Deb and I flew to Rochester, New York, to see our friend Steve Rifkin and his work with a play called *PeaceChild*, a musical about Russian and American kids dreaming about the end of the Cold War. The moving stage action wasn't the only entertainment in store for us that night.

Steve had told us that he had someone he wanted us to meet: Stas Namin, the foremost rock star in the Soviet Union at that time (with sales of reputedly forty million records). As it happened, Stas and his band were part of the evening's entertainment, on their first tour of America. After the play ended, they took the stage.

Wearing a light blue silk shirt and dark blue vest, the long-haired, bearded Stas said in broken English, "Excuse us, please. We have no pyrotechnics, so we just jam for you." The band was good and the songs were catchy. Later, Steve took us backstage to meet the rock star he insisted was Armenian. No way, I thought, not with that name of his. When we were introduced and Stas spoke to me in Russian (through an interpreter), I asked him about being Armenian. Yes, he said he was. But what about the name? I asked. Namin was his mother's name, he replied, and "Stas is short for Anastas."

"Like Anastas Mikoyan," I offered.

"Yes, he was my grandfather."

"That's amazing!" I went on. "My father has photographed Mr. Mikoyan." And just as my hands were making the rectangular shape of the portrait, Stas's eyes opened wide.

"I have that very portrait in my apartment!" he said excitedly.

Two unlikely Armenian acquaintances from thousands of miles apart, we fell into a big bear hug. Stas handed me his business card and invited me to call him next time I was in Moscow. Arto and Lucie howled with amazement when we told them about our unexpected encounter. They remembered a young man clad in blue jeans in the Mikoyans' *dacha* some years ago.

INNER JOURNEYS

IN THE MIDST OF THE EUPHORIC SUCCESS I WAS EXPERIENCING during this time were the less visible signs of career stress. The light that shone on my professional work didn't filter down to the inner spaces of my being.

At first it's hard to know what's troubling you when, by all exterior markers, you seem to have it all and should be ecstatic. (You have no business feeling sad or troubled, I told myself, with some guilt. If *you* can't be happy, who can?) But, of course, inside is where we live. Gradually I began to take stock of the things about myself that were puzzling me and seemed contrary to the person I thought I was.

Already inclined to examine my behavior, I caught frequent glimpses of what was bothering me. I don't mean the disagreements and arguments we all have with others from time to time, but rather the way I related to people and situations. Like my father, I had the habit of seeing what was wrong or missing in things at first glance. This trait made me a very demanding person with perfectionist tendencies. At times I thought this was merely how artists saw what was missing in the world so that they could make their mark and add their perspective.

Hard as I was on others, I was hardest on myself. I was deeply insecure and worried constantly about what people thought of me. In social situations, if I said one thing that might have sounded stupid or embarrassing in some way, I spent the next day or two thinking about it and feeling ashamed. And yet, at the same time, I felt a peculiar contempt for others, a feeling difficult to place, but probably the arrogant flip side of insecurity—a grudging intolerance of other ways, as if I knew best.

When Bonnie, Bert, Deb and I were planning one of the early albums, I recall being upset when the three of them were having too good a time—as if we had to do serious work before we could have fun, as if the two were mutually exclusive. It was just how I was, unable to relax and be in the moment. I had a controlling disposition that kept a tight grip on things, and I often got very upset when they didn't go my way. Mood swings left me wondering if I was manic-depressive. From the exhilarating highs I would come crashing down, sometimes losing my motivation for two or three days.

On top of all this, I still had a propensity for feeling easily insulted and offended. Punctuality became an obsession, as if someone being late was an insult to my busy schedule. I generally avoided confrontation, possibly because I was afraid of the anger in me and its possible consequences. If I was upset by something at work, I'd want others to feel that way too. This put a lot of pressure on my co-workers.

I was so absorbed with my role in the limelight and so accustomed to being the center of attention that it was often hard to find balance offstage, at work or at home. It was hard for me to be in a conversation that didn't revolve around me or my work. Although I talked often and at length to Deb about her work, her professional world sometimes felt remote and secondary to me.

At Troubadour there had been much talk about the child as a whole person and the factors that affected the child's well-being. Deb would tell me about kids in kindergarten who were already exhibiting symptoms of problematic behavior, and our conversations touched on issues such as the home environment and the quality of parental care. Wanting to be knowledgeable about my young audience, I became fascinated with how human behavior was shaped from the beginning of life.

What was the making of a person? What made a child a healthy person, and how did the idea of wholeness apply to adults?

For the first time, I started to think in depth about my own childhood and adolescence. And perhaps for the first time I started to see the effects of my own upbringing on my current adult behavior.

The child development books I was reading pointed me towards books on psychology. It was not Freud's ideas, but the work of Carl Jung that captured my interest, as did the work of Jungian analyst Marion Woodman. I was deeply moved by her writings about the struggle to become conscious, and the role of dreams; about the wisdom of the body and the search for personal identity; and about her celebration of the feminine both in men and women. Reading Woodman brought me face to face with matters pertaining to my inner world that were calling for attention.

In yoga classes we had often discussed the problems posed by the self-centered ego and the need, instead, for us to feel a broader kinship with the vast mystery of Creation—each as a child of the universe. Yet the very process of "self-realization," even with its goal of realizing one's divine heritage, involves focusing on the self, and the ego has a way of barking loudest when you think it has been quieted. At the very least, it wants praise—for meditating, for being good, for being on a spiritual path. To make matters worse, it can feel superior and self-righteous. We were therefore taught to be wary of spiritual pride.

At the same time, we also learned there was no point getting in our own way, curbing the ego to the point where our personal power was diminished and self-doubting created other kinds of problems. That I could understand.

So maybe the idea was for the ego to avoid the low road of petty personal politics in favor of acting in service of a higher road—a healthy ego aligned with "higher self." But how did you get there? I wondered. How did you achieve that kind of balance? And where did personality fit into this? *Be Here Now* (a classic book on spiritual consciousness by Ram Dass) was good advice, but just reading it over and over and practicing the idea wasn't enough. And we couldn't all go to India and hang out with gurus.

For all the spiritual books I had read and the meditation and yoga I'd done, I still had many questions about being *in* the world and not *of* it. Spiritual work raised life's moral and ethical questions with a view to transcendence, though in my experience it didn't delve into the everyday character of the psyche and childhood's role in its formation.

I was starting to wonder if spiritual work really changed you all that much. Sure, it felt good to acquire some positive habits on the path, like being less judgmental and more compassionate, and your external behavior might appear to be different. But did it change you deep down inside? Did it really bring a shift on an emotional level, or were you just walking around with a new lingo and new airs?

By comparison, psychology was about accessing the experience of the early years of childhood for what it might bring to adult awareness. It involved intense inner work, a process of illuminating acquired emotional patterns with the goal of transforming the negative core beliefs underlying those patterns into a healthy experience of self (a more modest goal than attaining Nirvana). I felt that this was where I could begin a renewed journey that would provide fertile ground for growth.

This sense was confirmed when I got together with Tanis Helliwell, an unusual counselor who was as comfortable dealing with spirit as she was exploring the psyche. I felt an immediate trust with Tanis. I could see that she was committed to working with what I brought forward, rather than imposing her ideas. Her way was to ask me what *I* thought about what I had just said, or what *I* understood about a dream I'd just had. Of course her clear and honest feedback helped me sort things out and provided wonderful insights, but she always looked to what came out of my own words and reflections. Tanis gave me the sense that it was me who was doing the uncovering work. And because it was safe to say absolutely anything I needed to say, including challenging anything that she said, I felt completely accepted for who I was. Hungry for understanding, I made the decision to pursue emotional growth with a passion. We worked together for a number of years, off and on, whenever we were both in town. It was to be a path of boundless learning.

Even after my first session, a couple of important realizations dawned on me: first, within myself I had not really made peace with my parents as I had thought; and second, despite being happily married and a successful entertainer loved by millions, I felt a growing sense of aloneness.

By my mid-thirties, I thought that my reasonably good relationship with my parents meant that my feelings towards them were okay and, I supposed, "grown-up." They were very happy with Deb and me, and we saw them often, mostly for lunch on weekends. And they loved attending my Toronto concerts. The public display of my success made them proud and gave them a great deal of pleasure. But for me, learning about what children need in order to grow into healthy and loving adults opened the way to examine the parenting I myself had received.

Although the feeling of aloneness was harder to get at, Tanis found a way. I had been telling her about my positive thinking and went on and on about how much was positive in my life. She was able to discern that I had painted myself into a somewhat unreal "everything's fine" box, albeit now with a murmur of discontent. Tanis said that when we take a positive quality and overplay it, in its excess it can become the opposite of its value. A strength becomes a weakness.

Over the previous few years I had fashioned an image of myself that was brimming with positives, underlined by getting accolades for making responsible, upbeat music for children and families. What Tanis showed me was that my public persona, the role model I had become professionally, couldn't express my whole being, warts and all. She explained that the persona of a public figure, if not integrated with other aspects of the self, could be a bigger problem than for most people because it played on such a large stage. Nevertheless, what was repressed would eventually, often through dreams and the unconscious, want to surface.

Along the way, Marion Woodman's writings both stirred my psyche and comforted me. Like the sessions with Tanis, where I felt accepted and understood at a deep level, I found in Woodman's book *The Pregnant Virgin* (which Bonnie introduced me to) guiding principles for authentic being that rang true, page after page. Her words spoke to me about the lack of personal boundaries in my family as I was growing up, the suffocating maternal love and the dominant paternal love that obscured my sense of self:

> The child, whether seven or seventy, can only break that unconscious bond with the mother world when it realizes it has a soul of its own, which has been born onto this earth through the body of the mother but does not belong to her (or to anyone else).
>
> At the deepest levels, most children know they do not "belong" to their parents; they feel their sense of unity with all life.

The words reminded me of a piece from *The Prophet* by Kahlil Gibran, one that made an impression on me when I first read it, and one that speaks to me still. It's the passage where he says that our children are not our own, but that they are "the sons and daughters of Life's longing for itself." Gibran writes that children come through us but not from us, and that we may house their bodies but not their souls.

As for a wholeness of being, I learned that it was vital to look within at one's shadow side—the "not nice" side that we all have, the dark places where we have locked away the demons that trouble us and the parts of our psyche that we don't like. As Woodman says, "Since the natural gradient of the psyche is toward wholeness, the Self will attempt to push the neglected part forward for recognition."

Tanis confirmed what my readings were telling me. To be aware of the emotional patterns that drive us in adult life, we need to understand the adult modeling that we internalized in the early years, primarily that of our parents.

I learned that alongside the many gifts of being born into my family, negative aspects of my "internalized parents" could (and did) thwart my best intentions to be myself. If I wanted to disarm them, it would help to access my "inner child" and allow that child's feelings, long buried in the unconscious, to be felt and expressed. I had read that most people have difficulty with doing this because at some point it involves feeling the anger of that child towards the parents, yet they continue to defend their parents' past actions rather than aligning with their inner child.

However, it is important to emphasize that the idea is not to blame parents for the sake of blaming. It's just that in order to heal the childhood trauma, the shame and anger stored in the psyche and in the body needs—for a while—to be directed at its source, which is almost always the parental dealings with the child. I was greatly relieved to learn that such articulation does not have to happen face to face. It can be poured out in a journal or in a letter written and not mailed or, ideally, shared with a therapist. The point is to acknowledge and feel the emotions, and thus vent them. Without doing this, ironically, the *subconscious* blaming of parents continues and the victim mentality prevails.

Prompted by such reasoning, I delved further into the process. Looking at a small black-and-white photo of me on the beach when I was four, I began a dialogue with this melancholy child, "Little Raffi" as I called him. I would talk to him and he would speak to me, answering my questions. It was amazing how much this helped me access the memories and feelings of those early years that I had forgotten. I recalled how it felt for me to grow up in my family. Previously, I'd simply been telling Tanis the facts of my upbringing and how my parents dealt with me, and I had noted the sadness of that sharing.

Now, hearing Little Raffi, I cried—for the first time in years—for that frightened little boy, and began to take stock of the considerable anger still inside me, not far from the sadness.

In the safety of my therapy sessions, I continued to cry. But I also roared my wrath like a lion, like a protective mother bellowing at anyone who might hurt her cub. To my astonishment, feeling and expressing such explosive anger didn't bring the world to an end. On the contrary, the feelings subsided after they were brought fully out into the open. What lay underneath was a powerful self-love that would not be denied.

The thirty-eight-year-old that I was knew it was now up to *me* to claim the love I needed and deserved and, in the same breath, nurture Little Raffi as he began to heal. I wrote a rebirthing song for him and sang it every day for weeks. I saw that child for the beautiful innocent he was, comforted him with assurances of my love and the love of God (the Divine Parent) that brought us here. In my unconditional acceptance, the child broke free of the internalized judgmental realm that had bound its every move. It was a feeling of growing up—this transformation from a punitive relationship with my inner child to a loving and accepting one.

In what felt like a joining of spirit and psyche, I was able to see my mother and father as children of the universe too, here by divine love, but very much the product of their own upbringing. Realizing that my parents were incapable of seeing me in childhood as I needed to be seen brought, along with sadness, a great release. I cried for them as well, and for their own difficult path in the world (and that of their parents before them). Within this wider understanding, I knew that it was my newly claimed wholeness that would nourish me—adult and child. Once I grasped that, I no longer looked to Arto and Lucie for self-approval or idealized them. I came to accept them for themselves, for the people they were, perhaps for the first time in my life.

Sharing any of this with my parents wasn't possible, as I found out even the first time I tried to broach the subject. I could see that neither of them was interested or capable of appreciating what I wanted to say. That stung a little, but it was all right; I had made the effort to communicate. More importantly, I knew I had done the work where it most counted—within myself.

Throughout all this I also learned that the subconscious continuously orchestrates events, failures and successes, setting up situations full of opportunities for emotional growth. Like in the Rolling Stones song, you get what you need (whether you want it or not). Whatever your core issues, events give you the chance to replay them—either to repeat existing patterns or to recognize and learn from them, growing in the process.

But the road home is full of pitfalls.

For a perfectionist, the spiritual path offers an irresistible high road of noble conduct against which you can always feel inadequate. I once asked a noted actor if his guru of many years (whom he was always talking about) was the center of his life. Quite agitated, he said, "No! I wish I could answer yes, but that's what I'm striving for." He then added, "It's like an onion, we have so many layers to peel off," implying spiritual growth was an unending task. I could see that my question had really distressed him. What about loving the whole onion as you go, I asked, so that you're not postponing self-love and peace of mind?

The offerings of the professed New Age field do not, in my view, necessarily bring insights into the emotional realm. Take "wellness" for example. There's not supposed to be anything wrong with you— if there is, blame it on toxins, physical and spiritual and do a cleanse, drink wheatgrass, and slow down. Or maybe it's "past life" stuff—try hypnotic regression, change your "channeler" and wake up. Even the idea of "joyful bliss" can be as heavy as any cross you choose to bear, if failing to achieve it leaves you plagued by inadequacy. You can lose yourself to perpetual healing, get stuck in victim mode, and workshop till you drop.

The psychological path can be just as confounding to those on a quest for unconditional self-love and personal integration. If we do the inner journey thinking that at some point we should "have it together" or have fewer problems, we're only creating another barrier to self-acceptance, living in the future instead of in the present mind-body onion.

I learned that living in the present means trusting that the storms we encounter are part of the experience, knowing they'll clear, and looking with love at how we respond to the dynamics of everyday life. Once we stop whipping ourselves for mistakes and start understanding what's going on within us, the learnings will come, guilt will subside and we'll breathe a lot easier.

It took me years to realize I had acquired a career that allowed me to give children the kind of consideration I lacked as a child. At times I felt I couldn't do enough for my young audiences. With the children, I would be so gentle, patient and understanding. For ten years I greeted my fans after every one of my concerts, for periods often longer than the show itself. (It was exhausting.) In the studio, money was no object when I was striving for the quality I wanted to give to my fans.

Of course it's wonderful to be so caring and attentive, and there's nothing wrong with striving for excellence. But I began to look at the motivation behind my behavior. Did it spring from the joy of being? Or was it coming from a drive to prove something, to earn love or win approval?

At the height of my career, my personal identity was so wrapped up in work that I seldom could read a book without relating it in some way to my fans and my career. I felt I had to make use of what I was learning, and it was hard to do anything just for the simple pleasure of it. Gradually, however, I began to see how vital it was to bring some balance and proportion into my life.

Another source of insight that came my way during these years was the work of Alice Miller, psychoanalyst and author. In books such as

Thou Shalt Not Be Aware, The Drama of the Gifted Child and *For Your Own Good,* Miller has written extensively of early childhood and the origins of violence. From *The Drama of the Gifted Child*:

> [We] gain our lost integrity by choosing to look more closely at the knowledge that is stored inside our bodies and bringing this knowledge closer to our awareness. . . . We become free by transforming ourselves from unaware victims of the past into responsible individuals in the present, who are aware of our past and are thus able to live with it.
>
> Most people do exactly the opposite. Without realizing that the past is constantly determining their present actions, they avoid learning anything about their history. . . . They are driven by unconscious memories and by repressed feelings and needs that determine nearly everything they do or fail to do.

Miller shed light on the prevalence of child abuse in Western society and broadened its definition to include not only physical and sexual abuse, but also emotional maltreatment. She viewed the traditional child rearing our parents and grandparents received as "poisonous pedagogy," a manipulative and humiliating upbringing of children with little or no regard for their feelings. This pedagogy, she explained, is unconsciously passed on from one generation to the next, unless the parent understands how the child in him or her was treated, and takes the liberty of feeling the outrage of that childhood coercion in order to heal the old wounds.

I had previously read a book that eloquently expressed how adults misinterpret children's behavior (Eda Le Shan's *The Conspiracy Against Childhood*) and another that warned about the effects of accelerated adult experience on kids (Marie Winn's *Children Without Childhood*). From these I had already learned much and done considerable reflecting on the issues they raised.

So, by the time I got to Alice Miller, her explanation of poisonous pedagogy gave me an "Aha!" insight into the epidemic of child sexual abuse and the widespread defamation of the child in our society. As Miller says:

As long as this child within is not allowed to become aware of what happened to him or her, a part of his or her emotional life will remain frozen, and sensitivity to the humiliations of childhood will therefore be dulled. (*For Your Own Good*)

In order to become whole we must try . . . to discover our own personal truth, a truth that may cause pain before giving us a new sphere of freedom. If we choose instead to content ourselves with intellectual "wisdom," we will remain in the sphere of illusion and self-deception. (*Drama of the Gifted Child*)

The societal tragedy involving the violations of childhood began to make sense to me. I felt a profound sadness for the countless wounded souls who, as a result, suffer such twisted lives in all manner of reaction and rebellion. I thought a lot about the prolonged effects of such intergenerational violence on our social institutions, and the almost unimaginable toll on the human spirit and the welfare of the common good.

In my own observations, it became clear that in spite of all the advances we'd made (less corporal punishment, more caring fathers), children were still a minority group unlike any other. We are still largely unaware of the biases we hold towards children. What other members of society do we still openly laugh at, in their presence, even if what they say is not meant to be funny? For who else is it still acceptable to use derogatory names like "monster" and "rugrat"? Why are caregivers and teachers of the very young the lowest-paid teaching professionals and shown little respect? Why are they not accorded the status and prestige of, say, college professors? Given that childhood forms the person, what does the above say about how society sees children, and—just as important—what does this mean for the adults they become?

The empathy that I had felt for children at the start of my work had come a long way. Child development professionals and psychologists had opened windows on the growing child and its struggle for dignity. In these windows, I saw myself and fought for life.

The experience of pain and recovery turned into a gift greater than my personal healing—it was the gift of a deeper empathy with the colonialized minds and hearts of all children. Self-esteem, the centerpiece of character and the soul's agent in this world, was what I knew I would defend and strive to promote for children in any way I could.

CAREER CHOICES

THE WHIRLWIND OF SUCCESS CAN BECOME A HURRICANE THAT sweeps you away if you are not grounded in the center of yourself and your purpose. I suppose that might be true in any business, but it is especially so in show biz, where you are front and center in the spotlight. Throughout the rise in album sales and public acclaim, I was tested by the winds of fame and fortune. Fortunately, from the beginning, I wasn't interested in the fast track to riches and celebrity. Even my earlier folksinger dreams had been modest, so when a trickle turned into a stream and the stream into gold and platinum, I managed for the most part to stay grounded.

The material seductions were certainly there. Troubadour had lots of money in its cash flow, and Deb and I had a lot in our bank accounts. Business lunches became common and the restaurants got better and better. It was a lovely feeling, being able —without a second thought—to warm up a dreary winter's day with a meal at Fenton's in midtown Toronto. Fine wines and savory dishes have a way with you and, when you work hard to achieve success, you tell yourself that you deserve it all. I got to taste the power that comes with money and privilege.

After my initial look at economics in university, I hadn't learned much more about money and how it moves. Other than having a basic understanding of cash availability, profit margins, interest rates and bank loans, I knew little else about the world of economic and financial activity. I didn't go in for fancy investment schemes, preferring to keep to modest gains from the bank's various term deposit plans. One day when our coffers were full and I was given another large bonus, I had a talk with Mike.

"Let me see if I get it," I began. "If this money is invested, it'll get more money, right?"

"Right."

"And then? If I invested *that* successfully, there's *more* money, right?"

"That's right. Raf, what are you driving at?"

"I'm not sure. It's just . . . what's the money *for?* Beyond a certain point, what *good* does it do?"

I wasn't really going anywhere with this. I was just frustrated with the idea of capital accumulating towards no apparent end. It was a concept that baffled me.

At Troubadour, we were constantly faced with choices to do with my career and where we wanted, as a company, to put our energy. I stressed that we needed to go slow enough to understand and emotionally process the changes that success was putting us through, not only in work relationships, but in the personal ones too. I hadn't started Troubadour to make money, and I became aware that I was involved in children's entertainment as a calling. This was where my musical gifts were meant to flourish, in the work of giving children songs they could make their own, with recordings and concerts that respected them as whole people.

When it came to promotional opportunities, we always asked if they fit into the Troubadour philosophy, which was shaped but not limited by my personal idiosyncrasies.

For a long time I avoided entering my name for the Junos, Canada's entertainment awards (akin to the Grammys in the U.S.). Quite simply, I didn't see much point in having a competition for "best children's recording" when children knew what they liked and could care less about a subjective selection of "winner" by an obscure process open to personal politics.

My abstention was not smart by conventional reasoning. Not only was there an opportunity cost to me and to Troubadour in passing up a chance for free publicity (and hence increased visibility and sales), but the competition gained the advantage we relinquished. I was aware of all this, but just couldn't bring myself to take part in something I didn't value. And besides, sales were excellent.

Many times I withstood Mike's impassioned pleas and those of A&M and took a pass on the Junos. While it didn't feel good to see the award go to others, I held on to the comfort of not "playing the game." Whether this meant I was not very competitive or extremely so, I'm not sure. I do know I didn't like the idea of losing. (I remembered my father did not enter his portraits in photo contests, saying he knew the value of his work and didn't need the validation of a contest that might devalue his art.)

So, even with what I felt were two of my best albums—*One Light, One Sun* (1985) and *Everything Grows* (1987)—I didn't compete for Junos. Both albums were recorded at Eastern Sound, a mid-Toronto studio where Gordon Lightfoot and Anne Murray had hit albums. There, engineer Peter Mann's fine talents guided me to great results, first with Ken Whiteley co-producing and then on my own. *Everything Grows* was my first album solo, done with arranging help from master musician Jack Lenz. And like its predecessor, it sparkled in players and repertoire. Both albums earned Parents' Choice awards in the U.S. and won the praises of critics and fans alike.

One unusual award came out of the blue. It was from the American Bowling Proprietors Association for my "contribution to Youth Bowling," in recognition of *The Bowling Song* that I wrote and recorded on *One Light, One Sun.* (The plaque still hangs in my office.)

To put it simply, I felt society was already too competitive, and that the arts were not the place to make it more so. That's better left to sports. More than once, interestingly enough, record industry people told me in private that they admired my position on the Junos.

We went through a similar process declining offers for commercial endorsements. (I had long felt that for artists to do endorsements demeaned their art.) No matter what products or monies were involved, it was our company mission that prevailed. In the long run, what we may have forfeited monetarily turned out to gain Troubadour a reputation for integrity—a prize all its own.

Credibility was worth much more to me than anything to be gained from selling fast food on TV. I wanted to be believed when I said that I cared for my audience and that I made music from my heart. And I wanted to set an example for children, to say that *purpose* was paramount in life.

By staying true to what I believed, I avoided becoming a caricature of myself, a cartoon character superstar in one marketing deal after another, with TV shows, movies and a hundred non-music products for sale—all the trappings of climbing the conventional ladder of suc-cess as a children's performer. Entertaining little children, however, had limitations I had known from the beginning. So, when I was advised to sing at New York's 18,000-seat Madison Square Gardens, with huge video screens to be installed for the benefit of those in the faraway seats, I quickly said no. Such a show might have created a media sensation, but it wouldn't have provided a quality experience for my young fans.

BIGGER AND SMALLER

SINGING WITH A DOZEN CHILDREN IN A NURSERY SCHOOL IS different than giving a singalong concert with a hundred people in a library, which is different again from performing before a full house in a 2,000-seat theater. Each situation requires different skills of the singer, both musically and socially. In a small group, there's an easy interplay and spontaneity that's awkward to match in a bigger group and almost impossible to achieve with a large crowd.

My folksinging experience served me well in performing for family audiences. Knowing how to weave the right variety of songs into a concert program was something I was familiar with. But it took some growing as a performer to get comfortable on the stage of a large theater.

I learned from experience that you could ask a small group of children an open-ended question like, "What song shall we sing next?", but, if you put the same question to a large audience, all you got was an indecipherable din. That's why in preparing for large concerts, I had to mentally go through the entire repertoire and think about the between-song patter very clearly, to avoid creating any dilemmas that might interrupt the flow of the show.

Getting ready for my first large performance, I remember looking out at 2,000 empty chairs and wondering if a participatory concert with that many children and adults could actually work. Somehow I had faith that it would and took some steps towards that goal—like going up to the balconies and checking sightlines, remembering how small many of my audience would be. I kept in mind the practical technique of projecting my performance out into the theater, and in meditative prayer I asked for blessings that the show might serve the greatest possible good.

The biggest threat to a large concert came from the littlest members of the audience—those we called the "under-two quotient." Many parents kept giving my recordings to younger and younger children and also brought these underage kids to concerts.

On posters and in media interviews, we usually advised that the concerts were for children three years old and up, and that parents should use their discretion in deciding whether their child was ready for a first concert experience. It did not occur to many parents that an infant's enjoyment of my songs in the familiarity of the living-room would not automatically translate into an enjoyable concert experience in a large auditorium.

In fact, so many children under two were brought to the concerts that the generally acceptable background noise that invariably comes with a sizable audience of young children just got too loud.

This was a problem in a number of ways. Not only did the noise affect the audience's overall experience of the show, but it made *my* job that much harder. It was tough enough to hold the attention of the very young for almost an hour of music. But when the show very much depended on the audience to sing and clap along and a great many of the fans just weren't old enough to do either, the challenge was even greater. And when I wanted to sing a quiet song (they can't all be exuberant), again it was difficult to set the right mood. Try as I might, the good strategy of "let's all take a deep breath together . . . and *gently* let it out" could only go so far.

Over the years, I talked about the problem of the under-two quotient with Deb, Bonnie and Bert more times than I care to remember. All the explaining in interviews failed to stem the tide of babies and infants. I knew that for some parents it wasn't possible to bring a four-year-old and leave the younger child at home. But my heart went out to the little ones who were simply out of place—and let it be known by their shrieks and frequent toilet sorties during the show and their sleepy, teary eyes afterwards.

A major contributing factor to all this was the popularity of my concert videos. Among my fans, video made me a TV star, despite my not having a TV series.

In 1984, Troubadour arranged for a multi-camera video shoot of a weekend of my concerts in Toronto. The finished product was a forty-five-minute video entitled, "A Young Children's Concert with Raffi," with me in a solo concert playing guitar and kazoo, sporting a dark-blue

Hawaiian shirt and beaded moccasins. This clap-happy singalong aptly captured the warm relationship between me and my fans, and the well-lit audience was as much the star of the show as the singer.

Glenn's suggestion to work with Toronto-based Devine Videoworks was a winner. Producer David Devine and associate Richard Moser put a great deal of thought and planning into this project, both during the actual shoot and in the editing process. This, along with Troubadour's input and the Committee's fine counsel, resulted in a video that offered the viewer a true taste of being at a Raffi concert. Judging by the response, we may have succeeded too well.

The Disney Channel took a liking to the video and, in early 1986, agreed to run it in its entirety. During a tour of California, shortly after that first airing, I encountered an interesting situation. When I greeted my fans after the show, I could tell those who knew me by my audio recordings from the ones who knew me because they'd seen me on Disney. How could I tell? The fans who'd seen my video considered me a TV star and, with an extra-wide look in their eyes, asked if they could take my picture.

The public's response was nothing short of phenomenal, as A&M sold over a hundred thousand videos within a couple of years. A&M president Gil Friesen had been right when he'd said that a video would broaden my audience considerably. Soon the fan mail we received echoed what Disney's viewers had written to them: families loved the video and children wanted to see it over and over again. We received this last bit of feedback with mixed emotions.

Of course, we were delighted that we'd created something that gave such pleasure and encouraged singing. But given Troubadour's concern that children were watching too much TV as it was, we had hoped that the video would be used sparingly—say as a once-a-week treat—and we said so in the parent-teacher notes packaged with each copy.

Imagine our surprise, however, when letters arrived from all over the U.S. and Canada saying, "Our two-year-old is a big Raffi fan, just adores your video, and won't go to sleep unless we show it," and

"Dear Raffi: my Mommy's writing this cause I'm only one-and-a-half, and I've been your biggest fan since I was nine months old and first saw your video!" Not exactly what we wanted to hear.

Before long, everyone was clamoring for another Raffi video. Initially, I toyed with the idea of deliberately *not* doing a second one, in part to make the strongest possible statement about children and TV. There was something about my fans' hunger (and the media clamor) for another video that irked me. Maybe it was the way TV was used so much as a babysitter, and the feeling I got from many of the letters that parents just couldn't say no to their kids or set limits. With more and more "my kid won't go to sleep if we don't play your video" letters, I wondered who was running the household—parent or child?

I had looked into the effects of TV viewing and was troubled by what I learned. Surveys revealed that young children were watching, on average, more than four hours of TV every day. This is a concern— especially for young viewers—for several reasons:

- TV viewing takes time away from children's normal developmental activities, like free time for daydreaming and imaginative play; it alters the brain waves of children, who often show aggressive behavior after the set is turned off (no matter what they have watched);
- fast-paced and quick-edited shows alter children's attention span and the ability to concentrate;
- viewing requires no skill, and is antithetical to visual skills needed for reading; what's more, children often see hostile, violent and sexually inappropriate imagery;
- so-called educational shows primarily teach children to love TV, and any learning that occurs is much thinner than that gained through interpersonal activities;
- young viewers are pitched thousands of commercials, yet they lack the discernment to evaluate them sufficiently; they absorb the invisible suggestion to grow up to be consumers; and
- the issue of "quality programming" obscures the more important issue of *quantity of viewing* regardless of programming.

This last point is all important and still not widely understood. Bert first told me about it in relating Neil Postman's idea that "it's not what they watch, it's *that* they watch." Postman, a communications professor at New York State University, was saying that no matter what the program, as long as kids watch the bright color lights of the electric screen, the physiological experience is the same.

I pondered the idea at length. When I finally got what Postman was saying, a lot of things about the frenzied behavior of "modern" kids came together. In any TV viewing, our brain waves are slowed down, imagery hits the psyche unimpeded, and we are affected far more than we realize. It is interesting to compare children who watch a lot of TV to those who are relatively TV-free and whose lives do not center around the tube.

Unlike their vid-kid counterparts, TV-free kids I know have a centered energy to them. It feels like there's somebody home in their bodies, rather than the vacant look I see in so many TV junkies. Not only are TV-free kids more capable of self-directed play, that play doesn't refer to TV but springs instead from their own imaginings. They can actually carry on a conversation using extended sentences and expressing complex thought. They also tend to be avid readers. Far from bored, they are still wonder-filled. Their curiosity is intact.

Was my video now contributing to TV's hold on children? The thought didn't sit well with me. What's more, I believed it was my video success that was causing the average age of children at my concerts to drop from four years old to about two. Parents watched their diapered infant-toddlers love every minute of the video-concert, and I could understand that they wanted to give them the real thing. But it made for a situation that could neither have been foreseen nor remedied.

The under-two quotient challenged my capacity as a performer and tried my personal patience. It was some years before I was able to resolve the matter.

TRANSITIONS

FUNNY HOW A WORD LIKE "SUBURB," WHICH SOUNDS SLIGHTLY subversive, can come to describe something quite different. Although North York was its own city, everyone (outside of its own city hall) considered it a suburb of Toronto, which it very much was.

Deb and I had moved there in 1976 to be closer to her work. We rented a place for the first few years and then bought a small house a few blocks away from the first Troubadour office (and even closer to the one that came later). We took possession of it in the spring of 1979. Then, with our stuff still in boxes, I took off for a one-week yoga retreat in Morin Heights, Quebec, an hour north of Montreal. The retreat was something that our yoga teacher had talked about for a while and I was really keen on going. Deb decided not to join me and wasn't pleased about being left behind to unpack.

The Festival of Lights, as the gathering at the Sivananda Ashram was called, featured a number of speakers and yogis from all over the world. Many people from yoga class were there, for a week of meditation, chanting, yoga and time spent talking about spiritual matters. One swami joked about not overdoing it, lest we get "spiritual indigestion." I was glad for the laugh in an otherwise intense week, the first two days of which I had a splitting headache brought on by the abrupt withdrawal from coffee.

The whole experience was an eye-opener. For one thing, the anticipated "manifestation" of the long-departed Swami Sivananda did not materialize, at least not convincingly enough for even his dearest followers. And sleeping as I was in my newly customized van, the mental will it took to wake up at 5 a.m. and have a cold shower en route to morning meditation left a lasting impression on me: you *can* do most anything you set your mind to. I made it through the showers by jumping, yelling and chanting to take my mind off the cold.

During the long drive home at the end of our stay, a few of us dropped into a highway eatery for a snack. It was like we'd landed on another planet. So attuned were our thoughts to the yogic world, its conscious diet, and a heightened awareness of every act of being that this commercial enterprise seemed sterile in comparison. Compared to the ashram, the restaurant had a totally different vibration. So much so that, after a quick look around, we just had get out of there and be content with the muffins I had in my van. The experience underscored for me that one's created environment has a huge impact on what one calls normal.

Back home, I found I was much less sensitive to cool weather than before, something I attributed to my recent routine of cold showers. For some time I continued the bracing habit, before inertia and comfort had me turning on the warm water again. Meanwhile, Deb had been busy and the house was now mostly organized. Soon we were planning renovations for a new kitchen, garden deck, a backyard fence for Bundles, and a carport.

After that work came endless repairs on the kitchen skylight that leaked. It was a rude welcome to the world of renovations, but apparently we were hooked. Phase two gave us a fireplace, an open-plan living room and hallway, "Bundles doors" to keep our beloved pooch off the furniture, a whirlpool tub in the bathroom, two small bedrooms made into one with a skylight installed over the bed, heat pump and air conditioning, and on and on. It was all mostly at my urging: we had the money, and what else was it for if not for the good life?

It was as if I had caught some affluence bug, perhaps a case of having a disposable income and wanting something tangible, something other than seeing the bank account grow. It may also have been a case of going with society's mantra that you can have it all. On the one hand, I rationalized renovation by thinking that it created work, kept money circulating in the economy and created beauty. On the other hand I was, without noticing it, living up to an affluent dream that permeated business life, especially if you got successful.

Within a few years, we were also renovating at Troubadour (again at my initiative), doing a thorough overhaul of the many rooms we rented. When we weren't touring, I spent a lot of time just planning and overseeing all this. And of course things were never quite right and seemed never quite finished. I used to get exasperated by deficiencies, by anything less than workers' best efforts. When I questioned job quality, I was told that contractors work to a "commercially acceptable" standard and that anything above that would cost more. It was enough to give a perfectionist insomnia. My dentist wanted to know if I was grinding my teeth at night.

* * *

During the mid-1980s, I was aware of a vast restlessness in me that I found hard to express. I imagine that I was a lot harder for Deb to live with than she even acknowledged at the time, given her love for me and her devotion to "the work." More than once I saw the reserve of quiet strength she drew on to see us through the tough times.

On one such occasion, when collateral was required against a bridge loan to finance a serious cash flow crunch at Troubadour, Deb and I put our house on the line. She was in tears at the thought of losing what we had, and yet she trusted my sense that Troubadour's work was meant to succeed.

If any couple ever loved each other, we surely did. We just couldn't imagine being apart, and counted how lucky we were to have found each other. But there's no denying that the demands of my career put considerable pressure on our relationship. Besides the time I was away on concert tours, it was the return to normal life that was difficult— not only for me, readjusting to life off the stage, but also for Deb, who had to get used to having me back in the house. It wasn't until much later that we figured out that my homecomings were more stressful than we realized at the time. I would have all sorts of exciting travel news to tell, and this often seemed to dwarf Deb's classroom stories. Often I wasn't able to appreciate her own local journeys.

We took trips together here and there, such as to lovely inns for weekends with friends, but my demanding ways often put an edge on things. The fact is, in this relationship I took up too much space. And perhaps, as the dominant force, I needed a stronger balance; it's hard to say. In the midst of a whole host of factors, the faded romantic elements were hard to retrieve, even while the affection between us stayed strong.

Our being engaged in individual counseling may have given us the feeling that we were dealing sufficiently with our issues. There wasn't a lack of communication between us; we talked about everything, openly and often. But sometimes, counseling can reveal that two shared world views have, over time, developed very different lenses. And two people can genuinely grow towards their life potential along different paths that do not become visible for a long time.

* * *

In the years after Deb and I left the yoga classes (after 1981), I regularly practiced the postures at home. To shed the extra pounds I gained from touring, I occasionally worked out at a local fitness club that Mike Mulholland introduced me to. I also played tennis as often as I could, usually with Mike or Deb. But try as I might, a 32-inch waist was fast becoming a thing of the past. Eventually I took up jogging on the oval track of a nearby high school in the summer months. As the sweat poured off and my lungs strained with the effort, I would think about heroic figures for inspiration. Archbishop Desmond Tutu of South Africa, Australian activist Helen Caldecott—I'd pretend I was running for them.

More often than not, weekends included invitations to my parents' or to Stan and Daphne's, and occasionally we'd have them over to our place. The Pike family had two newcomers courtesy of Deb's brother,

Tim, and his wife, Chris: two beautiful children named Amanda and David. Amanda made it onto a couple of shots in my first two videos.

The special bond I enjoyed with my sister since adolescence—when we used to commiserate about troubles with our parents—grew in the years that followed, and we maintained the close rapport that gave great comfort to both of us. Having a sister I could really talk to was truly a blessing, for she was the first in my family to have a clear understanding of who I was. Ani was a dear friend to both Deb and me and we would often socialize with her and the men in her life.

At my parents' place, the meals were getting better and better. Lucie continued to serve us veggie dishes that actually improved over time, and she took pleasure in trying out new meatless recipes. On one of our visits, Arto introduced Deb and me to Scotch. Dad liked it with ice and water. We took to the good stuff like Chivas and Glenfiddich, most often with ice, but sometimes straight up. Although the years of yoga had changed my diet, I still liked the occasional drink or two.

Watching my parents age was very difficult; I felt sad and bewildered by the changes I saw in them, but did what I could to give comfort.

I was on a concert tour when I heard the news that my father would need emergency quintuple bypass surgery. It seems that an annual heart checkup revealed trouble with Arto's primary artery. Sure enough, it was later found to be almost completely blocked—the surgery had come just in time. Arto recovered remarkably well, and before long he was in good humor. Compared to the fatigue we were used to seeing in him, now at family gatherings it was obvious he didn't miss a thing.

Lucie, though apparently in good health, was slowing down too. Sometimes, the day after she'd cleaned the house following an evening party, she'd be exhausted and say to me, "We grew old, didn't we?"

For exercise, Lucie occasionally walked a few blocks up Melrose, just like Peka Grandma had in days gone by. On one such outing, she stopped in front of number 554, the bungalow where we first lived in Toronto.

When she saw the residents, she couldn't help but let them know that this had been her first home in the new country. Then she added, "Do you know whose mother I am?" and went on to tell them all about me.

It seems that Lucie got such a charge out of telling people she was Raffi's mother that she would put the question to all sorts of people she met. When they expressed astonishment, she would smile and say, "After all, he had to have a mother too!"

Arto's health prevented him from driving the family car anymore. So, to help my parents get around town, I opened an account with a Toronto livery which supplied them with a car and driver on short notice. Arto and Lucie took a liking to this arrangement, enjoying both the practicality and the appearance of a chauffeured Lincoln sedan moving them about.

Not long after Arto entered semi-retirement, the Colonnade went through a lengthy refurbishing, during which time the Cavouks left Bloor Street. It was a difficult transitional time for my parents, and also for my brother, who took a much-needed break from the business for a few months. Arto continued, with Lucie's encouragement, taking a few photographs at the family home, but after a while he wasn't able to do any more portraiture at all.

Onnig soon set up shop in his own home, the name Cavouk once again passed from father to son. Arto now knew that his art was in Onnig's hands and he commended the growing confidence he saw in his son's work. Among Onnig's first successes was a portrait of then Chrysler chairman Lee Iacocca.

Although the Order of Canada was something that eluded Arto, 1985 brought an equally important accolade—one addressed to both my parents. It was a medal from the Armenian Church, awarded under proclamation (a *gontag*) by Catholicos Vazken I. Arto and Lucie were cited for bringing honor to the Armenian nation and to the church through the great success of their artistic endeavors. Arto was moved to tears. He told Onnig he wanted *him* to wear this medal too, to wear it with pride.

The first really good restaurant to open in North York (called Fiasco, of all things) had the Troubadour people in a buzz. By this time, Bert and I used to enjoy a martini together now and then: a dry vodka martini with olives or twist of lemon, or both. As Bert liked to say, "Halfway through the second martini is about as good as life gets." We were fond of our business dinners, where we actually did get a lot discussed, in splendid fashion. And when Deb and Bonnie joined us it was fabulous. The suburban gang of four, out on the town.

The four of us did truly have a great time whenever we got together. Simpsoni (as Deb used to refer to "B and B") were very bright and funny, and they loved children. They introduced us to *The New Yorker*. They were our best friends. In their contribution to the work of Troubadour, they played their role as members of the Committee with great kindness, humor and generosity. Never presumptuous, always there to help, Bonnie and Bert warmed our lives for many good years before the changes that later found us.

Given that Deb and Bonnie had done team teaching together and that Bert was also a primary teacher, our talks often included children and education. If it wasn't letting off steam about school politics, there were the endless stories about what certain kids had been up to or some child's unique rendering of our national anthem—"Oh Candada, gloriutz and free!" I also considered Deb, Bonnie and Bert to be as progressive, compassionate and dedicated as teachers could be. With our personal sharing and ongoing talk of childhood development, our friendship was vibrant on all levels. So, when we got together on Troubadour work, the ideas flowed.

Eventually, after Bert and I had done a good deal of "pretend talk" over Scotch (good for that kind of thing), the talk came true and Bert left teaching and joined Troubadour. Fortunately for us, Bonnie came on board a short while later.

After eleven years of teaching, Deb was also voicing tired grumblings from the schoolyard. I knew there was a growing discrepancy between my broadening touring experiences and her classroom environment.

Was it time to give teaching a break and join Troubadour? Wouldn't she like to join me on the road? We talked it over and gave it a lot of thought. When she accepted my invitation, I was elated.

Now, with the Committee's full-time engagement, our work really moved along. One immediate result was that the book side of our operation, which we called Troubadour Learning, picked up steam. Though Bert had primary responsibility here, Bonnie and Deb were also a part of the splendid *Songs-to-Read* series of picture books that New York publishers Crown did around the most familiar of my recorded songs. I got a kick out of our expanded weekly meetings, which often held as many laughs as work details. I felt uplifted to have this new level of support; it helped me face the very full agenda of my thriving career.

On tour it was a different matter. The rigors of the road—the fatigue of concerts and travel and endless interviews—were, on the one hand, comforted by Deb's presence, but at the same time made touring difficult for her. There wasn't a defined role for her to play, other than generally supporting my being in the limelight, and I didn't fully understand how tough it was on her. It didn't help that sometimes people called her Mrs. Raffi. And it certainly was unromantic that my needs (as performer) always came first during these shared travels. Spending so much time together left us with little fresh to talk about whenever the schedule allowed for a private dinner. Conversation would too easily drift to work, or to the personal dramas within our touring entourage.

* * *

The news from Los Angeles that A&M had put my name forward and got a Grammy nomination for *One Light, One Sun* as Best Children's Album bowled me over. It seemed the right time to take leave of my past awards trepidations and go for it. The New York trip was a blast for Glenn, me and Deb, and Bonnie and Bert. Losing the prize didn't dampen our spirits too much, and we had a great time at the A&M party, dressed to the nines and sipping fine champagne. That golden moment, in retrospect, seemed short-lived. A challenging time lay ahead for all of us in the coming months.

The concert touring season of October 1987 to May 1988 was, in many ways, the most challenging of all. At the height of my career, with many gold and platinum awards and sold-out concerts everywhere, there were stirrings within me that I hardly recognized. Although a change in my touring Rise & Shine Band brought a new sound to the old songs and gave the show a fresh feel, the grind of the road and the sheer number of concerts and promotional appearances wore me down.

I was hungry for days off without travel or interviews. However, the cost of touring a band with our own "sound and lights" gear and technical crew made every day on the road an expensive proposition. A family concert involved the same costs as any other theater presentation, but only half the ticket revenue, since prices needed to be kept low enough to attract a family of three or four. This meant that, on the road, days off were hard to come by.

One day I let it be known that I was considering taking some time away from touring. For the execs at A&M Records to get this news was one thing; for Deb, Bonnie, Bert and Glenn it was something else altogether. I was very much aware that my decisions affected everyone I worked with, and that the people I employed depended on me.

It's not easy to convey how tough the pressures of an entertainment career can be, especially when it's in high gear. Showbiz success gives you a most unusual form of relationship—a scale of millions to one—and celebrity's perks are certainly offset by its considerable demands. Constantly being in front of the camera, always expected to look and act your best, has an effect that can't adequately be explained to those who aren't up there on center stage. And, what's more, a children's entertainer—maybe more so than other entertainers—has to be a model of good behavior. In the times when I was very tired and stressed to the limit, it was hard to be nice to everyone.

After much thought, I told my inner circle that I wanted to take a large chunk of time away from touring. Looking back, I'd say it was burnout, even if I didn't call it that. After many seasons on the road, I had a need to stay home and watch the leaves turn color in the fall, to feel the rhythm of shortening days fading into winter and, most of all, to have very little planned. I needed a time of not knowing what came next, a time to hear my inner voice again. Deb was very understanding and supportive, even if the news may have given her cause for concern about my career. Bert and Bonnie felt the same, and we held a weekend retreat to talk about what I called "Troubadour without Raffi." I wanted to see what creative ideas we could come up with to keep my name visible in the marketplace while I was personally unavailable. I was definitely saying time out, let's take me out of the picture for a while.

I decided I needed a year—a full year—of "not knowing." That meant not planning again in six months what I'd be doing the day after the time was up, or even talking about what would come next. Although A&M was worried that sales would be in serious decline, we at Troubadour were confident all would be well. This was confirmed in the coming year, when our 1989 U.S. sales climbed to an all-time high of 900,000 units in one calendar year.

Near the end of one of these exhausting tours (whose audiences had the greatest number of children under two), there was yet one more project "before I sleep." We had decided to do another concert video after all.

In the years since the release of the first one, our many discussions about its home enjoyment brought us to accept the fact that how people used the video (that is, how often their children viewed it) was not our responsibility. And two videos, we concluded, didn't amount to "too many," and so we thought it might be fun to chronicle the musical fun of my touring band experience. This video would feature Raffi veterans Dennis Pendrith on bass and Bucky Berger on drums, and newcomers Nancy Walker on keyboards and Mitch Lewis playing guitars and mandolin.

We once again teamed up with Devine Videoworks to tape a weekend of shows from which to weave a second singalong video. Shot in the 600-seat Markham Theatre in the town of the same name (near Toronto), the concerts got good performances from both singer and audience. The band sparkled and Dave Devine's crew caught the action beautifully.

During the summer of 1988, I worked very hard to complete the editing and sound mixing of this video, a meticulous task made bearable by my good friend and engineer par excellence, Peter Mann (who had worked on the *One Light, One Sun* and *Everything Grows* albums with me). Peter's conscientious work and great sense of humor got me through a project that I sometimes doubted I could finish. All this effort paid off. The success of my video debut was about to be eclipsed by this sequel, entitled "Raffi in Concert with the Rise & Shine Band."

It seemed like a good way to enter my sabbatical, giving my fans what they'd been clamoring for and giving A&M something new to market. Totally drained by the end of the video post-production, I shifted into slow gear and wound down.

What a relief it was to slow to a halt. A pause. Some rest. Except that, at precisely this time, Deb and I moved into a new and very large home. This elegant place, with its cathedral ceilings and spacious grounds, took some getting used to, for ourselves, our friends and especially the aging Bundles. Nevertheless, we had felt we needed more space and, with business doing well, this house fit the bill. Also, it was close to Bonnie and Bert's.

Just when I most needed to rest, I had made more work for myself with the move. It was symptomatic of the unrest within me, one that was to affect Deb and me more than we could know at the time.

Things were in a state of change at work as well. We parted with Glenn, my manager of nearly ten years. Deb was now Vice-President of Troubadour, running the day-to-day operations and working closely with both Bert and Bonnie. Bert was now Director of Troubadour

Learning, while Bonnie, when she wasn't co-planning or consulting on any number of daily matters, worked with California consultant and workshop leader Shirley Handy on a *Teacher's Guide* to facilitate the use of our books and music in the classroom.

As for me, I spent a lot of time reading, meditating, following world news and mowing the lawn. Occasionally, when I couldn't keep my mind from wandering to work, I pondered the idea of entertaining older children. I needed relief from playing to underage children. My original children's recording had said on its cover "For ages 3-7." But the phrase "the very young" by now seemed to mean one- to four-year-olds. I wasn't about to get into baby music, and I felt that creatively there was little else I could do in concerts unless we addressed this issue. The Committee and I discussed whether an album aimed at older kids would be a new way for me to go. With nine albums, two concert videos and several songbooks and *Songs-to-Read*, I had achieved everything I'd set out to do in children's music (and much more).

There was a feeling that Troubadour was poised to take its success to new levels. Impressive as our sales were, we knew Raffi was not a household name in homes without young children. The Canada and U.S. markets, we felt, were not anywhere near saturation, and the overseas markets were completely untapped. We were looking for a new manager for me, and the company needed both new promotional representation and a new attorney.

Meanwhile, this whole period of change wasn't exactly smooth sailing for Deb. She was working on a number of things, but the lack of one specific area of responsibility made it hard for her to have a sense of personal accomplishment. No matter how much I stressed to her that this was *our* work, it didn't make up for what she felt was missing for her.

It's not easy to say why two people with great love for each other drift apart. By the time it was evident that our marriage was in trouble, it was clear to me that we had to go our own ways. It was the most difficult realization of my life, the path that took me away from Deb and the life that we had built together. In the midst of the crushing pain and the flood of tears, there was a quiet and firm knowing that I had to pursue a new life.

My move to a midtown apartment was the beginning of a trial separation that would become permanent. I filled the walls of my new empty spaces with the first paintings I had done since my youth, oil pastels, mostly abstract images, many female nudes. It helped to have these fledgling expressions of my emergent self greet me in these trying days.

When I broke the news to my parents, they were heartbroken for both of us. They loved Deb so much, and Lucie kept asking why this had to happen, as if to ask once more would bring a better answer. I asked her to accept that for some things there is no adequate explanation. As I sat in the living room with my head in my hands, Arto came and sat down beside me. He put his arm around my shoulders and we cried. I was deeply touched and comforted by this, and wondered how within such pain there could be such rare gifts.

Given the tight blend of our personal and professional lives, Deb and I had a great deal to untangle. Fortunately, we did it amicably. We both wanted to hold onto the best of what we knew of each other, and this helped to overcome the pain we felt. What's more, we didn't want an adversarial separation, and our personal counsel (a long-time friend of ours) supported our wish to steer an agreeable course. Doing so was an immense help to us during such a difficult transition.

V

EVERGREEN EVERBLUE

You give us each day our daily grain,
kissed by the sun and kissed by the rain.
Teach us now to find a way
to care for you in our work and play.

"Our Dear, Dear Mother"

TROUBLED WATERS

IN DECEMBER 1988, I HAD ATTENDED A SLIDE SHOW AT THE
Toronto Science Centre. The soft-spoken woman at the podium was
Leone Pippard (from Ile d'Orleans, Quebec), and she was speaking of
the plight of the population of beluga whales in the St. Lawrence River.
Living among the belugas and studying their behavior during a three-
year period had given Pippard a glimpse of something terribly wrong.
The estimated 5,000 whales at the time of World War II were now
down to around 450. Even worse, autopsies of dead belugas washed
ashore showed that the creatures had died painful deaths from cancer
and other internal failures, their flesh covered with lesions and so
riddled with toxins that the bodies were rendered hazardous waste sites.

I was stunned by the news.

I ached for the beautiful belugas whose very existence was threatened by their polluted river habitat. In fact, it was Leone Pippard who
made people aware that these whales were now an endangered
species. Baby belugas were drinking the poisoned milk of their
mothers who, at the top of the marine food chain, ingested the accumulated toxins of the entire family of marine life. And, as Leone said,
if this was happening to the whales, what was happening to the millions
of people on both sides of the river who shared the same ecosystem.
How had things gotten so out of whack?

Our beloved Baby Beluga, poisoned. I felt like I had been kicked in the stomach.

How could I sing that song again? Would it ever be the same?

Leone's presentation was a pivotal event for me. It was a clear wake-up call. My environmental concerns of previous years, muted then by many distractions, were now rustling for attention. I flashed back to songs I had written and environmental issues I'd heard about, such as the hazards of nuclear energy (which had always frightened me), the scourge of acid rain and the growing hole in the ozone layer. I reread my environmental books, bought new ones and scanned newspapers and magazines to see what else was going on.

In those weeks of paying attention, I noticed that a day didn't go by without some news of environmental disaster from some corner of the world. In an unprecedented move, *Time* magazine put our beleaguered planet on its January 2, 1989 cover—in place of its Man of the Year— along with the words, "Planet of the Year: Endangered Earth." It was all too obvious that serious environmental problems were everywhere, and many were of a global magnitude and transcended political borders.

It was then that I wrote the song *Evergreen Everblue*. The clearing of vast areas of the Amazon rainforest was making news, with projections showing that, at current rates of destruction, in a few decades not much of it would be left. I learned that tropical rainforests were not only the lungs of the planet, taking in carbon dioxide and emitting oxygen, but also vital regulators of global temperatures.

The mighty Amazon forest, the "jungle" that had been a source of awe in my youth, was now being destroyed—cut and burned with no regard for its indigenous people and its wildlife or for the health of the entire planet.

What kind of world would it be without the beluga and the Amazon? Would all the money in the world mean anything if they were gone forever? What kind of madness were we engaged in?

Not long after hearing about the fate of the belugas, I attended a briefing at the Four Seasons Hotel in Toronto on the state of the

Amazon rainforest. The presentation was part of a world tour by the singer Sting and an indigenous man, Chief Raoni of the Kayapo people, to focus the world's attention on the deforestation problem in South America and elsewhere in the world.

As Chief Raoni made his way into the conference room (followed by the pop star), I watched with fascination this man from another world and time—his mysterious eyes, black hair, colorful feather headdress and protruding lower lip were unforgettable. In the question-and-answer period after the presentation, the Chief made it clear that the Amazon was home to his people, and he said he felt sorry for the culture that was out to destroy it, for surely that meant those people must have lost *their* home. To me it was an astounding and profound perception of Western society—as an uprooted and homeless culture now inflicting that state on anyone who got in the way of economic ventures.

Chief Raoni's words hit me like truth arrows piercing ready flesh. I wanted to learn more. Back home, I sang *Evergreen Everblue* again and again, knowing it was in tune with all this. The song had the feel of an anthem, and stressed personal responsibility in its chorus:

"*Evergreen, everblue*
As it was in the beginning we've got to see it through
Evergreen, everblue
At this point in time: it's up to me, it's up to you."

Soon after, I came across a CBC radio show hosted by the respected Canadian geneticist, ecology advocate and broadcaster, David Suzuki—a five-part series called *It's a Matter of Survival.* (For over twenty years Suzuki had been host of a CBC TV show called *The Nature of Things*, enlightening viewers on the many wonders of the natural world, stressing the interdependence of all life and sounding warnings about pollution issues that affected our lives.) The radio special painted a graphic outline of the hazards of the global warming that would follow the significant destruction of the world's rainforests. From the vantage point of the year 2039, Suzuki looked back at a chain of events that led to unpredictable climate changes, and presented interviews with scientists from around the world to explain the cause-and-effect scenario.

I learned that increased carbon dioxide emissions from industry increase the greenhouse effect in the atmosphere around our planet, letting in sunlight but not allowing the usual amount of heat back out. Deforestation compounds the problem by reducing the number of trees available to soak up the carbon dioxide and effectively diminishes the cooling aspect of the globe's temperature regulation. It's this combination that causes global warming. And because life on Earth exists in an intricate balance that has evolved over millennia, a sudden and dramatic change in its processes could raise the overall heat levels, bringing climate changes that may be irreversible.

While we can't know this for certain, the point Suzuki made was, can we gamble the future security of the entire human race for lack of hard evidence? One-hundred percent proof might only come when it's too late to respond. Given these serious grounds for concern, wouldn't it be prudent to err on the side of caution when the stakes were humanity's very survival?

Irreversible! The word sank in. Suzuki and the other scientists explained that unpredictable climate change (of which global warming was only one aspect) had the potential to wreak havoc on human societies. A very slight sustained increase in global temperatures could mean rising ocean levels, resulting in widespread flooding of coastal and low-lying regions and the possible migrations of hundreds of millions of people seeking higher ground. And the disruption of dependable growing and harvesting cycles the world over would imperil human food supplies everywhere and shatter life as we know it. Irreversible—the word gave me the chills.

This radio show was a first: finally, an eminent broadcaster and scientist had the vision to connect the dots and present a global picture of crisis. What's more, seeing the scale and urgency of the problem, he had the courage to call it *a matter of survival.* Some ecologists were saying that we had a ten-year window of opportunity to turn things around before it was too late. The 1990s, they said, was "the turnaround decade." If that was true, we didn't have a moment to lose.

I felt this message in every cell of my being. It really frightened me. I feared for my future and for my loved ones. I thought of my niece, Kristin, and my nephew, Sevan (then eleven and seven). What kind of world would they inherit, and what hope could they have for their future if adults couldn't be bothered to heed the many signs of danger? If I didn't respond to the challenge of these times, what could I ever say to them if they asked me, Why?

Thinking of all this, I was overcome by enormous sadness. It seemed the more I learned about the state of the Earth, the sadder I got: sad for the threatened beauty in the world, and sad for our children who faced a perilous future.

What could I do to address the global crisis, I wondered. Thinking about this day and night soon produced a new song, *Our Dear, Dear Mother*, a ballad of love and respect for our planet. I also thought of some other songs I'd already written, like *Big Beautiful Planet* and *One Light, One Sun*, and some I had not yet recorded, and soon got the idea of making an album of environmental songs for older children,

When the Committee mulled this over, we didn't reach any decisions except to note my need to work with an older audience for a change. This was unsettling for Bert, Bonnie and Deb to consider. Their experience was with younger children, and it wasn't easy for them to hear both my deep concern and my strong sense of a new creative initiative. Previously, all my work with children had come from our group synergy, and although in recent albums I had shown increasing confidence—producing the last one, *Everything Grows*, by myself—I had still relied on my wife and close friends for all kinds of advice. But now there was a change: I was talking about a new direction and they were a little taken aback. A step into the unknown was always hard, and when one player took the lead, it shook up the rest of the team.

STARTING OUT AGAIN

SADNESS TURNED TO ANGER AND DESPAIR AS I STRUGGLED TO hold on to my rapidly changing personal world while worrying for the world at large. The breakdown of my marriage, the awkward response the news elicited from friends and associates—all this was deeply unsettling. Combined with my growing awareness about the global eco-crisis, it led me to question *everything* in life all over again: identity, relationship, love, trust, politics, society—the whole works.

I had last gone through something like this in my early twenties. Now, with twenty more years behind me, I was again looking at the world with new eyes. I was wide open and hurting. Colors and emotions seemed intensified, as if the big tear in the fabric of my life allowed unusual perceptions. And yet, I have to say, I felt completely alive. It certainly helped to keep a journal, writing this stuff out, getting it out of me.

In the summer of 1989, when Deb decided to leave Troubadour and Toronto, our break was complete. I started to see a new therapist who helped me wade through my tumbling emotions, and to realize that these storms were in fact part of life—that much learning and growing would come from all this. There were only two choices: sink and shrivel up or swim and be stronger and wiser for the experience.

This felt like the right time to accept an invitation to visit Mendelson Joe, the Toronto painter-musician I first met in the Colonnade building some years before. I had long admired Joe's art and when I stood before the paintings in his studio, they had a direct impact on me. All I could see was the love behind his fierce truth-telling.

A stout bohemian with his heart on his canvas, Joe was given to saying things like "I paint everything from puppies to politicians," and "the name of the game is results, not schmaltz." The visit did me good.

In some jangly way, life moved on.

I turned my distress into words for a new song called *What's the Matter with Us*, a compelling number with a reggae beat, asking, "Why do away with our woodlands, nothing to be gained from that, Why waste the best of our farmland, where's the logic in that?" Then I went into a studio and made a demo of this and five other songs, including one called *Clean Rain*, a song about acid rain that recalled an earlier time "when the rain fell clean." I felt they sounded fresh and my voice sounded strong.

Troubadour's new counsel, New York lawyer Ron Feiner, was one of the first to see the potential for an environmental album. His feedback helped a lot. For the first time I was creating an album on my own, and though my Troubadour colleagues knew about it, this was clearly something born of my need to respond to the global eco-crisis in a personal way.

The song *Evergreen Everblue* got such a strong reaction every time people heard it that I later decided to make it the title track of the emerging album. On one occasion, during a benefit for world hunger relief at the home of Peter Yarrow (of Peter, Paul and Mary) in New York, I sang the song to a very enthusiastic reception. In those days, I could barely get through the second chorus without my voice breaking from an impending onset of tears.

Soon I was in Vancouver being introduced to David Suzuki by our mutual friend Cathy Chilco, the producer of my two CBC TV specials in the early 1980s. It was great to finally meet the charismatic man with the sonorous voice, whom I had long admired and whose courage had ignited my existing environmental concerns into action. On the verandah of his house, overlooking Vancouver's waters and mountains, I shared with him the impact his radio special had had on me, and he was glad to hear about my new songs.

At the A&M offices in Los Angeles, the reception was different. The execs were lukewarm to the news that my next album was not for little kids. As for their suggestion of making an environmental album for young children, I had a number of things to say. I felt that my new music needed to be aimed at an older audience, not only because the content of the new songs was unsuitable for little ones, but also because it wasn't *their* job to rise to the challenge of the eco-crisis. It was up to adults to protect the planet for the children who would inherit her. What's more, songs like *Baby Beluga, All I Really Need* and others had already been on the nursery school "playlist" for years, and those were fine for that age group. Now, I needed to speak with a stronger voice, to sound a wake-up call with my new work.

When I took my "year off" in September 1988, little did I know what lay in store for me, personally or professionally. I can only say that I did hear my inner voice once again, in a time that was uncluttered by career demands, and I responded honestly to its calling. In the turmoil of the times, doing children's concerts was the farthest thing from my mind. (But I never said I would no longer sing for children, as the press contended on a number of occasions.)

The more I thought about it, the more I realized that the message of the new songs had to get out to the widest possible audience. That meant a "cross over" into pop music. When Troubadour hired Linda Goldstein to be my new manager, we figured she would be the one to make this happen. She'd had great success producing a hit for Bobby McFerrin with the song *Don't Worry, Be Happy*, and was well known in the pop world. We went into the studio to do some new demos, thinking that she would produce this new album. But when her other commitments slowed down my momentum, I knew this wasn't going to work—I needed another producer. By this time, I was feeling very frustrated at the many obstacles to getting this album done.

I was feeling pretty lonely too. Being a single man again for the first time since my mid-twenties was a strange new experience, and I likely made a fool of myself here and there with women I met.

I also felt quite exposed. Raffi, the smiling children's entertainer, wasn't supposed to be depressed, or angry, or lonely, sitting in a restaurant by himself, pining for company but often feeling too vulnerable or too low to call anyone. I tried hard not to let it show.

Visiting friends in Vancouver during the summer of 1989 and taking in the excellent folk festival, I was again so smitten by the city's spectacular natural setting that I felt the urge to find a little place where I might retreat from Toronto. An apartment with a view appeared on my very first look around and I said yes to it immediately. Over the next few months, I escaped on occasion to the West Coast to embrace its beauty, and took comfort in the company of old friends from my years performing at the Children's Festival.

That same year, I got a call from A&M President Gerry Lacoursiere that tickled my fancy. He said my name was on a short list of those being considered for the Walt Grealis "Industry Builder" award, a special Juno given each year for outstanding contribution to the Canadian recording industry. I was speechless. What Gerry wanted to know was "If you were selected, would you accept the award?" Composing myself, I asked if I'd have to compete for it. The answer was no. Then I'd be delighted to accept, I assured him.

I was genuinely pleased, as were all of us at Troubadour, when I was in fact chosen to receive this Juno recognition.

* * *

During my sabbatical, the only exception I made to the "no planning" rule was accepting an invitation to perform a benefit concert at Carnegie Hall in September 1989. It was tough to commit to singing in New York during a time when I was struggling to hold myself together day to day. But I did, and in June tickets went on sale for two shows. They sold out in two days.

Meanwhile, again bending my own rule, I started to imagine doing a very different Raffi tour around the release of *Evergreen*

Everblue, one in which the shows would be aimed at older kids and would start at 8 p.m. The Carnegie Hall date, though a matinee, seemed to offer a transitional outing towards that end.

With New York in my sights, I set about designing a show that presented a new Raffi. I would come onstage without a guitar, wearing a white linen jacket, and sing the first four songs on a hand-held wireless microphone. (Since, in all previous concerts, I had performed sitting down, this would be quite a change.) I also added a number of my environmental songs to the show, including the new *Evergreen Everblue*, yet to have its concert debut. This was a bold move. Family concerts can only be so long, and with fans wanting to hear their familiar favorites, inserting an unknown song into a one-hour show was risky.

The weekend before the one in the Big Apple, we had concerts in Windsor and Hamilton, Ontario. Despite having just said a final farewell to my ailing Bundles (then fifteen years old), I did perform well in these shows, and that gave me a boost heading into New York. No matter how much you calm yourself by saying that it's just two more concerts, playing in New York always has a unique buzz about it.

On the network morning TV shows, I talked it up. The excitement grew, and on the big day I was ushered into the renowned hall and up to my dressing room. I felt such an intense mix of emotions, having this moment to share with Bonnie and Bert, but not with Deb. Being able to feel it all and crying a few tears was my way of getting through it. It was so helpful to have Ron Feiner in our camp, and Linda Goldstein was also on hand. The support of my band members Dennis, Mitch, Nancy and Bucky was tangible but never intrusive, a laugh or two when it was needed, or an arm around my shoulders. Backstage, waiting for the show to start, Bucky was on his knees with salutations, "The king is back, the king is back!" And then came the big moment.

I walked onto the famous stage to thunderous applause—the air was electric. The linen jacket added a sense of occasion, a grown-up look, as if something had changed. I did feel different, and I sang those first four songs, including *Big Beautiful Planet,* full out, superbly backed by the band. Then I took the jacket off and the crowd went wild (I figured it was the young moms). Next up was *Evergreen Everblue.* I told the fans why I had written it, and they actually listened. The song got strong applause and I couldn't believe people singled it out for praise after the show. As they say in New York, "Who knew?"

What a concert. The band played great, I was proud of them. The rest of the day is a bit of a blur, except that I remember a reception where I met a select group of fans and posed for a photo with Susan Sarandon. It was such a dreamspell, the whole thing.

THE TURNAROUND DECADE

Our dear, dear mother, daily provider, Earth be your name;
The time has come to honor you, to know you and to show our love.
"Our Dear, Dear Mother"

ON A CRISP JANUARY DAY IN 1990, WALKING FROM A LOCAL BAKERY to my new Vancouver apartment (my occasional getaway), I was swept away by the sight of the snow-capped mountains and tugboats in the sun-kissed bay. Like a gift, the beauty of the moment turned into *Where I Live,* another song for the upcoming album.

To produce *Evergreen Everblue,* we hired Billy Bryans, a Toronto producer who was hip to "world music" and pop. He flew to Vancouver and we got right to work on what was to become the most expensive Troubadour album ever. Billy's experience was crucial to getting the sound of this recording right, since it had to be more radio-friendly than any I'd made. If we wanted the songs to be played on radio and music video stations, they had to grab your attention and hold it.

While still stubbornly protective of my creative process, I gave Billy more license to shape my music than any collaborator in the past. I was in new territory and it was a humbling experience. Billy helped change a melody line or two, rerouted chord progressions slightly, and taught me a lot about how these little moves made a big difference. I learned, for example, that just because I had written a song and thought it was great, that didn't necessarily make it so. It was the recording that would determine whether people liked it or not. I finally got it that the production decisions—from the physical layout of the recording sessions to the selection of musicians—would affect the finished sound as much as what was played and recorded.

Like any growth experience, working on this new album was at once exhilarating and frightening. At times I felt fearless in doing what I had to do, and at other times so vulnerable. It was as if destiny were pulling me along.

For the reggae-rap tune *What's the Matter with Us?*, Billy insisted we cut it with a reggae band to get the authentic feel. At first I resisted, but soon realized he was right. He lined up the Toronto band Messenjah.

Our rehearsals were quite something. I'd never hung out with reggae players before and I was nervous. What would they make of me, an off-white guy singing in their style? Would they dig the tune? When I got to the studio, there they were, dreadlocks and all, accompanied by their rapper friend Devon. After the initial introductions, I played them the song. When they all said they liked it, I told them how relieved I was "because I'd been really *dreading* the session." That broke the ice, and we got down to making music and had a good time doing it.

To check the idea of this alternative Raffi tour of 8 p.m. concerts, I sang the new songs to a focus group of fifth- and sixth-graders with Bert and Billy looking on. The kids liked the songs, sang along with some and offered several poignant comments. After I sang *Clean Rain*, a ten-year-old boy said, "I'm glad you made that song, because maybe kids don't know what there was before acid rain." It seemed I was on the right track.

In February, I traveled to Los Angeles to attend my second Grammy Awards show, and for the second time I lost out in the Best Children's category. Fortunately, there was other business to attend to. This trip also included meetings with a number of record company execs to discuss distribution of my music. The deal with A&M was nearing its end and their people were not enthused about my new ambitions.

Of the different labels we approached, MCA gave us the best hearing. At lunch in the Universal City executive offices, my VIPs (Bert, Bonnie, Ron and Linda) and I met with President Al Teller and many of his VPs. It was evident, both by their numbers and by my being seated next to an ecologist they had brought on staff, that they were taking this meeting seriously. When it came to clout in the music business, MCA's size made them a prime candidate on our shopping list—and it didn't hurt that Linda personally knew Al Teller and Geoff Bywater, Marketing VP.

Speaking passionately about my concerns over the state of the Earth, I said it was time for all of us to do our part and insisted that if my music was distributed by MCA, it could not be in the wasteful packaging known as the "longbox" (a 6 by 12 inch cardboard box containing a CD or cassette, already housed in its own container).

The MCA people said they admired my stance and would support it. They had listened to the recent songs and liked what they heard. We even talked about doing a music video of the title track. I made it very clear that Raffi was now pursuing a new path and *Evergreen Everblue* had to be our priority. That said, of course, we wanted MCA to market the children's catalogue vigorously, subject to Troubadour's ethical constraints. The meeting was a great success and, in the following months, we signed a lucrative six-year distribution agreement for Canada and the U.S.

36 The Colonnade studio show window, with the Cavouk portrait of Queen Elizabeth II.

37 A glimpse of the gallery-studio.

38, 39, 40 Cavouk portraits: the Queen Mother (1975), Governor-General Vanier (1960), and the Armenian troubadour Hovnanian with his wife, Agnes.

41 Lucie and Arto awaiting the arrival of dinner guests, among them
   Ruth Kilgour and son Arthur, and the Micheners.

42 My hair and beard at their longest.

Portraits by Cavouk:
43, 44 U.S. Vice-President Hubert Humphrey, painter and sculptor Ervant Kochar (above);
45, 46 composer Aram Khachaturian, ballerina Lois Smith (below).

47 Father and son in the Colonnade studio.

48, 49 From among Onnig's portraits: Lee Iacocca, past chairman of Chrysler (1982);
Catholicos Karekin I, head of the Armenian Church (1997).

50 The family marking Cavouk's 50 years in portraiture (1982).

51 Glenn Sernyk, Gerry Lacoursiere, me, Ken Whiteley and Joe Summers
with early gold and platinum awards.

52 At the *Baby Beluga* listening party: the Honolulu Heartbreakers trio
with engineer Daniel Lanois and co-producer Ken.

53 Troubadour celebrating a half million units sold. *Left to right:* Joyce Yamamoto,
Tina Hann, Rob Williams, me, Deb, Mike Mulholland and Glenn.

54 Onstage in 1984, with Hawaiian shirt and moccasins.

55 The Cavouk portrait of Deb and me
with the Order of Canada medal.

56 Backstage in Los Angeles
with John Candy.

57 With Soviet rock star Stas Namin,
Rochester, New York, in 1986.

58 A sign of the times, from our 1980s concert tours.

59 Bowling with concert presenter Carol ("Orange") Schroeder in Madison, Wisconsin.

60 An after-show autograph for fans, circa 1983.

61 With Jan Bruton and Lynn Kelly, bookstore proprietors and concert presenters, Portland, Oregon.

62 On tour: Dennis Pendrith and me playing table hockey, Nancy Walker supplying organ sounds.

63 Carnegie Hall sound check (1989) with Mitch Lewis, Nancy, Bucky Berger and Dennis.

64 With the Raging Grannies and Sarawak natives Unga Paran, Mutang Tu'o and Mutang Urud (far left), at the video shoot of "Evergreen Everblue."

65 Severn Cullis-Suzuki and me (wearing a plumed Kayapo headdress) at the 1992 Earth Summit in Rio.

66 Senator Al Gore with indigenous leaders at the Earth Summit in Rio (Mutang Urud, again far left).

67 At the Vice-President's office with the Gores, April 1993.

68 Making rainstorm sounds with Mikhail Gorbachev in Washington, DC (1993).

69 With a Gabonese child, Kyoto Global Forum.

70 Teens backstage in Canada's
    banana belt, 1994 concert tour.

71 A conference call *avec* banana fans.

72 With Garth Brooks
    at a *Crook & Chase*
    TV taping in
    Nashville.

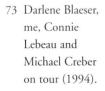

73 Darlene Blaeser,
    me, Connie
    Lebeau and
    Michael Creber
    on tour (1994).

74, 75 My young friends: the
Beezer (left) and Robin.

76 Kristin and Sevan,
all grown up, Vancouver.

77 That's me, kayaking in Troubadoria.

* * *

My still struggling personal life got a boost when I summoned up the courage for an unusual meeting with my parents. I wanted them to know something of the person I had become, and since communications were never easy with Arto and Lucie, I decided to show them instead.

The next time I was invited over for Sunday lunch, I told my parents I would bring the oil pastel paintings I had done in past months, and they sounded keen to see them. When I told Ani what I was up to, she agreed to come with me.

I would have been more nervous to show my paintings (and especially ones of nude figures) if I hadn't first been very clear about why I was doing it. I knew that I wasn't needing my parents' approval; instead, I was saying, "This is who I am—it's important for me that you know." Naturally, I hoped that they liked the artwork, but that wasn't the important issue. I wanted respect, and was prepared to take my paintings and leave if my parents were less than courteous.

After a delicious lunch, we relaxed in the family room over Armenian coffee. Then I could put it off no longer—it was time to show the goods. With a glance over at Ani, I unzipped the black portfolio and took out the first painting.

"Ahem," my father said, leaning forward for a better view from his oversized chair. "Can I make a criticism?"

Since he had put it as a question (rare in itself), I asked, "Can you wait until you've seen a couple more?"

"Yes. Why not."

The next painting drew a couple of positive sounds and throat clearings from Arto and a remark from Lucie about good colors. The third piece was even better received; they liked its energetic, strong lines. My God, I thought, this was going well, though I did notice a few beads of sweat on Ani's forehead. Arto quite liked the following piece with two full figure nudes, but Lucie let out a girlish giggle; she even asked what a certain obvious anatomical shape was. I calmly told her.

"Raffi, *why* so many nudes?" she brusquely wanted to know.

"Ma, you know how it is. Art's full of them," I answered. She gave me a conciliatory sigh.

Up next were a couple of abstract paintings: one showed strong forms and colors, and the other had a comparatively airy look, but with a vivid tension at its center. By now, Arto was really enjoying this show and said so, with a couple of "bravos" thrown in. And Lucie was enjoying it too, in her own way. Pointing to one abstract work, she wanted to know what it meant.

"Well, Ma, it's more a feeling, I suppose."

"What feeling?"

"Freedom." The word spoke itself.

After I had shown more than two dozen of these paintings, I turned to my father.

"Ba, what was that criticism you wanted to make?"

"Oh, it's nothing." he said, "You've done well. Very, very well."

* * *

Around this time, other uplifting experiences bolstered my confidence.

In Reno, Nevada, I sang before an audience of 300 educators at a reading conference. Billed as a "Song-Talk," my hour-long presentation was a blend of talking about environmental issues and singing my new songs. The teachers were a wonderful audience. From their faces, I could see they were more than a little curious about what I was up to. They listened to me attentively, provided rousing accompaniment to songs like *Clean Rain* and *Evergreen Everblue* and, at the end, wanted more. This was perhaps the first time I had shared my new path with an audience, and to be so warmly received meant a lot to me.

In New York, Linda introduced me to Noel Brown, Regional Director for the United Nations Environment Program (UNEP). After talking with him, I felt I was on the right track with my new album.

Noel was quite taken with my environmental fervor and I got braver as the meeting went on. "Why doesn't UNEP and the UN proclaim the '90s the 'Turnaround Decade'?" I offered. He received the idea graciously and invited me to sing at the UN's upcoming Earth Day event.

Earth Day 1990 was perhaps the most widely publicized peace-time event ever, attracting participants in countries all over the world. Twenty years after the first Earth Day (and twenty years after Greenpeace was formed in Vancouver), I found myself in the General Assembly Hall, with the familiar marble podium I had often seen on TV when ambassadors addressed the world. There, Noel Brown give an impassioned speech on the many threats to the health of ecosystems worldwide, himself sounding the call for this to be a "turnaround decade."

Again I felt confirmed in the path I was taking. As the finale at the UN that afternoon, I performed three songs from my forthcoming album. With the help of a wonderful children's choir and my friend and master musician Jack Lenz, I sang *Evergreen Everblue, Our Dear, Dear Mother* and *Big Beautiful Planet,* backed by the instrumental mixes of the recent studio sessions. It was a thrill to hear my songs fill the hall on such an auspicious occasion.

After I finished singing, I was approached by a delegation of Cree from northern Quebec. They had traveled by canoe to Manhattan to speak at the UN about how the massive James Bay II electric power project proposed by Hydro-Québec posed a threat to the Cree and their homeland. They asked for my support and that I not forget them. I promised I wouldn't. It was just the fuel I needed to return to Toronto and finish the album.

Sometimes during this often trying and lonely time, it was hard to go into the studio for one more overdub or one more vocal. With Billy's help—and the voices of David Suzuki, Noel Brown, the Cree and others ringing in my ears—I persevered. Bit by bit, we were getting it done.

In midsummer I made a trip to Vancouver, where I met with Jeff Gibbs, the young mover behind the Environmental Youth Alliance (EYA), a national network of high school and college students concerned for the Earth. Jeff loved my new music and introduced me to the local EYA youth.

I found the spirit and energetic naiveté of these kids refreshing. They were planning a demonstration in support of the Penan, an ancient hunter-gatherer tribe whose millennial home in the rainforests of Sarawak (in the Borneo region of Malaysia) was being destroyed by round-the-clock logging. I was invited to join their public protest outside the Malaysian consulate in downtown Vancouver, and the next day I found myself on the street, holding a sign.

It felt strange coming out as an activist, but reminded me of my early twenties when I was on the streets selling counterculture newspapers on Toronto street corners. Hardly anyone took notice of me in amongst these teenagers. Getting my first taste of supporting indigenous people on the other side of the globe, I felt the youths' yearning for justice, so like my young idealism years ago. I decided I would not hide in my new hometown but instead would let my passions be visible in the community.

During my sabbatical year, I had become newly aware of the magnitude of the many crises our society faces—child abuse, drug addiction, street gangs, violent crime, educational malaise, teen suicides, environmental disorders, and more. After years of hearing such depressing items in the news, I began to wonder if they weren't linked to each other.

In 1990, it was with some fright (and, strangely enough, some relief) when I realized that the dozens of problems dubbed "crisis" actually revealed the breakdown of an entire social system, the undoings of an unworkable, outmoded social paradigm and that throwing money here and there wasn't going to solve anything—no more than retreating to romantic notions of bygone eras would, be they the 1950s or thousands of years ago.

There doesn't have to be total anarchy in the streets, I thought, before the signs of system breakdown are apparent. Statistics are just one way to see the magnitude of social problems, although quantifying is such a dispassionate assessment of the real pain and suffering in everyday life. The difference between 10% and 1% unemployment, say, and between 25% and 5% living in poverty, is substantial; but, regardless of the number, the distress of the disadvantaged is total, and the social costs are borne by everyone.

I pondered at length the relationship between personal and global issues. Needing to make sense of the broader picture, I left no stone unturned.

I was attracted to a day-long "Women and the Earth" conference. One of perhaps a dozen males in a packed hall of 500, I was deeply touched by the proceedings, as speaker after speaker made connections between society's treatment of people and its treatment of Mother Earth. When I considered patriarchal society's dominance of women and its subjugation of the Earth, it was as though a veil had been lifted from my eyes, allowing me a clearer view of how our conditioned biases played out in the world. (I had just read *A People's History of the United States* by Howard Zinn, with its reversed portrayal of the good guys and bad guys—written not from the conquerors' perspective, but through the eyes of the oppressed.)

Did the dominance mode in patriarchy and the need for control stem from a culture's separation from nature? To learn more, I bought a book called *Healing the Wounds* (edited by Judith Plant), a collection of essays from an eco-feminist perspective. I was now able to link the human rights aspirations of feminism to the ecological concerns affecting all of us.

That summer, I made a trek with friends through the giant Sitka spruce of the Carmanah Valley on Vancouver Island. Just before we got to Carmanah, we drove past a long stretch of clear-cut landscape, a dead zone of lifeless stumps as far as we could see. The contrast between this and what greeted us at our destination was devastating.

With backpacks on, we slowly descended into the majestic glory of a complex forest with trees hundreds of years old and hundreds of feet tall. It was my first time in such awesome company, and I walked silently, eyes wide, mouth open. My guides showed me the natural cycle of decay and rebirth all around us in the fallen "nurse logs" that hosted the growth of many young trees. The moss-laden scene made a huge impression on me, one that lasted long after the overnight outing.

As I continued reading and reflecting about the Earth, I realized how the health of our planet's ecosystems is the very basis of all that we do. Every business depends on planetary resources (and creative people) for success in the marketplace, and every family depends on quality nourishment for healthy life. As one country's pollution and deforestation easily affect the welfare of another, and since all countries have an interest in clean air, water and soil, I could see that here was an issue that brought individual and community together. The ecological context is where self-interest and the common good merge.

It occurred to me that the learning I had pursued since I left university had become a search for an integrated theme tying a whole range of subjects together—a multi-disciplinary look at life. If I had a method, a way of learning, it was simple: I asked a lot of questions and I looked for answers that made connections between issues.

Some people look to religion for a unifying meaning by which to live. Since leaving the church, I had done my share of spiritual inquiry, mostly in the Eastern traditions. By this time, however, I wasn't interested in salvation for its own sake, or earning "good karma" points for a better next life, and I didn't see the indwelling spirit as something apart from matter. As well, I was looking for what people of different faiths could celebrate together.

With the Earth now front and center in my attention, a unifying principle started to take shape: the same attitude we have towards nature is likely the same attitude we have about other people and perhaps ourselves.

I thought about this idea while eating my organic cereal one morning, grateful for the age-old farming practices being revived. How can we live in harmony with the Earth if we can't make peace with each other, and how can we do that if we can't find peace within ourselves?

In her book, *The Chalice and the Blade*, author Riane Eisler writes of a basic choice people have between domination and partnership as ways of being. It made me think about how a need to be in control blocks the benefits of "living in process," of participating in a dynamic cooperation with others and with the natural world. Sharing, respect, working together—that's what we try to teach children, I thought, even if individually and collectively we may not model it very well.

As for inspiration, in addition to Gandhi, Martin Luther King and Helen Caldecott, I was also finding new heroes. One of these was Buckminster Fuller, American philosopher-architect *par excellence*, designer of the geodesic dome. Bucky, as he was known, was a great integrated thinker and lived in reverent celebration of the universe and what he called "spaceship Earth." His books overflow with visions inspired by the designs in natural systems; Bucky adored Creation's omni-textural elegance and elevated the wonder and majesty of the phenomenal world to an art. Every child, I felt, would benefit in Bucky-immersion from an early age.

Living alone, I had plenty of time to read, and I harvested from an excellent crop of non-fiction books, like Fritjof Capra's *The Tao of Physics* and Michael Talbot's *The Holographic Universe*. I loved having a number of books on the go at once, littering my living room. As I would read one, another would call to me. Invariably, I would pick that one up and find that it echoed the content of the previous book.

I soon became enchanted by the quantum physics view of Creation. Compared to the old reductionist view of an objective world pared down to bits and pieces and then analyzed, quantum physics reveals a highly relational world whose parts can only be understood in relation to the whole. (That reminded me of a unique product of one branch of photography: the holographic plate—an image whose broken segments each contain the entire picture, the whole in every part.)

Research on subatomic particles has shown that the very act of observation changes their apparent nature—an electron can pose as particle or wave depending on the "photographer." This to me was a unifying idea unlike any other: the very act of participating affects what we find.

I was excited by this notion of a participatory world, where we indeed co-create our greater reality in an evolutionary dance with all the other species, a dance far too complex for step-by-step analysis. It's *dancing* that matters; as the Bard said, "the play's the thing."

TROUBADOUR WEST

My next major decision was to call Vancouver home. The wheels of change were turning and, with Bert leaving Troubadour (Bonnie had already done so), I decided to move the company out west, where I wanted to be. The West Coast and its forested mountain glory were calling and I couldn't say no. I put the big Toronto house up for sale and informed my staff of the decision. I would miss Tina, my assistant of many years, Mary Ann, our receptionist, and, of course, Joyce, who had been there from the beginning. They had been a tower of strength for me in those last few weeks, but I knew I had to move on.

It was a big leap, this wading into new waters without my old team to guide and nourish me. Throughout this period, my family kept me in its embrace. Ani and Onnig stayed in touch regularly, and Lucie and Arto, even as they struggled to make sense of my actions, kept me in their prayers and offered encouragement. And it was always a special comfort to remember my longtime friendship with Bonnie and Bert, each a distinct source of understanding and ongoing support. I trusted that we would always stay connected, whatever the distance or time between us.

Walking along Vancouver's West 4th Avenue one day not long after my move, I saw an old accordion in the show window of Reliable Cleaners, a small family-run dry cleaning and laundry business. I went in, tried it out, traded some cash for the old gray Hohner, and took it home. Its warm tones brought back memories as I fumbled my way through a few songs I used to play (in secret) years ago on my father's accordion in the upstairs bedroom on Melrose. What I lacked in technique I made up for in attitude, imitating Arto's emphatic style on the few pieces I recalled from his repertoire. I got very sad, thinking that here I was reclaiming something of my father—something that for so many years remained distant—and now we lived 3,000 miles apart.

Soon after, I bought a small red Camerano accordion in a used furniture shop a few blocks down from the cleaners. Now this looked and sounded just like a miniature version of my father's accordion. Oh, I loved this little *bambino*, everything about it, including the worn black shoulder straps. Even though it only had one voice and a limited keyboard, it was lightweight and portable in a canvas shopping bag.

When I called Arto and Lucie to share the news of my new passion, they were excited. Arto asked if I would play his accordion next time I visited. His speech was now slurred from the Parkinson's disease, and conversations on the phone were a challenge. Any news that made him happy was a gift to all of us in the family.

Not long after, I took the little red accordion to Toronto, and played it for Arto as best I could. It brought tears to his eyes. He wasn't hearing my mistakes; he was watching a part of himself from long ago. God only knows the fullness of what he felt, for he wasn't able to say. Lucie asked Arto to play the little accordion too. But even this undersized model proved too much for him. He just couldn't get it going, and it was painful to watch. I would have given anything to be able to comfort him. I soon took the instrument from his shoulders and promised to play it anytime I was visiting.

Then I got a better idea. Would he like it if I had his own accordion repaired, the very one he'd had since the 1940s when he played at

King Farouk's wedding reception and other functions around Cairo? We got it out of its case, and clearly it needed work—it would require some visual restoration and the reeds would have to be tuned. "Leave it to me," I promised, "I'll bring it back like new."

A few weeks later when I returned the restored instrument, there was a joy in Arto that's hard to describe. His physical vulnerability had brought with it an emotional tenderness that took some getting used to. I felt I had access to a part of him that I had longed for in my youth but was unable to find. Now that he had lost his strength and was almost totally dependent on others, our parent-and-child roles had got reversed.

Arto was in Lucie's constant care, and she devotedly ministered his medication, exhorted him to get his daily exercise and generally fussed over him. Lucie was in such a bind though: the round-the-clock care-giving was draining her, and yet she wouldn't accept anyone's help. What's more, she no longer had the bon vivant husband to take her out on the town. On the occasions they did socialize, she did the work to get them both ready. You could see the toll it took on her— on them both—but she would summon her pride and insist she wasn't complaining. "*C'est la vie*," she'd say.

Onnig was almost a daily presence in their lives, and this was also complex. He didn't live far from Melrose (he was recently divorced), and they regularly needed him to do this or that. Personally and professionally he needed them as well. However, in the many matters unresolved and the things that couldn't be said or improved between the three of them, friction so easily won the day. Ani and I would get distress calls from all concerned to help sort things out, but we could only help so much. Often we'd end up comforting each other, knowing that after the long conversations we would dutifully have with everybody (by phone and in person), things weren't likely to change. The patterns were too deeply ingrained.

And so, exasperated, I continued to play the accordion full out, with attitude and flair, and with mistakes.

When I mentioned to my Vancouver friends that I was looking for someone to open the new office, that someone immediately appeared in the person of Lynne Partridge. Lynne had made a name for herself in PROCAN, a performance rights organization that collected and paid out royalties to songwriters and music publishers. It seemed she needed a new challenge and Troubadour fit the bill.

Thanks to Lynne, we were soon up and running. Within two months of our meeting, she had us established in a wonderful second-floor space not far from my home. With the assistance of Joyce and Tina, who flew out from Toronto to help us sort through the voluminous files, the move was complete. Troubadour West was open for business, though not business as usual. The children's troubadour had turned eco-activist—it was business *unusual.*

After a long time in the studio mixing and remixing the songs that took a year to complete, *Evergreen Everblue* was finally finished by October of 1990. When the album's media launch in Los Angeles was underattended, I got the feeling that my new path would be an uphill climb. It was. It didn't help that my manager, Linda Goldstein, and I weren't getting along.

Evergreen Everblue was off to a shaky start. Many retail chains would not carry the CD in its basic "jewel box" format; they demanded the wasteful longbox. To make matters worse, there was no indication on the front or back cover that this was for older audiences (this was noted only on the inside).

The front cover had a dramatic computer-generated color rendering of a black-and-white photo of my face, colored to show blue sky and clouds in my forehead and eyes, and forests in place of my beard. Although this didn't look like the cover of a children's album, I insisted that we still needed to state clearly on the cover that the album was different. I was really upset when this didn't happen, and we got reports of angry parents making a purchase only to realize later that it wasn't what they expected. Even retailers were putting it in the children's bins. Maybe all this would have happened no matter what we said on the cover, but in any case, at my request MCA did finally add the phrase "an ecology album for the '90s," albeit a tad too late.

On top of everything, radio programmers weren't keen on the *Evergreen Everblue* single MCA released. It seemed that my name was just too synonymous with little kids to be hip enough for radio. More than I realized (and as people kept saying), Raffi was an icon in children's entertainment and not easily suited for a makeover at retail, on radio or on TV.

There was, however, some good news: the shooting of the *Evergreen Everblue* video came together in a magical way and attracted many people on my wish list. For a director, MCA suggested Michael Patterson, who had some recent pop video successes. We met and mapped out the idea of using a crystal ball being passed from hand to hand as a metaphor for our planet and the future in our hands. We also compiled an assorted cast to sing with me, among them my young friends in the Environmental Youth Alliance and a group of grandmother activists called the Raging Grannies. I was hoping for David Suzuki's involvement, but knew he had a very busy schedule. I also thought it would be great if aboriginal people were represented.

Wonderful synchronicity lay just around the corner. While Michael was in town for video planning, I took him to a Rainforest Benefit at the Hotel Vancouver. The program included three captivating speakers that night: environmental activist Thom Henley, ethnobotanist Wade Davis and, as luck would have it, David Suzuki. Both Michael and I were very moved by their presentations. We also learned that Vancouver would soon be visited by three people from the endangered rainforests of Sarawak, located on the Malaysian island of Borneo. When it was announced that the tribesmen would be in Vancouver four weeks later—the very weekend of our video shoot—I knew we'd been handed a gift.

The next day I called Thom and asked if the Sarawak delegation might agree to take part in the video. Assured of my commitment to proceed with integrity, he agreed to ask them.

Not only did we get a positive response, but a kind of synergy took hold of the project.

Early in the morning of a crisp fall day, we went to an old-growth forest on Vancouver Island to shoot footage of the pristine stand. By a waterfall, I sang over and over again on-camera, meditating in the warm sun between takes. In amongst giant Sitka spruce and Douglas-fir, I walked the soft forest floor, sang to the dappled leaf canopy and hugged the moss-covered trunks. We then moved from this paradise over to a clear-cut area, a shaven slope of stumps that felt cold and devoid of life. How strange to step through the charred remains of a recently vibrant forest. It was eerie to sing where the heart did not want to sing.

From there we regrouped in Vancouver's Stanley Park, where Thom introduced us to the Sarawak natives: Mutang Tu'o and Unga Paran from the Penan tribe, and Mutang (Andy) Urud of the Kelabit tribe. Mutang and Unga were the first Penan ever to travel outside their habitat, and Andy accompanied them both as supporter and interpreter. I was immediately struck by the gentleness in their faces and the serenity of their being.

Both Unga and Mutang wore a colorfully woven straw hat with a feather at the back and carried with them a survival tool from home: a six-foot-long wooden blow-pipe with a spearhead at one end. They used these, I was told, to blow poison-tipped darts at targeted prey in the Sarawak rainforest.

We shook hands and I tried to imagine the culture shock for these nomadic hunter-gatherers, jet-powered halfway around the world. Colonial contact had long been a fact of life for the Penan, even though many had conserved traditional ways. Now they were out in the open, on a controversial world tour, appealing for help to protect their rapidly diminishing forest home. To help them make sense of the day's proceedings, I gave them a cassette of *Evergreen Everblue*. They took it, smiling, eyes darting between the cover photo and me.

We walked in an open field, Mutang, Unga, Andy and I with my EYA friend Jeff Gibbs, joking about the blow-pipes while squirrels quickly scattered. Arm in arm, we posed for photos. I then welcomed the other members of our diverse cast: the Raging Grannies, excited teenagers and a number of my Vancouver friends.

As the shoot progressed we got more good news: Suzuki would try and make it sometime that afternoon. I was very happy that Anne Whonnick and her daughter Jojo (Squamish people, Natives of the land now called Stanley Park) were able to take part. I took heart from the day's many blessings and kept working. The Sarawak trio were terrific: Andy was a delight, and Unga and Mutang even braved the cold to pose bare-chested for one important scene. All the while, the shooting expanded possibilities in director Patterson's mind. When Suzuki and family finally dropped by, I knew we were in for a very special video. We even got David to sing on camera.

The rough cut looked promising. All of us at Troubadour who saw it were very excited, and every time we watched it together, we got all choked up.

I flew to Los Angeles to join Michael for the finishing touches. The results were superb—the final version gave me goose bumps. I felt that the challenges of my new direction would soon get a much-needed boost, and that all the hard work and the often-lonely uphill climb would soon bear fruit. This video was sure to touch the hearts of all who saw it on the music video channels.

The people we showed it to raved about it—activists, teachers, parents and kids alike. We made arrangements for further viewings in schools and at conferences.

But in the commercial world, our hopes were dashed. The best the video did was a get couple of plays on VH1. No go on MTV. No better on Canada's MuchMusic. Even the Suzuki content didn't bust their cool.

What crazy irony. I bristled at the thought that all the kids who had grown up with my music could watch junk-sex footage and macho-rap, but not my eco-video.

WHAT'S THE MATTER WITH US?

JUST WHEN I WAS ENGAGED IN THESE VARIOUS PROFESSIONAL battles, war broke out in the Persian Gulf. The "mother of all wars" and the PR campaign of all deceptions hit me hard.

For weeks I had watched TV reports of the escalating rhetoric between President Bush and President Hussein, whom, oddly enough, Bush always called by his first name. It was reported in *Harper's Magazine* that the U.S. knowingly allowed Hussein to advance on Kuwait, and that Iraq might have been provoked by the recently volatile supply-price politics of oil. Whatever the known terrors of the Iraqi leader, it seemed to me there had to be some alternative to all-out war. Stephen Lewis for one, Canada's ambassador to the UN, had urged that comprehensive economic sanctions be imposed on Iraq.

In a letter to the *Globe and Mail*, which the paper printed, I voiced my disgust at a predicament that could have been avoided if we, in the West, had pursued energy self-sufficiency in the '70s and '80s. I also pointed to the alarming fact that western nations had, for years, sold weapons to Iraq, supposedly to address the region's balance of power, and that those weapons were now to be used against Allied soldiers. The previous year, the enemy of the day had been drug king Noriega; this year it was the terrorist Hussein. How long would this reprehensible game go on—doing business with thugs and murderers, only to turn on them when things turned sour? The hypocrisy was all too clear. I was resolutely opposed to the war option.

Nevertheless, here we were on the brink of global conflict, with consequences no one could predict.

Besides the usual horrors of war, this one had others with the potential to scar the region severely as well as cripple the environment of the globe. Not only was there the danger of an enormous black cloud of smoke if Kuwaiti oil wells were set ablaze (as Hussein had warned would happen), but there was also the threat of the Iraqis using chemical warfare and firing missiles with small nuclear warheads.

Although the latter danger was mostly speculation as to what madness Hussein might unleash as a last resort, it was enough to get some American pundits themselves talking of a U.S. response to the Iraqi threat with small "tactical" nuclear warheads—as if the fallout from such mini-nukes was of no concern. What was all-important, apparently, was to protect the principle of national sovereignty and "liberate" Kuwait, an oil dictatorship that did not even respect the liberty of its own citizens. Both sides were engulfed in a galloping madness, yet the propaganda worked so well that in the U.S., 80% of those polled were said to support the war. And in Canada, sending combat troops to the Gulf also won wide popular support.

I thought back to the energy crisis of the mid-1970s, when there was talk about pursuing solar and other renewable energies during the Carter Presidency. The promise of energy self-sufficiency through non-polluting, ever-abundant sources was exciting then. But the U.S. relied heavily on fossil fuels for its armaments and automobiles, and vested interests resisted fundamental change if it meant cutting into their profits.

I woke up to a flood of revelations.

A culture that thrives on instant gratification and short-term profit cannot embrace such vital and long-term issues as renewable energy and world peace. We all know, on some level, that violence cannot cultivate lasting peace. And, what's more, we are societally engaged in and profiting from the means to do violence, then the impetus to work for peace is severely compromised.

By engaging in international arms sales, many countries, including Canada, were perpetuating the conditions and the means of the very violence they sought to avoid. This was a remnant of the old territorial thinking of deterrence through strength, which perhaps applied when conventional armies did not threaten vast eco-regions or when the world was not faced with the nuclear threat of "mutual assured destruction."

That old paradigm was also entrenched in a notion of national wealth (Gross National Product) so perverted it counted among its tallies of goods and services the production of death machines that could annihilate the whole world. I now understood the toxicity of an economic system that only valued activities measured in dollars, regardless of their impact on personal and planetary health. I began to see how, through the mind's unconscious beliefs, we maintained old patterns in the world, unable to leap to the changes that our hearts desired.

The night I heard that the first Iraqi Scud missiles had been fired and the war had begun, I was so frightened I was shaking. I stood in the kitchen in a panic, stuffing my face with potato chips, bread and mayonnaise. Finally I rang my friend Tara Cullis and went over for a visit. We commiserated over some wine, and I was able to calm down.

Over the coming days and weeks, I was glued to CNN. I found the incoherent images from the military "theater" mesmerizing, like some kind of video game in "night vision" green. The sterile jargon of contemporary war coverage fried my brain: "triple A," "ordnance," "collateral damage"—it was all too reminiscent of Orwellian doublespeak.

It's hard to forget the televised images of this surreal war, its Scuds and Patriots, gas masks, and cormorants in oily agony. The most massive aerial bombing in history was brought by TV into our living rooms, and still the Allied Commanders refused to comment on the possible numbers of Iraqi casualties.

The thorough destruction of a far-off country's infrastructure and the suffering of its people, themselves victims of a ruthless regime, were hard for Westerners to imagine. We hadn't had a war on our soil in recent memory, insisting—as we had in Vietnam—that the bombs fall elsewhere. "War game" maneuvers were one thing, simulating battle conditions to see how the expensive war toys did. But a real war, with bombs and blood, death and destruction? Not in the West.

As the weeks went by, I was shocked by the media war groupies reporting every aspect of machinery deployment. Round-the-clock analysis of the "kill potential" of both sides, like talent comparisons for the Super Bowl. Meanwhile, into the Persian Gulf leaked the largest oil slick in history, many times the size of the *Exxon Valdez* spill. It made my blood boil.

It occurred to me that every day we let the profiteering of the worldwide weapons industry go unchallenged was a day that contributed to the next armed conflict. In Vancouver, where there were several protests against Canada's involvement in the war, I took part in a large demonstration in front of the Vancouver Art Gallery and sang *This Little Light of Mine*, holding only a small candle in my hand.

More than ever, during this terrible time, I realized how our choices at home affected the outside world, and the phrase "think globally, act locally" took on new meaning. I thought about the fact that the world's nations spend about *one trillion dollars* each year making weapons of destruction, and I tried to imagine the benefit to all of humanity in shrinking that horrible account. Certainly it was heartening, at long last, to see substantial cutbacks in the nuclear arsenals. But it was clear to me that we still needed to vigorously challenge the deep-rooted assumptions that kept armed forces spending at levels often surpassing funding for all our social programs. I racked my brain for something else I could do.

What I came up with was the idea for a second video from *Evergreen Everblue*, of the song *What's the Matter with Us?* The title seemed to address the current madness head on, and I thought the song could generate some critical thinking at this time.

Our distributor, MCA had other thoughts. The U.S. execs were nervous about Raffi releasing an anti-war video amidst popular support for the war, and they didn't want to fund the project. Undeterred, Troubadour let MCA know that we would use our own money to make the video, and I defended my right to speak out. They relented somewhat, approving our ambitious video concept and even agreeing to pay most of the costs.

With that, Toronto video producer Jim Banks was hired to shoot the video in two locations, Toronto and Jamaica. Lights, cameras, dancers, dry ice, makeup—we were off. In a Toronto club with Messenjah and Devon for a full day's shooting, then on to Montego Bay. But even in the island's stunning splendor, this was not a happy time for me. With the grief of the war and discomfort from a hernia I had developed in the last year, I found it hard to keep my spirits up. Somehow I got through it and we shot the scenes we needed. Back in Toronto, Jim brought all the elements together into a visual romp. It was well shot and directed. To the point.

The feedback from MCA was hopeful for a while. It seemed that this video got farther down the MTV selection process than the last one, and we waited for word the video channels would put it in rotation. Once again, however, it was not to be. MuchMusic was a little kinder. I did a MuchWest interview in Vancouver and, amid jokes of Rasta Raffi, the video did get a few plays before dropping out of sight.

BRANCHING OUT

THE COMMERCIAL FAILURE OF THE VIDEOS AND THE LACK OF ANY play on radio were demoralizing to the max. Some days I seemed to be hurting all over and really low in energy. I'd have my dinner and then feel exhausted, needing to rest. Rest from what, I wasn't sure. It bugged me enough that I finally went to the doctor for blood tests. The results said Epstein-Barr virus, associated with Chronic Fatigue Syndrome.

Not a lot was known about this condition at the time and some people totally discounted it. For me, though, the diagnosis shed light on the previous six months, a time when I'd been generally very tired and hadn't known what to make of it. Fortunately, I hadn't got it as bad as some people who were bedridden or couldn't go to work. I had been able to will myself to do the work I felt compelled to do, even if at times the effort left me drained and depressed. It turned out that my cholesterol count was way up too, which surprised me, because I thought I was eating well. I figured out, though, that I had been treating myself to foods for emotional comfort. Even the veggie treats weren't great for the body if they added up to a lot of fried food: samosa, tempura, falafel, potato chips. No wonder things were out of whack.

I followed my good doctor's advice to take it easy whenever I needed to (I was lucky to be self-employed). I also heeded the recommendation of a homeopathic practitioner to give my body a rest and my immune system a boost with a dietary cleanse. What did I have to lose?

It was time to cut out the junk. For the first two weeks, I took Chinese herbs, drank special teas and ate organic brown rice with steamed veggies and little else. (It was boring, but I stuck to it.) Then, for the next four weeks, I followed a maintenance diet in which salads and fruits were okay.

By the end of these six weeks, I was feeling much better and the aches in my muscles and joints had subsided. I remember that it wasn't just the diet that did it, however. I had also experienced an important mind shift. I was actively caring for myself, going to the health food store, grateful for the Earth's harvest of nutritious foods and feasting my eyes on the treasures in the bulk bins. I know that these thoughts produced a more positive frame of mind and helped restore my energy.

The last eighteen months had been an action-filled time. Was I doing too much? Excerpts from my journal show some of what I had been up to:

- In Vancouver, heard a chilling lecture on global warming by Stephen Lewis, Canada's Ambassador to the UN. He explained that if India and China opted in the 1990s to fuel their economic development by burning coal, the negative impact on the atmosphere would be so great that it would negate whatever the rest of the world might do in curbing CO_2 emissions.

• Joined teens in a street rally through the streets of Vancouver, chanting and beating a drum. The Environmental Youth Alliance was in loud voice that day, even if the hundred or so who turned out were far fewer than the numbers hoped for.

• In Ottawa, the EYA invited me to their national conference and, in the middle of my one-hour performance, attendees gave *Our Dear, Dear Mother* a standing ovation. For me and these teenagers who had grown up with my music, it felt like a magical reunion of old friends. In among the eco-songs, they especially wanted to hear *Brush Your Teeth*, a childhood favorite; we sang it together.

• Did a performance at Wheelock College in Boston, billed as "Feel the Soil, Touch the Earth" (subtitled "Raffi speaks out for radical change"). Got a rousing reception.

• Donated my time singing benefit concerts for a number of environmental organizations and conferences.

• In a huge ballroom at the Las Vegas Hilton, presented my "Feel the Soil, Touch the Earth" song-talk to 1,500 educators at a conference of the International Reading Association. Enthusiastically received.

• At the opening of the Vancouver Children's Festival, sang and did my "radical" talk. It wasn't the most comfortable feeling, this new Raffi in the kids' tents. I felt like a preacher out of place, and sensed the audience's discomfort.

• Flew to L.A. to record *Raining Like Magic*, a song I wrote for the animated film *FernGully: The Last Rainforest*. I had made the demo of the song in Vancouver, and the producers liked it so much that we used a number of the demo tracks in the final recording. My first time singing in a film.

• Took part in a "Greening the Playground" party at a local elementary school.

- Was invited to give my radical song-talk before 2,000 teachers at a Reading Conference in upstate New York. Half of them walked out during my opening forty-minute talk, offended by my feminist perspective with its buzzwords like "patriarchy" and "women's holocaust" (referring to the burning of witches in Europe). The remaining brave souls really got into the music that followed. Conference organizer Ardith Cole stood by me.
- Gave the opening night address at Teen Summit USA in Princeton, New Jersey, in front of 250 outstanding teen leaders from all over the U.S. Thanks to the advice of Ron Feiner and his assistant, Lee Moskof, I blended the songs and the talk to make it a more musical presentation from the outset.
- Sang at a conference on sustainable agriculture in Asilomar, California, and was followed by innovative ecology advocate and author Jeremy Rifkin. Had a chance to visit organic farms and learned that food production touched on all kinds of pollution issues.

By and large, the press's response to my environmental activism in the early 1990s was to serve me up as some kind of madman. Sympathetic articles were few and far between. Had I just been talking about recycling, I might have fared better. But I was responding to the urgent call of many for a fundamental change in society—a radical turn of heart and mind towards changing the priorities in our lives.

Time magazine's two-page profile of me (November 1991), set up with the dour headline "No More Clapping Hands," was full of inaccuracies, out-of-context quotes and misrepresentations. My attempt to highlight the interconnected nature of social and environmental issues got branded "frantic and indiscriminate." During the interview for the piece, I do remember asking the writer one question (for which he had no answer): How can I communicate my heartfelt message to readers via an admittedly cynical journalist and medium?

A *Washington Post* feature in 1992 dismissed my awakening as a mid-life crisis and complained that the biographical information in my press kit was too thin. The article accused me of turning serious and of breaking away from the consumer society that had made me rich and famous. I was criticized for giving up my "affluent lifestyle to live in a barely-furnished apartment in Vancouver," and even for having a modest car and sometimes taking the bus.

That same year, the *World Scientists' Warning to Humanity* was issued by the U.S.-based Union of Concerned Scientists. Endorsed by over 1,600 of the world's most prominent scientists—among them 104 Nobel Laureates—this document outlined the damage that humans have inflicted on the natural world, and listed the steps needed to avoid a global catastrophe. Sent to 160 world leaders, it said in part:

> We the undersigned, senior members of the world's scientific community, hereby warn all humanity of what lies ahead. A great change in our stewardship of the earth and the life on it is required, if vast human misery is to be avoided and our global home on this planet is not to be irretrievably mutilated.

The warning received little media attention.

In the context of the times, Maurice Strong, the Canadian who organized the Earth Summit in Rio de Janeiro in 1992, spoke clearly about the need for a sustainable direction: "The stakes are high [and] the evidence is strongly persuasive that we must take fundamental action . . . moving ahead to what I call lives of sophisticated modesty" (*Maclean's*, December 16, 1991); and "Frankly, we may get to the point where the only way of saving the world will be for industrial civilization to collapse" (*The Province*, Vancouver, May 10, 1992).

I repeatedly referred to people like Maurice Strong and Noel Brown in talks with reporters about the fate of the Earth. They not only ignored the credibility of my sources, but remained deaf to my plea to make a change for our children's future.

GORE IN THE BALANCE

ONE PERSON WHO DID HEAR ME WAS U.S. SENATOR AL GORE. In late 1991, David Suzuki called to ask if I knew that Al Gore had just written an excellent book called *Earth in the Balance* (he'd been reading an advance copy of it before doing a TV interview with Gore). Also, Gore wanted to know where he could contact a person named Raffi, whom he had just read about in *Time* magazine! I was intrigued. David gave me the Senator's office number in Tennessee and a meeting was arranged. In February I was to meet Gore in Toronto, after his TV interview.

Before leaving for Toronto, I got *Earth in the Balance* from David and read it cover to cover. I found it to be a remarkable work, a very intelligent look at the challenges to global ecology and a pressing call for nations to make ecology the central organizing principle of society. I was truly amazed by this vision and took heart. But why did the Senator want to see me?

We met for almost an hour and a half in private, drinking herbal tea. Gore said he gathered from what he read that I had gone through a personal re-evaluation of my life, adding that he admired my courage to make a bold change as a result. He went on to tell me that his six-year-old son, Albert Jr., had nearly been killed in an auto accident a few years before. The experience had had a profound effect on Al and his wife, Tipper, prompting them to take stock of their lives and reprioritize what was of primary importance. His son's brush with death had brought about a change in Al—yes, a *mid-life* change—a sharpening of vision that drove him to write that:

. . . Complacency has allowed many kinds of difficult problems to breed and grow, but now, facing a rapidly deteriorating global environment, it threatens absolute disaster. Now no one can afford to assume that the world will somehow solve its problems. We must all become partners in a bold effort to change the very foundation of our civilization.

In the passionate introduction to his book, the subtitle of which is "Ecology and the Human Spirit," Senator Gore also wrote:

The ecological perspective begins with a view of the whole, an understanding of how the various parts of nature interact in patterns that tend toward balance and persist over time. But this perspective cannot treat the earth as something separate from human civilization; we are part of the whole too, and looking at it ultimately means also looking at ourselves. . . .

. . . As always, it is easier to see the need for change in the larger pattern than to address the need for it in oneself. Nevertheless, with personal commitment, every individual can help ensure that dramatic change does take place. I have therefore come to believe that the world's ecological balance depends on more than just our ability to restore a balance between civilization's ravenous appetite for resources and the fragile equilibrium of the earth's environment. . . . In the end, we must restore a balance with ourselves between who we are and what we are doing.

As if this weren't enough, Gore used the metaphor of a dysfunctional family in his book to show how we must heal ourselves—psychologically and spiritually—in order to heal our ailing environment. This bowled me over. Finally, *someone* in politics was making that connection.

To my knowledge, this was the first time a senior politician in Canada or the U.S. had displayed such an astute understanding of personal and global interdependence. (Suzuki wished Al could run for political office in Canada, citing a vacuum of deep thinking in the Mulroney government of the day.) I was impressed by what I read and told Al that *Earth in the Balance* could be the most important book of the 1990s. It would mean a lot to countless volunteers who had worked so hard to promote ecology issues for so long.

Al asked me about inviting songwriters to compose songs on various environmental issues, such as global warming, to provide another avenue for popular awareness. He wondered if the many songwriters in Nashville (the capital of his home state) might be approached in this regard.

I wasn't sure that what he was asking for could be done, for two good reasons. First, not many songwriters have an understanding of these issues, let alone a feeling for them; and second, a song is not like an information booklet—you can't just sing about an environmental issue using the correct words and expect anyone to listen to you. If the song preaches, you lose most of the audience, and if it isn't a good song, forget about the rest.

Nevertheless, I admired Al for trying to find another way to get the word out as far as he could. That's just what I was trying to do with *Evergreen Everblue.* We had a really good visit and clearly resonated on the important themes. When I asked him if he was thinking of running for President again, he said no, citing family reasons.

I was glad to have had this time with Al, and when he invited me to perform in Nashville a couple of months later, I was delighted to accept. It was for a weekend conference he convened on dysfunctional families, called "Family Re-Union."

The concert was a challenge in that many conference delegates had brought their kids to see me, though I was expecting an adult audience. I quickly went through a mental adjustment and embraced the situation, saying hello to some of my fans while tuning my guitar offstage. A warm welcome ushered in a wonderful evening of singing the mixed repertoire of my Earth songs and a few kids' favorites to everyone's delight.

At dinner, seated between the Gores and joined by a small number of their friends, I felt fortunate to be in this circle of genuinely warm people. I liked Tipper instantly and was interested to hear about her photography and her interest in mental health. Al was, by this time, on the short list of prospects as VP running mate for Governor Bill Clinton (the Democratic Party's nominee for President) and he was giving it consideration.

The table talk was an exchange of views on how to face the many challenges in contemporary society. After listening for a while, I said that beneath the visible issues we were discussing, I perceived a deep and widespread societal malaise, one that we knew was there even if it was hard to talk about. Around the table there was quiet agreement.

On Earth Day 1992, I was invited to a screening of *FernGully* at the UN (a first in the General Assembly Hall), along with Olivia Newton-John, a Goodwill Ambassador for UNEP. Though I was concerned that a few of the scenes would scare little kids, I felt overall that this beautifully animated film was a strong voice for preserving our ancient rainforest treasures. How could it fail to move all those who saw it and heard its call? At the end of the film, Noel Brown called a few people forward for presentations. To my surprise, I was one of them, receiving an Earth Achievement Award for making *Evergreen Everblue* and promoting ecology awareness.

THE RIO SHUFFLE

Losing my future is not like losing an election
or a few points on the stock market . . .
Severn Cullis-Suzuki

WE WERE IN A YEAR UNLIKE ANY OTHER FOR THE PLANET. FIVE hundred years after Columbus stole ashore in the Americas, the world's nations were invited in 1992 to Brazil to chart a course towards finding a balance between human development and environmental protection. The gathering was called the United Nations Conference on Environment and Development (UNCED), also known as the Earth Summit.

It felt exciting to be living in such an important time. Humanity was at a crossroads, and the path we took could lead to either disaster or restoration. I wanted to do all I could for a sustainable future.

Buoyed by my recent UN recognition, I wondered if there was a contribution I might make in Brazil. By now Ron Feiner was acting as my manager. He approached MTV and MuchMusic about my filing reports to them from Rio, but got nowhere. I had even been pushing my video producer friend John Love to join me in Rio with a camera crew, but costs and on-site logistical challenges made us reconsider.

Despite these frustrations, I couldn't help but recognize the unique moment at hand and wanted to respond appropriately. However, taking into account that a role hadn't come my way (and troubled by the growing discomfort of an abdominal hernia), I began to wonder if I should go at all. And then I heard that Severn Cullis-Suzuki, the daughter of David Suzuki and Tara Cullis, and three of her friends—Michelle Quigg, Morgan Geisler and Vanessa Suddie—were raising money to go to Rio as a youth NGO (non-governmental organization). These twelve- and thirteen-year-olds planned to give speeches and set up a booth at the Global Forum part of the conference. It dawned on me that I could go to Rio simply to support *their* voices. They liked the idea, as did David and Tara. When the kids asked me to sing with them, I agreed, even though I was not taking my guitar with me.

The year before, I had joined the David Suzuki Foundation, a non-profit organization formed by David and dedicated to making fundamental changes in the way we think about ourselves and our planet, and promoting solutions that would put us on a sustainable path.

A centerpiece in the Foundation's thinking was the "Declaration of Interdependence" written by David and Tara with help from a few friends; I was delighted when they included some of my suggestions as well. The piece ended up on the back of a 1993 calendar named "Endangered People, Endangered Places," advance copies of which were to be distributed to key participants at UNCED.

In the previous three years, though I had learned a lot about ecology, I still felt like a newcomer around those who had worked on the issues for a long time. There was a whole new language to this advocacy work, from names of pollutants and chemical elements to acronyms like NAFTA and GATT. And, as was the case with my work in children's music in the late 1970's, I went through a similar learning curve with this ecology work. The recognition I received from organizations and colleagues in this field helped me to value my own perspective. Whatever naiveté I brought to the work may not have been a bad thing; sometimes it takes an arrow from the heart to pierce dense policy debates and intellectual elitism.

From the first time I heard about sustainable development, back in the summer of 1989, I disliked the phrase. I saw "development" as a word burdened by the old baggage of the linear expansion of consumer society. Apparently this was the one phrase that would "bring Business to the table" around ecological issues. While I understood that strategically, I still thought that the phrase was of dubious value—a compromise that obscured the deeper process of fundamental value change. My concern was that the phrase put the emphasis on development, however we chose to describe it.

I couldn't deny that the term "sustainable" was useful. Scores of politicians, economists and business people were, perhaps for the first time, thinking in a whole new way, with the notion of sustainability helping to trade short-term myopia for long-term thinking. But if the very idea of development itself was not questioned, then how would we break free of the economic growth model of "bigger-and-newer-is-better"? The root cause of regional problems—often brought about

221

by development and then dealt further development fixes—might never get analyzed or resolved.

Packing for Rio, I was filled with mixed feelings. I had heard that scores of street kids were being rounded up and taken out of town so visiting dignitaries would not see them. Everyone talked about the crime levels, the need to be extra careful, how tight security would be. Yet I'd also heard about the beauty of the place, with its evocative names—Copacabana, Ipanema.

During the ride into the city from the airport, it was hard not to notice scores of young soldiers with automatic rifles, lining avenues and bridges all the way. It turned out that my hotel was almost next door to the one the Suzukis were staying in. I managed to hook up with Tara and we hurriedly left to catch a talk by David and the kids that morning. My spirits were up, but the stifling heat had me wondering if I would make it through my nine-day stay.

We got to the Speaker's Tent just in time for David's speech. After briefly setting the context of the global eco-crisis, he introduced Severn and her friends. Each of the four girls spoke articulately, expressing how it felt to have a dark cloud hovering over their future, and imploring adults to live up to their duty of protecting the Earth for their children. Their words brought tears to the eyes and they received a standing ovation.

We then went to the kids' booth. With a colorful sign, and cards and materials to hand out, the Environmental Children's Organization was now ready for business. The Suzuki Foundation materials were there as well, among them many copies of the Declaration of Interdependence.

Down by the bay—Guanabara Bay—was Flamengo Park, the site of the Global Forum. While UNCED was the political part of the Earth Summit, the Global Forum was where the NGOs operated. This is where I intended to spend most of my time. I walked the grounds and soaked in the pulsating human heart of the world's citizens, beating in tents and booths. There were people of every color and mind, dressed in all kinds of clothes, with some wearing little more than a large plumed headdress.

The list of names for the Speaker's Tent—from David Brower and Vandana Shiva to Jacques Cousteau—was a Who's Who of the world's environmental thinkers. With this compact "Global Ed" course before me, I set about attending as many sessions as my energy would allow in the Rio heat.

Jacques Cousteau's talk was jammed to overflowing. This beloved oceanographer had seen the degradation of the oceans in the last two decades, and he sounded a warning about the collapse of marine ecosystems and the danger that posed. Again it all came down to an interdependent world. If you damaged one part of it, you affected the rest. He cautioned humanity to change its ways, unless we wanted our children and grandchildren to "live like rats."

When Senator Gore came into the Speaker's Tent and we exchanged greetings, he invited me to a reception later that evening. Among the attendees were Noel Brown, activist Bianca Jagger, and Tom Van Sant, the inventor of a new photographic representation of the Earth, achieved by compiling crystal-clear images shot from a high elevation on cloudless days. A seven-foot-high model of the Earth made of these images sat as a centerpoint for this gathering and, in a strange twist—a message perhaps?—during one of the speeches the globe fell from its base with a thud.

The reception thrown by the Canadian Ministry of the Environment was what I expected, if not all I'd hoped for. I was glad to see Jim Fulton, then parliamentarian and Environment Critic. The Canadian NGOs were strongly represented by, among others, Vicky Husband of the Sierra Club, Colleen McCrory of the Valhalla Wilderness Society (who had just won the prestigious Goldman Prize), and Elizabeth May, Cultural Survival's impassioned advocate. A question period produced little to cheer for from the government side. Most of the inspiration came from comments made by NGO members.

Another aspect of the conference was the Earth Parliament, ostensibly a forum for indigenous peoples to voice their perspectives. (However, to many, separating these people from the main proceedings looked like another divide-and-conquer tactic.) I was there on two occasions. The first was with Severn, Vanessa, Michelle and Morgan, who spoke onstage during a designated Children's Day. After their speeches, I joined them to sing a song on global warming (one that I co-wrote at a Vancouver Children's Festival songwriting symposium with a group of teenagers).

A gathering of indigenous leaders brought me back to the Earth Parliament a second time. Representatives of many of the world's First Peoples were standing shoulder to shoulder, and each spoke in turn about the threats that development imposed on their culture, and the storehouse of human wisdom that was in danger of being lost forever. Among those assembled was Mutang Urud, now leader of the Sarawak Indigenous Peoples' Alliance. It was good to see Mutang again. I hadn't seen him since his role in the *Evergreen Everblue* video.

An invited, non-indigenous guest joined the leaders. Wearing jeans and a green T-shirt, Al Gore spoke in passionate support of indigenous peoples and their "intellectual property rights," calling specifically for an end to the commercial exploitation of their lands without compensation. Gore's speech earned vigorous applause. Though my mind drifted to the continuing apartheid-like situation of the indigenous peoples of both the U.S. and Canada, my heart again wanted to believe in this flicker of hope represented by this respected Senator.

The end of this story is an act of courage by a twelve-year-old girl and her supportive family and friends.

At the official UNCED plenary hall on the last day of my stay in Rio, I had the privilege of hearing a talk that rang from the heart and soul of Severn Cullis-Suzuki. In a speech that she edited at the last minute to include the sentiments of her friends, Severn said:

We [came] 6,000 miles to tell you adults you must change your ways. . . .

At school, even in kindergarten, you teach us how to behave in the world. You teach us: not to fight with others; to work things out; to respect others; to clean up our mess; not to hurt other creatures; to share, not be greedy. Then why do you go out and do the things you tell us not to do?

Do not forget why you attend these conferences, who you are doing this for—we are your own children. You are deciding what kind of world we will grow up in. . . . You grown-ups say you love us. I challenge you, please, make your actions reflect your words.

Their professional reserve temporarily shed, 200 diplomats couldn't stop clapping and found themselves standing in unison to praise the clear admonition of this young voice.

I was reminded of the full power of children speaking their mind, and resolved to go back to Vancouver and find a way to support them in expressing their own hopes and dreams. During dinner with David, I voiced that sentiment, though I did not yet know how to pursue it. He encouraged me to rejoin my fans and make more music for family audiences. Images of performing again, this time perhaps sharing the stage with children, danced before my eyes.

* * *

When the Clinton-Gore ticket won the 1992 U.S. Presidential election, Washington was abuzz with the hope that we might see a change in politics-as-usual. Environmental campaigners were excited too: the Environmental Protection Agency would again be held in esteem, Al Gore might be able to act on the themes in his book.

In December I got an unusual Christmas present—an invitation to sing with President-Elect Clinton the following month in a Disney Channel's TV Special, "Inaugural Celebration for Children."

I was to perform two songs at the top of the show and then return to lead the finale.

What a way to start a new year: at the Kennedy Center in Washington, DC, rehearsing for the event with Kermit the Frog, Fred Rogers and others for the Inaugural Special. It all went so fast. Before I knew it, host Markie Post introduced Hillary Rodham Clinton, who explained to the children what a Presidential Inauguration was. Then it was my turn, singing *All I Really Need* and *Baby Beluga* to the very vocal capacity crowd.

A variety of performers led to the appearance of the beloved Mr. Rogers who, when he was done, calmly brought out a surprise: the President-Elect himself! Standing ovation, rhythmic applause—the place went wild. After things calmed down, the two men chatted for a while and Mr. Clinton answered questions submitted by children, such as "Do you ever get angry?" and "How many washrooms are there in the White House?" Clinton was his affable best.

To close the show, Markie and I came out to lead the finale with Mr. Rogers and the President-Elect. When I shook hands with Clinton, he noticed my flamboyant tie and said, "That's a very nice tie." Turning to the crowd, he said, "Isn't that a nice tie? I used to wear ties like that before I ran for President!" With that spark, *This Little Light of Mine* caught fire, and we were joined by Hillary Clinton, Kermit and the rest of the cast to sing it home.

In the Inaugural Parade the following afternoon, I was part of the procession. Waving at the crowds lining both sides of Pennsylvania Avenue warmed my heart on that cold day. I heard their voices singing *Baby Beluga* all along the way.

VI

HOMECOMING

*Only recently have we
become aware, fully aware,
from our studies of healthy people, of the creative
process, of play, of aesthetic perception . . . that
every human being is both poet and engineer,
both rational and nonrational,
both child and adult,
both masculine and feminine,
both in the psychic world
and in the world of nature.*

Abraham Maslow

THE COMEBACK TRAIL

THE ROAD BACK TO CHILDREN'S MUSIC WAS A MEANDERING ONE.

In the fall of 1992, when I told Lynne Partridge that I was ready to tour again, she was very pleased and got on the phone right away. Before long she had contacted tour manager Bob Silk and come up with a list of musicians for me to consider in my band.

For the new kind of concerts I was considering—where singing children would join me in the show—I wanted a different sound, ideally with a smaller band. The key would be to find a versatile keyboardist who could fill the air with a variety of sounds and accompany me in a number of styles. I called my Vancouver friends to help me track down the right person: a talented musician with a sense of humor, and someone who would enjoy performing for family audiences.

Keyboardist Michael Creber came highly recommended. He had toured for years with the Irish Rovers and, more recently, had been in k.d. lang's band. I called him up immediately and invited him over to play a few tunes on my electric piano. I ran him through a selection of songs and he played beautifully to my singing. This good-natured man certainly had the touring experience, the musical chops, and lots of jokes. Michael got the gig. I asked him to go on the road with me, starting November.

For the first time since 1988, I was booked to go on tour again. It was both exciting and a little scary. Would the audiences sing with me like they used to? Would I be up to the task? Would it be fun?

The concert we were planning was something new for me. I designed a show that would play to a broad family audience, meaning that the ten-year-old and the seven-year-old would enjoy the outing as much as the younger children and their parents. It was billed as a *family* concert and would start at 7 p.m. In media interviews, I said that this show would be a celebration of life on Earth and would include environmental songs. I chose my words carefully to give a clear sense of the program and, I hoped, to draw the appropriate audience to sing with.

No matter how many times Lynne, Ron and our New York based publicist, Marian Rivman, suggested that I add *Apples and Bananas* and *Shake My Sillies Out* to the repertoire, two favorites of the very young, I simply wasn't ready to sing them. I knew I couldn't just pick up where I left off in 1988. I had to be who I was now, and that person very much wanted to share his concerns for the planet with his audience.

The "comeback tour" that began in November of 1992 in Seattle played in sixty cities in the U.S. and Canada before it was over a year later.

Down the West Coast we went and across California, through the heartland of the American mid-west and onto the Eastern seaboard, playing before huge crowds.

From the moment I walked back onstage in Seattle, fans gave me a warm welcome and sounded very happy to see me. Still, I was quite a changed man from the person I had been a few years ago, and the show reflected that change. It contained a number of my *Evergreen Everblue* songs, both singalong ones like *Big Beautiful Planet* and *Clean Rain* and the more grown-up *Mama's Kitchen*.

Though I loved singing *Baby Beluga* again and hearing my fans belt it out, I was not ready to jump solely into unabashed play. After the song, I briefly talked about the belugas' plight in the St. Lawrence River, hoping that the disclosure would give the older members of the audience something to think about. Then I lightened the mood with imitations of how others would sing *Baby Beluga*: Bob Dylan, U.S. Presidential candidate Ross Perot, and Elvis. Dylan's gruff style drew howls of laughter; Ross, well, he didn't quite sing it—he talked about it, something about finding a team of experts to go out and protect that little whale; and Elvis sang the song to the tune of *Don't Be Cruel*. The bit was a hit, and even my littlest fans laughed to hear their Raffi sounding so silly.

In concert, I sported a tie, the one President-Elect Clinton had admired at the Kennedy Center—and fans all across the continent enjoyed its wild colors. Another twist was that, for the first time, I had youngsters onstage with me. These were a dozen kids between the ages of eight and ten, chosen ahead of time in each community I visited, from the local chapter of an American group with members around the world. The group was called Kids for Saving Earth (or KSE), and had been started by eleven-year-old Clinton Hill, a boy with a passion for the planet, who died of cancer a few months after he set up the first KSE club. For his mother, Tessa, KSE became a full-time calling. It seemed like a good fit to have KSE kids sing a couple of songs with me to acknowledge young people's concern for the Earth and highlight an example of positive action.

Bassist Connie Lebeau (of Victoria) had joined the tour in Los Angeles. Connie's fine vocals and cheerful presence were a welcome addition to the show, adding harmony and texture to the songs. Michael and I appreciated her solid playing and all-round musicianship. She even played the accordion on a couple of numbers, much to our delight. On top of that, she was great company.

Fans were so excited about my return to the stage that they packed the theaters. The 4,300-seat Fox Theater in St. Louis, for example, was completely sold out—the promoter said we could have had at least one more packed house.

People sang, clapped and stomped along, just like in the old days. The KSE kids got a warm reception and I enjoyed hearing their voices.

Concert-hungry fans sang *Day O* and *Down by the Bay* at the top of their lungs, and gave Michael and Connie a big hand. They may not have heard as many infant songs as they might have liked, but the overall mix was enthusiastically received, judging from the response both during the program and at its rousing encore finale. All this was music to my ears. So was the news the following April that the Recording Industry of America was putting an end to the wasteful CD longbox.

During the fall of 1993, we performed in a number of Canadian cities, from Montreal to Victoria. One day I even had time for a wonderful visit with entertainer Al Simmons and his family in their rural home north of Winnipeg. I well remember the golden light on the prairies that autumn. It contrasted sharply with a federal election campaign devoid of Earth imagery, let alone echoes of Rio only a year after the Earth Summit.

A few dates into the tour, Ron's assistant, Lee Moskof, had an idea: why not bring the show to Broadway? At first I was taken aback. Broadway and its musicals weren't exactly me. But I began to see that here was a chance to take our environmental message to the heart of the big city. And when Ron negotiated a video deal for the show with MCA—a deal involving video-maker John Love and pop legend Phil Ramone as producer—it was a go.

A New York director, Phil Adelman, flew to Toronto to go over the lineup of songs with me and make some adjustments. (Phil was a fan—he had sent me that tie I'd been wearing.) We did keep the basic repertoire, but Phil's suggestions made it a better show and for that I was grateful.

A big ad in the *Sunday Times* announced "Raffi on Broadway: At the Gershwin Theater." Six shows nearly sold out the next day. The Troubadour gang and Michael, Connie and I were very excited. Few Canadians got to make this kind of noise, and we were wowed by the opportunity.

Of course, it made my life crazy for a couple of months.

Ron and Lee attended to the infinite details that went with mounting a Broadway show and, on top of my already-busy concert schedule, I had meetings with John and the two Phils to go over the creative aspects. They found a terrific group of kids to sing with me and, before I knew it, I was in New York for the rehearsals. Although by now I was very familiar with the show, there were new elements like TV camera angles to consider, stage moves to "block," the kids to meet and rehearse with, and entrances and exits to choreograph. A tad more theater for Connie, Michael and me, and a whole lot more work.

And so it came to be: my Broadway debut. The concerts went very well and the audiences were warm and appreciative.

For many days after the excitement faded, I worked long hours with John and Phil Ramone to put the finishing touches to both the video and its soundtrack album. Our performances on the Gershwin Theater stage had been captured beautifully and we also had excellent footage of the audience to work with. Once again, frame-by-frame detail and audio frequency specs vied for attention along with the bigger picture of these recordings.

It was late spring and real drudgery to be indoors all day in closed rooms, directing electronic machinery through hundreds of moves. At the end of the day I'd return to the hotel mentally and physically fatigued, so exhausted that all I could do was veg in front of the TV. There came a point of diminishing returns, where health spas and massage could only help so much. And, as good as the take-out food in New York can be, I longed for the West Coast, to be home and be stilled by the mountains and the sea.

But there was no way any song on this video was going to get less than the full attention it deserved. Anticipating possible international release if the North American sales were good, we had taped two special songs to close the program.

One was *Haru Ga Kita*, a beautiful Japanese ballad about the coming of spring, which I had recorded (with vocals by my niece, Kristin) on the *Everything Grows* album. The other was a song I learned from a Pete Seeger recording. Pete also told me it was written by a four-year-old Russian boy in the 1950s, who wrote all four lines of the song on a drawing he made. This touching little song was called *Poost Vig Da Boodyet Solntse*, a phrase that means "may there always be sunshine." My performance included verses in four languages: Russian, English, Spanish and French.

To our great disappointment, the release of "Raffi on Broadway" in video and audio was fraught with problems. The product was late to arrive at retail and, once there, didn't catch fire with fans who really wanted a new studio album, not an eco-concert with many songs already on previous albums or videos.

Surprisingly, the Broadway angle didn't help sales either, making some people wonder whether I had changed my singing style. Though the media interviews I gave stressed the positives of this new work, it seemed that the public was less interested in the environmental message than in the Raffi children's songs it hoped for. And then there was the puzzling reaction of the CBC to my six sold-out shows on Broadway. National shows we approached for interviews on both CBC TV and Radio weren't interested and ignored the achievement.

Though the video was shown in its entirety on the Disney Channel and some time later on CBC, sales never clicked. I had to live with the fact that I'd busted my butt on Broadway on a very expensive project with a legendary producer, only to see expectations plummet. I comforted myself by remembering that not all creative ventures succeed commercially.

The winds of change were blowing again. A few months previously, Lynne Partridge had left Troubadour to pursue her dream of operating a bed and breakfast. In her absence, I had become closely involved in the company's day-to-day operations, ably assisted by Fiona Smith and Katherine Bellamy in Vancouver. After the mixed results of the Broadway release, I sadly realized that it was time to curtail the management services that Ron and Lee had provided. I knew I had to bring the direction of my career back within Troubadour's nest.

* * *

Around this time my sister was recovering from a health concern that came to a head in 1992. Luckily, Ani has the combined strength and drive of both our parents, a trait that served her well in the ordeal she faced when a tumor was discovered in her brain. It was determined that she would require brain surgery. To the great relief of the entire family, the procedure went very well and she was given a new lease on life. Not one to stay still for too long, a few months later Ani was back at her job full time. What's more, a year later she decided to write a book—the bulk of which she completed in a remarkable six months, a feat that still amazes me. *Who Knows: Safeguarding Your Privacy in a Networked World* (co-authored with Don Tapscott) was published in Canada in 1995. It became a best-seller and was published in the U.S. the following year.

SUNSHINE AND GORBY

IT WAS WITH MUCH SURPRISE AND GREAT DELIGHT THAT I RECEIVED an invitation to perform at the Kyoto Global Forum, which took place during the week spanning Earth Day 1993.

The original Global Forum of Spiritual and Parliamentary Leaders on Human Survival was born in 1985 when, on the fortieth anniversary of the UN's founding, a small group of religious and political leaders from all over the world met near New York City. Discussing critical survival issues that would combine the practical with the moral and ethical, they called upon colleagues from all nations to join them in a conference on global survival.

The first Global Survival Conference was in Oxford, England, in April 1988. Attending were parliamentary and spiritual leaders from fifty-two countries, as well as scientists, artists and journalists. Inspired by that first assembly, the Soviet government invited the Global Forum to Moscow in January 1990 for a conference on environment and development.

The Moscow Forum drew a thousand participants from eighty-three countries and was hailed by then-President Mikhail Gorbachev as "a major step toward the ecological consciousness of humanity." I remember hearing about that event, and thinking how far-sighted it was of Gorbachev to host it (something one couldn't imagine coming from George Bush or Brian Mulroney).

Before I had even left for Japan, my publicist, Marian Rivman, faxed me the news release of the daily briefing from Kyoto, which read in part: "President Mikhail Gorbachev was greeted by students from the Kyoto International School (KIS) who serenaded Mr. Gorbachev with a song *Dear Mother*, written by world-renowned children's entertainer Raffi. . . . President Gorbachev observed, 'I particularly enjoyed meeting with children from the KIS who sang to me . . . Their song *Dear Mother—Mother Earth*—gives me hope that our children will lead us in the value change which is so necessary if we are to save our earth—Our Dear Mother.'" One more "dear" would have got it right—but who was complaining? I was abuzz as I boarded the flight for Kyoto and a likely meeting with one of the most important national leaders of our times.

The theme of the Kyoto Global Forum was "Value Change for Global Survival." Another reason for my excitement about this event was that David Suzuki would be there with daughter Severn, who was scheduled to be the closing speaker. Back in 1989, David had been among the first to use the word "survival" in describing the seriousness of the threat to humanity's future. Now it appeared that survival was very much the context of these upcoming discussions.

The conference was memorable in so many ways.

At a luncheon reception for Gorbachev, I took advantage of the opportunity to introduce myself. His translator explained that I wrote the song the children from the International School sang to him and, as I shook his hand, I said in Russian, *"Poost vig da boodyet Gorby!"* (may there always be Gorby), which turned him and his wife, Raisa, all smiles and laughter. It made my day. That afternoon, amidst the pink and white April blossoms, Gorbachev presided over a tree-planting ceremony that included Severn among its special guests, as well as children from the African country of Gabon.

I learned from Marian that a Japanese choir was ready to sing with me in the forthcoming Earth Day concert, and that a visit to the International School would yield another singing opportunity with its choir for the conference's last day. She also had a surprise for me: I was among the few invitees to a dinner hosted by the Gorbachevs the following night. Apparently, Gorbachev enjoyed meeting artists and valued their perspective on issues. I could hardly believe my good fortune.

Gorbachev was in Kyoto primarily for his work with a new organization, the International Green Cross. This initiative grew from the Moscow Forum, where Gorbachev had urged the formation of a body to assist any state in ecological trouble. Its mandate was fourfold: to serve and collaborate with existing groups already working to foster a change of values; to advocate wise ecological policy and law; to prevent disasters; and to provide expert support and rapid response services in the event of environmental emergencies. (It was said that Gorbachev had been profoundly affected by the colossal disaster resulting from the meltdown of the nuclear plant at Chernobyl, and that the tragedy had been a turning point in his ecological awareness.)

In his inaugural address as head of the International Green Cross, Gorbachev gave a stirring speech, ultimately appealing to the conscience and moral spirit of the world to fashion an ecological imperative by which humanity would be bound. "What should we rely on in our struggle for the survival of mankind?" Gorbachev asked.

His reply included these thoughts:

> Without an ecology of spirit . . . all our efforts to save mankind would be pointless. . . . Life itself is the greatest moral value on which our civilization should be based. Today it is not enough to say, "Thou shalt not kill." Ecological implication assumes, above all, respect and love for all living things. . . .The philosophy of survival is based on this philosophy of diversity.

He stressed the need to move from the industrial age philosophy of conquering nature and reshaping the world to "a philosophy of limits," one that constrains human pride and human passions. He went on:

> The ecology of moral and spiritual health implies the rejection of racism, chauvinism and national arrogance in whatever manifestations. . . . A human civilization will be a planetary civilization. . . . We should form a new kind of ecological literacy, a new relationship with nature, a new meaning of some traditional values. . . .
>
> . . . The 20th century was, in effect, a century of warning. The 21st century will be either the century of total crisis, or the century of human recovery, the century of human revival.

When we got our breath back, Suzuki and I couldn't get over what a radical speech it was. Clearly a remarkable transformation had occurred in the life of the former President of the Soviet Union—an inspiring example of the value change he was talking about.

A colorful "Welcome Raffi" sign greeted me and my guitar at the International School the next day. The teachers and the kids were primed for photos, fun and learning a Raffi song. We rehearsed *All I Really Need* a number of times, the children's voices charming the warm spring day.

Before I knew it, it was time for dinner with the Gorbachevs. There were about twelve of us around the rectangular table, with

Gorbachev seated in the middle, Raisa to his left and then me, flanked by an interpreter.

I enjoyed a lengthy conversation with Raisa (with the interpreter's help). When she learned I was of Armenian descent, she spoke compassionately of the unfortunate armed conflict between Armenia and neighboring Azerbaijan. Her astuteness and considerable charm moved me. Charm was not in short supply with her husband either: Mikhail Sergeyevich had the ability to light up a room with his smile and abundant humor. He was very open and accessible during his Kyoto stay, and especially so at this dinner.

After spending much of the next day attending Forum sessions, I rehearsed in the late afternoon with the Japanese Children's Choir, preparing for that evening's concert. On our program was the song *Haru Ga Kita*, which all the children knew as a popular folk song in their country, and *Evergreen Everblue*, a new song for them.

As the Earth Day concert began, I waited backstage with my guitar, watching some of the performances and getting ready for mine. Suddenly appearing at my side was Hugh Locke, the man in charge of the Gorbachevs' itinerary, with a question for me. Because the Gorbachevs couldn't stay for the entire evening, would I mind if, at the end of my three-song set, they joined me onstage to say their good-byes? Of course I agreed.

Finally my time came and I was up singing the two songs I had added to my Broadway video: the Russian song (which I sang solo) and *Haru Ga Kita*, which I performed backed by the Japanese children.

Then, in my closing song, as the choir and I reached *Evergreen Everblue*'s repeated chant, "Help this planet Earth . . . oh, help this planet Earth," I saw a commotion below me in the hall . . . a herd of photographers, flashes going off, rushing towards me . . . and now the Gorbachevs were walking up onto the stage . . . the place simply ELECTRIC, the crowd all chanting with us, "Help this planet Earth, yea, help this planet Earth. . . ."

The next few elastic moments were of a rare and unexpected variety. The song ended and, during the applause, Gorby gave me a big hug. As I stood beside the choir, he praised my singing, and Raisa even suggested I learn some Russian "romances" (love songs). Those of us gathered in the hall that night were then treated to the warmth of an unhurried farewell from this remarkable couple. In his closing comments, Gorbachev thanked the conference participants for supporting the Green Cross, before embarking on his new mission. He and Raisa left the stage, shaking the outstretched hands of the excited choir children.

For the final morning session, the students from the Kyoto International School joined me in song. And Severn, as the Global Forum's closing speaker, gave a speech much like the one in Rio. As happened there, everyone rose to applaud and there was hardly a dry eye in the house. I wondered how the conference might have gone if she had been the *opening* speaker. Would the talk of this outstanding children's ambassador have set a tone that compelled the participants to address even more directly the points she raised?

These conferences have a way of keeping one's light shining. Though I didn't get out to visit Kyoto's ancient shrines, sharing the temples of our hearts those few days at the Global Forum rekindled a great deal of hope in mine.

One footnote to the Gorbachev story. Some months later, I was invited to sing in Washington, DC, at the launch of Green Cross USA. Once again I found myself in great company. Seated at the head table with Jane Goodall, Chief Oren Lyons of the Onandaga, Ted Turner, Jane Fonda and Yoko Ono, I was pleased to see Gorbachev right across from me. He greeted me warmly and asked if the gathering would be hearing my prayers that day. When I asked his interpreter, Pavel, for clarification, Pavel said, "Prayer, yes, that's what he calls your songs." I turned to Gorby; his face was radiant, beaming.

SOCIAL VENTURING

AROUND THIS TIME, I READ A BOOK THAT MADE QUITE AN IMPACT on my thinking about values, business and the business of money. Paul Hawken's *The Ecology of Commerce* took a fresh look at the unsustainable way most business is conducted, and outlined principles of sustainable commerce that would be required for a "restorative economy," one that would support the health of all living systems while providing for human needs.

Hawken challenged the notion of commerce conducted in a climate of maximum activity and minimum accountability. He called for a redesign of the financial and production biases that create the substantial hidden costs of social inequities and environmental decline. He surprised economists and environmentalists alike with his contention that business was the only mechanism powerful enough to reverse the world's social and environmental degradation. His solution called for integrating economy and ecology and operating within nature's biological design limits. Reading this book, I felt a broadening of perspective—it was just the kind of integrated thinking I cherish.

In Vancouver, I met with a money manager who handled "ethical investments," mutual funds with social and environmental "screens" by which money can be prevented from going into ventures that might be unsavory to the investor. This way investors can choose where they invest, to reflect the values they hold. (The idea originated in the conscientious actions of American religious groups that refused to invest their holdings in companies that dealt with South Africa.

Over the years the approach proved successful in its returns, and it grew in its scope of concerns.)

I found out that a fund could be custom-designed around one's concerns, as long as the highest interest rate wasn't the primary goal. That being the case with me, we designed a portfolio that would ensure my investments were not in companies that dealt with tobacco or military sales, for example. Knowing that this manager's firm had a good track record in ethical investments, I was excited to have found a new way to put my money where my mouth was.

The more I thought about it, the more I realized that ethical investment funds could be an important way to steer commercial activity towards good. Given its tremendous power in this world and the way it is worshipped and wielded, money is clearly a form of energy, not something neutral. And, if it is not directed towards good, it defaults towards the opposite—what might well amount to an indiscriminate and amoral power.

In 1994, I attended an unusual conference in San Diego, a three-day gathering of an alternative business community called the Social Venture Network (SVN). In its own words, SVN is "an international organization of successful business and social entrepreneurs dedicated to changing the way the world does business and to using our influence to promote progressive solutions to social problems." Member companies include The Body Shop, Ben and Jerry's, the *Utne Reader* and Reebok International. To join the network, member companies have to be successful (with minimum annual revenue) and have to show a track record in social responsibility. That way each member is proof that you can "do the right thing" and be profitable—or, in other words, "do well by doing good."

In the breakfast hall of the conference hotel that first time, I felt right at home. People looked relaxed, they were casually dressed and, from what I could see, they were having a lot of fun. Admittedly, many members either knew of my music or had children who were fans, so the connection I felt was not solely due to a shared interest in doing good in the world.

As it happened, one of the keynote presenters at this conference was Paul Hawken, who gave a very inspiring talk on transforming the way we conduct business. He spoke with quiet assurance of a shift from linear, growth-driven, wasteful, disemploying, environmentally destructive commerce to a circular, cyclical, efficient, employing and environmentally restorative economy. He expressed his ideas with an upbeat tone that suggested all this change was not only possible, it was inevitable. It sounded like the most reasonable thing in the world.

Another presenter that moved me was Marian Wright Edelman of the Children's Defense Fund (Washington, DC). She spoke with power and compassion about the huge number of American children living in poverty and under threat of violent crime, and the need for a personal and institutional response to this crisis. I knew the child poverty numbers were high in Canada as well, somewhere around one in five children. It gave me pause to think about the ways an unsustainable, irresponsible economy might be linked to the social misery of poor children—their diminished lives, their dim hopes for the future—and what the cost of this to society might be. I started to make more connections between issues.

At the conference "products expo," a large sample of goods from member companies was on display, including clothing made from organic cotton. When I learned that the global production of cotton uses vast quantities of pesticides, the organic alternative looked even better. During the three days, I also attended a number of talking circle workshops (groups of twenty or so people) where I heard ideas such as "multiple bottom line" (financial, social and environmental), and shared with others my passion for ecology.

Throughout the proceedings there was a good deal of lighthearted play, a great feeling of camaraderie, and the uplifting spirit of people making a positive difference in the world. Here were individuals who were actively seeking integration in their lives, who could talk about soul and business in the same breath. Ram Dass, a longtime board member, brought a spiritual perspective to the gathering and provided a forum of personal and group reflection in the Quaker-style meetings he facilitated.

The SVN members—like Gary Hirshberg, award-winning CEO of Stonyfield Farms, a thriving New Hampshire yogurt company— were, I thought, the cream of the '60s rebels: idealists who succeeded in the marketplace, but without leaving their ideals behind. I was easily cajoled into singing a few songs during the day, and then a lot more in a late-night hotel room singalong where we ran through them all— Peter, Paul and Mary, the Beatles, Joni Mitchell and more. I even revived my Dylan imitation. By the time the conference ended, I felt I had made new friends who would figure significantly in my life.

A POSITIVE EMBRACE

WORKING IN THE ARTS IS AN ONGOING CREATIVE DANCE. When one door closes, you look for another opening, another dream that might take shape. You constantly evaluate where you are and what opportunities arise and, if you're like me, you move from the inside out, doing your best to remember what's important to you and looking to express that in a new way. Directing an entertainment career is not unlike managing a string of political election campaigns. You want to "get the vote out" to support your candidate.

Up to the fall of 1993, I hadn't done a concert tour in Canada for many years. Where once the mere mention of a concert would have guaranteed a packed house, now we had to work hard to attract good crowds. Still, in many cities there were far too many empty seats.

On the plus side, the disappointments were balanced by wonderful audiences who stayed with me, note for note. There were many teens who came to the shows to sing along with their old friend, and that was very gratifying. I often met with them backstage. Some would get shy, quietly seeking an autograph; others were boisterous, approving my rap version of *Brush Your Teeth*. Some even said I was an inspiration and told me of their work in care of the Earth. I treasured these moments with kids who had grown up with my music—just the tonic I needed to get me through the ups and downs of life on the road.

One enduring aspect of this tour was a banana joke, a gag I did on stage with Michael, that turned into an idea for a song. The gag involved holding a banana to my ear as if it were a telephone. Audiences laughed when I talked on this pretend phone and I later dubbed it "bananaphone."

All through the tour I had boasted that the show featured bad jokes. Now it was time to take my punning nature a bit further. In the shortening days at year's end, it occurred to me to take the funster in me and let it go. I needed more fun—both on and off the stage.

It was the beginning of a return to play.

After coming through two years of painful changes, I was searching for a way to be. I wondered if there was an approach that didn't narrow life down to a superficial goodness, yet that offered the least turbulence in daily life—a state of inner peace.

I thought about how the ever-fleeting "now"—this moment—could feel unsafe even if there was no imminent threat of harm, and how the mind's worrying and projecting could keep anxiety near in the course of a given day. Living in the present, I knew, was the way to feeling joy in *every* day. If you removed anxieties that came from the mind's racing ahead (really a form of the worrisome ego in control), maybe the absence of such stress could open a space of stillness for the joy of being alive.

Once again, as I had done in my yoga days, I invited positive imagery into my personal life and continued my inquiry into the magical nature of Creation. In past years, I had tried various forms of affirmations to help me stay centered and in a positive vibe. But I really hadn't grasped how they worked, usually thinking, at some point, that saying daily affirmations couldn't be of much use.

What brought me close enough to see all this in a new light was Deepak Chopra's book *Quantum Healing*, which describes the body's cellular wisdom and the interrelatedness of all the living processes within our bodies. According to Chopra, "the immune system has a habit of eavesdropping on the thoughts of the mind." I warmed to the idea that the very quality of my mental vibrations might have an effect on my whole body and my overall health. The next step was to think about what state of mind I most desired and how I might access that on a day-to-day basis.

Remembering Gandhi's idea of *becoming* the change we seek in the world, I knew I wanted to access inner joy and peace. The real break-through came when I realized there was no need to postpone these feelings to another day when I would have such-and-such done and things would be better. *That day* is fantasy and does not exist. I could forever be postponing joy.

So, I took to writing an affirmation for myself, one that aspired to a viable way of being while acknowledging the storms that come and rock one's best intentions. I would begin and sometimes end each day with saying it (silently or out loud), thinking about its meaning all the while.

My goal was to have the mind and heart in concert, to spin kindness in as many ways as possible. Not that I was able to actualize this every day—far from it. But now I had some words to ring in the new day intentionally, to send a clear signal to all the cells of my being as to what I wanted. And when conflict did arise, I found I was able to choose a more helpful response than what might have come up before. This new "response-ability" allowed me to make more room for others and, in this growing tolerance, I found a measure of personal peace.

These days I was laughing more than I had in a long time, as if finally realizing that laughter was utterly indispensable, helping make light of things that might have otherwise bothered me. I liked this new lightness of mind.

BANANAMANIA

THERE WAS MORE GOOD NEWS. CONVERSATIONS WITH MY OLD friend and colleague Bert Simpson, who had come to see my Broadway show, led to his rejoining Troubadour. I knew that Troubadour could only benefit from our renewed collaboration. Bert would be a management associate, working from Toronto, or Troubadour East as we called it. To run the company in Vancouver, we hired Ruth MacPhee, whose creative energy, I felt, would more than offset her lack of music industry background. Given the need—for financial and logistical reasons—to look for legal counsel closer to home, we turned to Vancouver entertainment lawyer Ken Dangerfield, a seasoned and effective voice to guide the new team.

When it was time to record a new album, I thought it might be fun to work with someone who definitely has his share of laughs—my touring partner, Michael Creber. On the road, Michael and I had had such a great time with wordplay that I asked him to co-write a bunch of new songs with me for this album. I knew his strong musicianship would be a boon to the tunes I dreamed up, and so it was.

We got together at my place a couple of times a week all through January and February to write songs over coffee and biscotti, and with the occasional walk on the beach to help the lyrics flow when we got stuck. Michael was an ideal collaborator for me, coming up with inventive musical bridges in songs, confirming some of my ideas, and helping me move through hurdles both real and imaginary. And, what's more, he was full of jokes. We had "too much fun," as he would say.

Among the first songs we worked on was the title song of the album, *Bananaphone*. I was glad it came along when it did, because it was just the right idea-form to express, in a really upbeat way, the importance of stimulating a child's imagination. A comedic send-up of the "inter-active" high-tech hype, *Bananaphone* used puns galore to bravely go where no banana (since *Day-O*) had gone before—into the minds of just about everyone who heard it and said, "I can't get that song out of my head." (It drove them bananas.)

I had an early sense of a melody and lyrics, but they were a bit plodding and didn't really cut it. Then, out of nowhere, one morning I just put a few "rings" together in a row . . . and there it was, a very simple first line and verse idea that worked like a charm, in a musical style that sounded like a relaxed version of a 1920s Charleston. And the song's mocking mood conjured up a new word: "interactivodular." It had just the right stupid-smarts for Michael and me. Before we were done, we had managed to put pizza, the White House, Beijing and yin-yang into the darn song!

As for the rest of the album, time and time again, as we wrote lines to various songs, we encouraged each other to be bold. Why not have a ball? And have a ball we did, coming up with a wide variety of songs. *Shake a Toe* seemed like a *Shake My Sillies Out* for the '90s:

> *Everybody come shake a toe, from your head to your feet*
> *In the rhythm of the come-and-go, shake a toe toe toe*
> *Come together and shake, like a birdie on a wing wing wing*
> *Feel the rhythm and groove, shake a toe toe toe.*

The World We Love turned into a ballad in three-quarter time, an ode to beauty in the world. The song *Slow Day* was a real sleeper, written with my first sip of coffee, as I looked out the window one overcast morning. It featured some of my best scat-singing to date, Leon Redbone style. Lyrically, some of my favorite lines were in the organic farming song, *Naturally*:

See that soil with the good manure,
It's the living end, it's so darned pure —
Feeding the earth, naturally.

The album also included pensive songs like *The Changing Garden of Mr. Bell*, a moving piece written by Janice Hubbard, whom I met at the Disney Presidential Inaugural TV show. The song has a Zen quality that's hard to explain, an unsentimental yet compassionate rendering of passing stages in a man's life. The changing garden he tends is both real and a metaphor.

One song I'd been writing off and on for over a year, about indigenous people around the world, finally got done with Michael's help and encouragement. *First Peoples* was a delicate song to write, open as the subject was to sentimentality and romanticism despite one's best intentions. The lyrics we came up with celebrated indigenous cultures by naming a number of such peoples and paying tribute to their part in the human family. We recorded it with our friend Randy Raine-Reusch playing a number of instruments he had gathered from all over the world, and Michael playing the didgeridoo. And my young friend Severn (now fourteen) narrated two short descriptive pieces that I wrote to frame the verses. It was quite a production number and I was very pleased with how it turned out.

Bananaphone's repertoire included the Shaker hymn, *Simple Gifts*, C-A-N-A-D-A by country music great Stompin' Tom Connors, and *The Shmenge Polka*, my very first polka composition and a tribute to the late John Candy.

In the middle of this banana madness came a communiqué from Kenya. We got word that I had been named to UNEP's Global 500 Honor Roll for Environmental Achievement and invited to London to receive the award. Beijing had been the site of the awards the previous year, with Severn being one of the youngest honorees. I was proud to be the next Canadian recipient.

The United Nations Environment Program (UNEP) launched the Global 500 Roll of Honor in 1987 for outstanding achievements in ecology advocacy. On June 5, 1994, World Environment Day, this year's honorees assembled inside the Queen Elizabeth II Conference Centre in London. Presiding over the awards was UNEP's Under-Secretary-General, Elizabeth Dowdeswell, a Canadian from Saskatoon (then stationed in Nairobi, Kenya).

And once again it inspired me to meet people from all over the globe, doing marvelous work to preserve the world we love.

One example was Omar Castillo Gallegos, a young Mexican recipient who, since the age of eight, had rallied public opinion in Mexico for the protection of nature, working with indigenous peoples and walking and bicycling thousands of kilometers to raise ecological awareness. Another honoree was Bernadette Vallely of London, who founded the Women's Environmental Network (WEN), one of Britain's leading environmental pressure groups with broad grassroots support. Bernadette's tireless campaigns, tackling issues such as chlorine-free paper, minimal packaging, eco-labeling and tampon safety, met with great success in the fields of consumer information and health and brought her a number of awards.

I was also moved by a group of British youths whose work, "Mapping the Future," was displayed on the walls of the conference center. With colorful drawings and hand-written letters, children from all over England had expressed their hopes and dreams for life in 2012. They were as interested to hear about my music as I was to hear about their work. After we traded a few banana-puns, I praised their work and said I hoped they would continue to carry the ecology torch all their lives.

Back home, *Bananaphone's* eclectic mix was well received by both my fans and the press. Similar to *Baby Beluga* in its balance of playful and pensive, this album seemed to catch people's imagination.

It was great fun taking bananas with me on TV interviews and punning like crazy in every print and radio interview. The laughs came in bunches and the media got a kick out of the parody of high-tech. As I saw it, the bananaphone was a digital device of the information low-way: a cellular phone with a-peel, the soft-path in communications, an "*inner*-active" wonder tool.

The inner-active bit got attention.

I said that, in a child's early years, it was so important to activate imagination, and you couldn't do that with TV (and it's pre-fab images) or even CD-ROMs—which are TV-like but with more options for the user and therefore described as "interactive."

Storytelling and then books, I pointed out, have been the traditional way to stoke imagination's fire. Radio also allows listeners to conjure up their own images of the broadcast sounds. Recordings work in the same way, and for children they can provide countless hours of imaginative time. But this is not possible with TV. What TV is good at is showing you its image of things, things you might not otherwise see. But because the picture and sound are a complete package, there's nothing else to do while you watch. Manufacturers of video programming for kids countered the criticism about video's passive nature by offering the user options—clicking this or that. That makes it interactive, they said. Quite the sales ploy.

"Interactive" thus became the biggest sales slogan since "new and improved." Now parents were supposed to feel good about buying any video product for their child if it was interactive. What nonsense.

Anyone knowledgeable in child development will tell you that, in the formative early years, children need a primary connection with the natural world and with people, not the simulation of the electric screen. Childhood professionals agree that, developmentally speaking, stimulating the imagination has no substitute as an early experience that shapes the child's ability to be creative and to make appropriate choices in life. Imagination is the key to self-reliance and resourcefulness, strengths from which a great life can unfold.

When I said this to reporters, in person and over the phone, it rang true for them, though only up to a point. "But parents are so busy these days," they argued, "and often with both parents working, what's wrong with giving the kids something to occupy their attention while supper's being made?" You can't resolve that issue in two minutes.

I have great sympathy for parents trying to make ends meet. The economic system that creates absent parents is not the parents' fault—just as the family's financial predicament is not the child's fault. However, the child's needs are real and must come first. Given that we all buy into a system that takes parents away from their children, it's clear we need to reflect on the value of such an arrangement. The point is well made by author Penelope Leach in her 1994 book, *Children First*, which describes "what our society must do—and is not doing—for our children today."

That said, the problem with "interactive" is that it has become a guilt-releasing cure-all for parents who aren't there, and for parents who think they are giving their tots a competitive edge (as if that's why people have children). Einstein himself understood that imagination is paramount—more important than intellect.

And that's why I invented an imaginary phone that rings in the theater of the mind.

Are you going to make a *Bananaphone* video or CD-ROM? I was occasionally asked. No, that would defeat the purpose, wouldn't it? Then how is the album going to be promoted? Well, in all the other ways, I guess.

The Troubadour office went ape with marketing and promotional ideas. Working with Margaret Potyrala, who had recently joined us, Ruth and Bert started the Raffi Fan Club. Then they cooked up a whole bunch of ideas with MCA to catch the attention of retailers, the media and the public. A graphics design firm had come up with an eye-catching cover that showed a banana close up with a sticker on it. And who was on the sticker, wearing a red hat and holding a banana to his ear? You guessed it. Rounding out the image was a red maple leaf under the photo. It was great fun, and everybody loved it.

When the album was ripe for release, we sent CDs to the media in little paper bags containing four bananas, stickers and a press kit. A CD-sized cover image was on each side of the bag, the handles of which were tied with yellow ribbons. In the press release and the concert program, we proudly announced "an addition to the Troubadour family."

We worked especially hard to promote the album in Canada, where I had not toured for a few years. MCA Canada touted the news that "Raffi's back!" all across the country. Faith Carriere, a music-loving retail executive (and future marketing specialist at Troubadour for a while), organized special events and "bananaphone joke" contests throughout her chain of teacher's stores.

The twenty-four-city concert tour across the U.S. and Canada received a lot of media attention. Connie, Michael and I had a ball stickering the various airports along the way. I admit I started it, that first day at the Vancouver airport. I walked up to a food concession stand and, sighting a yellow bunch, put a sticker on the top banana. Michael called it "a walk-by fruiting." Bank machines, video arcades—anything was fair game for our merry prankstering. (I remember putting a sticker on an escalator hand-rail at Chicago's O'Hare Airport, watching it go away and then waiting for it to come back up—it did.)

As for the show itself, it was among my favorite concert experiences ever. Onstage I felt playful again and light on my feet. The 7 p.m. starting time actually kept the underage kids at home, and Michael and Connie were at their musical and charming best on stage. We even worked stage manager Mick Hatherby into the show. He brought out props every now and then (among them a giant red toothbrush), and that got additional laughs from the crowd. Mick's stage lighting and the excellent sound mixing of Paul Way didn't go unnoticed.

There were also a couple of firsts on this tour. In addition to colorful tour manager Darlene Blaeser, we had the help of Tracey Page, who took care of a number of tour duties and also assisted me personally on the road. Also, I agreed to give the fans something more visual than they were used to at a Raffi show. Onstage, we had a large screen on which we rear-projected slides of children's drawings to accompany the songs. Shiny cardboard maple leaves and bananas hung on either side of the screen.

From L.A.'s Universal Amphitheater, to Toronto's Roy Thomson Hall and across to Vancouver's Queen Elizabeth Theatre, the *Bananaphone* tour met with wonderful audiences and generated great press. In a prominent *Globe and Mail* feature article on children's entertainers, the lead photo showed *moi, avec cellular.*

The night before the Toronto concert, I was able to honor Arto and Lucie's request that our touring group come over to their place for some Armenian food. Lucie laid out quite a spread, nearly all vegetarian—delicious rice pilaf, several dips and other dishes she loved to serve. And then, while Arto was showing people his art collection, Lucie put on *Bananaphone* and started to dance, by herself, with me, with Ani, and even inviting my father to get up for a step or two. After we drank Armenian coffee, Lucie proceeded to "read" the grounds in our demitasse cups. Her readings were, to say the least, entertaining.

I'll never forget how my ailing father took to *Bananaphone.* He just loved the album and praised it all the time. My mother said he would listen to it every single day and do his exercise walks around the house to the music. She loved it too, and they both said there was something in my voice on that album that really moved them. Lucie especially loved the polka song and some days she would dance to it with Onnig's dog, Pasha, up on his hind legs.

Against all reason, there stirred in me the hope that maybe this new album would be a hot seller and achieve gold status, something my new releases had not done for years. To do it in a single fall campaign would create a buzz and get much-needed publicity. It was not to be. By Christmas the album had sold a respectable number of copies in both the U.S. and Canada—but was only halfway to gold. Compared to the mid-1980s, 1994 was such a video-dominant time in family entertainment that the amount of retail space for children's audio had shrunk dramatically.

However, back home in Vancouver at the end of the tour I got some good news. *Maclean's*, Canada's only weekly newsmagazine, had selected me to be one of twelve Canadians on its annual Honor Roll. My part of the feature had a large photo in which I'm surrounded by smiling kids, all of us holding bananas to our ears—a conference call.

NATURAL LEARNING, VALUE CHANGE

TO ME, ONE OF THE BIGGEST STORIES IN 1994 HAD TO DO WITH the crisis in public education. For years I had heard about the failure of schools in preparing students adequately for post-secondary education and the job market. I was also aware of declining literacy rates.

Then came somber news from the Ministry of Education in my home province of British Columbia: A 1993 in-school survey of students revealed a dramatic drop in students' motivation the longer they stayed in school. In grade four, for instance, 62% agreed that "what I'm learning in school is useful," 41% said "I feel that I am involved in my class," and 27% said "I feel cared about at school." For grade twelve students, those numbers dwindled to 12, 6 and 4% respectively.

Early in 1994, I had seen the smiling young face of Ilana Cameron on the cover of a local community magazine, highlighting the lead story, "A New Model in Education." I read it and was impressed with the novel approach described: child-directed learning or, in other words, "natural learning." My curiosity was heightened when I read that in Ilana's younger years, her parents had, at her request, taken her out of kindergarten and devoted themselves to home learning.

Brent and Maureen Cameron reasoned that if children possess the intelligence for that most complex task of learning a language at a young age (how they do it is still not fully understood), as they grow they must be able to learn anything they are interested in. I thought this approach showed faith: faith in the child and in the life processes unfolding in the child. Day by day, Brent and Maureen put this faith to work, simply letting Ilana's interests lead the way. Before long, Ilana's play had spun into a learning environment for about a dozen neighbors' children as well. The Camerons called this learning center "Wondertree."

The success of Wondertree eventually led to the growth of a new branch called "Virtual High," an alternative secondary-level learning center for about twenty teenagers. Instead of teachers and students, there were learning consultants and learners. In this model of self-directed learning, learners chose what and with whom they learned. They progressed at their own pace, according to their interests, and chose from among a number of "mentors" with whom to study.

I telephoned ahead and paid a visit to the center, located in an old mansion not far from my place. Over a cup of tea, I met Brent, Maureen, Ilana and learning consultants Sunder Green and Michael Maser.

The first thing I heard was about Ilana's learning to read at age ten. What? "How could she not read for that long?" I asked. Well, the Camerons said they didn't push it, confident that Ilana would read when she was ready. She was painting, going to the park, singing, creating poetry, having all kinds of fun. There were lots of books around and people read to her all the time, but there was no pressure for her to hurry up and read. Then, one day, she was ready. It took her little time to learn and in fact she picked it up so well that, three years later, she took a second-year university literature course.

Inside Virtual High, the mood was very friendly, definitely relaxed. A few learners I met smiled and said they had grown up listening to my music. The small "office" was a space where all were welcome. Pinned up in the kitchen were a roster for cleaning duties and reminders about house maintenance chores, which were shared by all. In another room hung a poster of the days of the week, with various activities and people slotted in. A pair of conga drums stood in the corner. Photos of Einstein with choice quotes lined the walls of the stairway.

The second-floor computer room surprised me with its preponderance of lap-tops. Oh no! Was there a high-tech bias lurking here? When I asked about the role of the computers, Brent said that kids were doing exciting work, designing their own programs and exploring entrepreneurial opportunities to earn personal income. But what was stressed most at Virtual High, he said, were relationships and personal interaction. Social isolation and heads buried in computers was not okay. Regular group meetings were one way that learners connected with each other.

It took a family decision for a learner to be enrolled here. The parents had to be involved, with a full understanding of the youth's choice and the center's commitment to him or her. Brent said the vast majority of parents who turned to Wondertree did so because their child was having difficulty at school, either academically or socially.

Critics—so-called realists bent on seeing academic work predominate above all else—don't see that the personal skills of emotional intelligence and management that kids learned here would serve them well in the outside world. They were learning to follow through on promises and keep agreements, to exercise choice and realize its consequences, and to be part of a caring community. In this way they would come to trust that their interests were important and their contributions valuable. It was accepted as a given that confident learners willingly make the effort required to excel in their chosen fields, academic, technical or artistic.

In my return trips to Virtual High, I got better acquainted with the community, took part in public events and sang at the Friday night coffee houses organized, of course, by the kids. I got to know many of them and over a couple of years saw a growing confidence in their abilities. I loved visiting the center, to soak up the openness of that learning environment and take part in the talks that always gave me a lot to think about. To see such a deep love of children at the heart of this new educational model made me very happy.

I remembered my own intuitive flashes years ago in talks with Deb, Bonnie and Bert. After we'd been discussing "whole language" and the child as a whole person, I would say, "So what this all means is that the *child* is the curriculum!" In teacher talk I may not have known all of what I was saying, but in another way I did understand something important. Maybe that's why I took to the natural learning idea so well.

Child-directed learning also seeks to give children an experience in basic democracy from a young age, so that exercising choice becomes second nature as one grows older. Choice is seen as both a basic right that carries responsibilities and an important part of community life. To me, there was something very healthy in all this if it made a person less tolerant of coercion and more like the active citizen we all say we need come election time. I couldn't help but think that student apathy in school seemed to mirror voter apathy in our elections.

At times I did wonder if the Wondertree program wasn't too open, too unstructured. We had many a conversation about that. On the other hand, I was all too aware of my own inner constraints, a residue of the demands of my highly structured upbringing.

The natural learning model does not claim to be a perfect system; that doesn't exist. As Michael Maser said more than once, this model may not suit everyone. What it does do, however, is offer a creative choice in education—an alternative to convention based on the premise of *confidence* in human nature. In my view, that's an experiment well worth supporting.

I have learned this much: The learning environment does shape the psyche of the young learner, at home as well as in school. As much as anything else, the social medium is indeed the message.

A phrase that Brent and his colleagues often use is "self-design," based on biologist Umberto Maturana's idea of "autopoeisis," or creating a self. For me, this notion resonates with what psychologist Abraham Maslow called "self-actualization," the psychological process also known as individuation.

At a time when I was having lively discussions with friends on these ideas, encountering Maslow's work both confirmed some of my long-held intuitive ideas and expanded my exploration of learning, education and optimal being. (Maslow is perhaps best known for articulating what he called a "hierarchy of needs," ranging from the basic biological needs such as food and shelter to the higher social needs—truth, love and beauty—which he viewed as later evolutionary developments.)

Maslow dedicated himself to the study of psychologically healthy people, "self actualizing people, those who have come to a high level of maturation, health and self-fulfillment."

He discovered that those who are in a positive state of health function differently than those operating in a state of deficiency. For me this was significant—it mirrored Maturana's suggestion that we are emotional beings who create our personal reality moment by moment, depending on our emotions. It is also the reason why Wondertree places such a high priority on emotional intelligence as the foundation of learning.

Maslow believed that psychologically healthy people were motivated not by the values imposed by religion or culture alone, but by values they developed naturally. His eternal optimism regarding humanity held that the highest possibilities of human potential are still to be tapped, and he even maintained that we had come to a point in biological history where we were now responsible for our own evolution. This appealed to me. It implied that just as evolution involves selecting, "self-evolvers" make conscious choices and decisions, according to what they value.

A central idea of Maslow's about human nature intrigued me. Human beings, he said, have the innate tendency to move to higher levels of health, creativity and fulfillment—a natural self-actualizing tendency, blocked only by neurosis. Psychological health, I understood, is indispensable to forming societies in which everyone can reach a high level of fulfillment without restricting the freedom of others.

Thus, as Maslow reasoned, self-actualizing people are not "well adjusted" in the naive sense of needing cultural approval. Instead, they resist enculturation—in many positive ways—and thus redeem the self from an unhealthy culture. This doesn't make them perfect (for there are, of course, no perfect people), but shows they are in conscious charge of their destiny, to the best of their ability. I felt I had been fortunate, through therapy, to access such a process.

It didn't escape me that Maslow's idea of cultural resistance is echoed in Theodore Roszak's book *The Voice of the Earth*. In this exploration of a recent branch of psychology called "ecopsychology," Roszak (who coined the word counterculture in the 1960s) points out that healthy being cannot be defined by an unhealthy culture. The healing journey, he says, continues beyond individuation, to a mature bonding with Mother Earth and the universe. I could see that, in light of the (mostly urban) context of psychoanalysis we have known until now—one concerned with being well-adjusted—we must now ask, Well-adjusted to what?

Individuating. Aspiring to higher levels of fulfillment. Cultivating a partnership connection with life on Earth. Each of these, it dawned on me, was related to a lifelong process of natural learning. I was reminded of the value change that Gorbachev, Suzuki and others were advocating and that young Severn implored of the adult world.

It all pointed to the need for an integrated approach to life— perhaps the very quality that was sorely missing for the B.C. students who said the classroom experience had little relevance for them.

Value change cannot "trickle down," I realized. Its seeds need to take root within and grow.

* * *

My experience with Wondertree inspired me to go through my old child development books and pick up a few others. At a time when there were so many newspaper articles about "techno-tots"—with photos of preschoolers in front of a computer—I was focusing on the value of primary experience for kids and looking more closely at the adult-child dynamic.

Among the books I turned to, the work of Joseph Chilton Pearce stood out. In his classic bestseller, *The Magical Child*, Pearce painted a cogent picture of the emotional and relational basis of human potential. He traced the developmental growth of a newborn from one "matrix" to another, stressing the importance of an infant learning the lessons of one phase before facing the challenges of the next. His description of inherent intelligence, of the vital bonding process at birth and of the societal constraints that impede the development of a child's innate creativity made quite an impression on me.

Increasingly aware of the value of volition and choice in early life, I found myself thinking about a child's need for reliable structure as well. Not being a parent, I didn't have to go through those daily situations that can challenge one's personal resources. Nevertheless, I did notice that my own interactions with kids were changing; for one thing, I was a good deal more patient now than I had ever been.

I came to believe that respecting the volitional instincts of a child had to do with understanding his or her emotional life, and that missing this link was likely the cause of many of the power and control issues between kids and parents. I began to see the theory at work in even the most loving families I knew.

Children have a strong volitional nature that they need to both experience and learn to control. However, because of their complete dependence on adults, they are continually presented with situations not of their own making. To provide children a comforting, tangible structure for exploration and play, the choices they are offered must be given within a context of firm limits, consistently expressed. Children's need to test their own strength will inevitably create power struggles that require the most loving hand, for kids simultaneously need to feel their own developing abilities while being reassured of their parents' superior strength.

Responding to a child's willful or accidental testing of the behavioral boundaries—"misbehaving," not keeping agreements—requires that parents be consistent. This is not about being obsessive, strict, heavy-handed or even disciplinary. It has to do with helping a child learn the outcome of his or her actions. And when it comes to optimal learning, *love* is the most effective enabling context. As Pearce puts it, "Anxiety is the crippler of intelligence." When children are not distracted by parental anger, they have room to consider the lesson at hand—the consequences of their own behavior. In this way, discipline can grow as an inner value rather than as something always imposed from the outside.

In my experience with close friends and their children, I found that next to giving encouragement and support to a child as positive reinforcement, responding early to a child's behavior provided the clearest signal as to what was acceptable and what was not. It also gave a clue as to the child's current aptitude for social interaction. If a child of four, given a choice between eating at the table with adults or eating somewhere else, chose the table (and rules of conduct were made clear), it seemed that misbehavior (playing with food, making all kinds of noise) was better addressed sooner than later. What's more, neither half-hearted nor escalating parental responses to several deliberate "offenses" did any good at all. If the child needed to be removed from the table, it proved far better to do it early for everyone's sake. The relieved tension alone made the meal much more pleasurable for the adults, and the child got a clear message about limits.

I have learned that in the demanding art of harmonious coexistence between adults and children, recognizing the child's emotional needs yields a tremendous harvest of insight and goodwill. As with any art, a combination of technique, materials and practice goes a long way to benefiting everyone involved.

RAFFI RADIO

AROUND THIS TIME, BRENT SHOWED ME A BOOK CALLED *THE POWER of Limits*, written by Gyorgy Doczi. It was all about proportional and reciprocal designs in nature and the simple mathematical basis underlying their form. Leafing through the illustrations, I was fed by the inspiration I saw on every page. I was thrilled with the discovery of such apparent order.

What really impressed me was learning about spirals. It was an Italian scholar, Fibonacci, who came up with the particular sequence of numbers that, expressed as ratios, describes the curve of a spiral.

Here was another way of beholding the magic of Creation. I already knew that DNA strands—the genetic blueprint of all life— appear in the form of a double helix spiral. Now I realized spirals were everywhere! My neighborhood walks were transformed: on pine cones, sunflowers and daisies, in the branches of a monkey puzzle tree, in snail shells and sea shells on the beach, I saw the Fibonacci ratio at work all around me.

Pregnant with song ideas, I knew there was another album in me. I wondered how I could enfold my new learnings into the body of that work.

Early in 1995, the question answered itself. Hot on the heels of *Bananaphone's* praise of inner vision (and a Juno to boot), I conjured up an album that would be a celebration of audio and, at the same time, would contain a metaphor for tuning in to the universe's grand designs. The concept would be called *Raffi Radio*, a pretend radio show and a state of mind. It would exist in a mythical place I called Troubadoria.

The title song was to set the scene. Ruth and Bert loved it when they first heard it. It was an invitation to come alive, to tune in to our inner mysteries and to the universe whose reflection we are by design. I wrote it in a contemporary country style:

In the town and in the country-o / Dance it up, do-si-do,
To the music of an all-star show / With a soul full of stereo,
    Chorus: Raffi Radio, woa woa woa Raffi Radio—tuning in,
        Raffi Radio, ooh ooh ooh Raffi Radio—tuning in.
With the colors of a studio / Paint the sky, paint the day-o,
Wing it up or take it slow / In a bowl full of stereo . . .

The bridge had references to other songs of mine that kids would know, and the song ended with a long fade of the chorus, now with the extended line "tuning in, tuning in to the universe . . ."

Just how and in what order these ideas came is unclear. But I did love weaving my everyday joys and explorations into my recordings. The new concept provided a huge canvas to paint on, and Doczi's book inspired two or three songs that Michael and I wrote.

Michael took to the radio idea right away and dug up some tapes of old radio shows for us to listen to. They were great fun to hear, these shows from the '30s and '40s, many with an element of zany comic mischief. Our friend Roy Forbes showed us a few of his old radios and lent us vinyl albums featuring vintage country music radio shows. The CBC had just come out with a boxed set of tapes commemorating sixty years of radio service, and we found a gold mine of inspiration there as well.

Raffi Radio was like no other recording I had ever done. How could we make a potpourri of songs, chitchat and a variety of segments in an adult format work for kids? The grown-up medium of radio needed a child-sized element to charm the youngest listeners.

Finally it came to me. Why not have a *dog* as my co-host? Yes, a barking, panting canine, full of wit and sound-bites. The character Sleido JazzDog was born, a cool pup with shades, into all kinds of music and occasionally prone to thinking it was *her* show. I was in the Vancouver Kids Bookstore when I first saw her: a white-and-gray shaggy dog puppet, with dark eyes, pink tongue and floppy ears. Two-and-a-half feet of big, fluffy fun. Her light-colored coat meant she would be very visible in stage lighting—I knew then and there she would be perfect to take on tour.

It was all coming together in my mind's eye. This pretend radio show would be commercial-free, but full of satire, weather, news of the day, bad jokes, interviews, kids and lots of brand new songs. Now all I had to do was convince Connie to supply Sleido's barks and yelps in the studio.

I knew that Michael's diverse talents would be ideal for this project. For a two-legged creature, he could do a lot of vocal tricks (and an excellent John Wayne imitation). So when we got together, the ideas started flying.

We did a spontaneous skit called "The Silly Panel," in which I interviewed a panel of silly experts (just Michael). We did one skit on the subject of time and another on audio, with Michael sounding like a huffed-up silly expert full of nonsense. Then there was Michael Creberchof, our roving reporter coming to us live from the Geodesic Opera House in Upper Troubadoria (where the famed tenor Raffarotti was about to sing).

The creative work took some lovely turns.

The upbeat *Kitchen Sing Sing* was a call-and-response song on the joys of cooking. Sleido, of course, just had to have her own song, so we came up with a jazzy, finger-snapping lounge tune. Then a brief minimalist phase produced *Coconut*, a toe-tapper with only one word—coconut—in it, and *Sunflower*, with just seven words. A ballad, *Ripple of Love*, became an ode to love's radiant energy. And the closing song, *Every Child*, said:

> *Every child, every child, is a child of the universe,*
> *Here to sing, here to sing, a song of beauty and grace,*

Here to love, here to love, like a flower out to bloom,
Every girl and boy a blessing and a joy.
Every child, every child, of man and woman-born,
Fed with love, fed with love, in the milk that's mother's own,
A healthy child, healthy child, as the dance of life unfolds,
Every child in the family safe and warm.

With its world-music bounce, the song "dreams of children free to fly, free of hunger and war."

During this project, the idea that continued to excite me was that all of Creation is filled with numerical design, projected into form on various levels, and differently perceived depending on the specs of the receiver.

It was fascinating to me that the same world of sound and light waves appears and is experienced very differently in varying species. For example, compared to humans, dogs have much more developed senses of hearing and smell, but are relatively limited in cognitive capacities. In humans, on the other hand, the brain development of the newborn is critical in the making of a broadly functioning and perceptive adult, abounding in spiritual depth, physical grace and emotional intelligence. What impressed me is that what we see in the world and what we experience as reality depends largely on our capacities—on our perceptual development.

At this point in my life, I saw Creation as a boundless vibratory field: an audiovisual projection open to infinite experience and interpretation, its waves shaping both the sound pictures and the color-light images that sing to us day and night—a rippling playground of pulsing vibrations.

That's why *Raffi Radio's* musical signature is followed by the word "vibration." You might say *vibration* takes the place of the call letters of this station.

As with *Bananaphone*, the demos we did for this album yielded keeper tracks we could build on. It was great to be working again with engineer Rolf Henneman and we had our hands full going from one available studio to another to fit our recording schedule.

Unlike other musicians who book a studio for weeks at a stretch, I liked to go in for two or three days and then have a couple of days off to reflect. Holding the functions of singer, writer, arranger and producer made my studio days (even with Michael's help) densely packed and demanding. I've always liked an intermittent schedule with built-in "down time" to rest up and stay on course. Even during mixing, the time away from the studio enclosure gives me a chance to be in the outside world and gain perspective.

Once more, Michael gathered a fine array of musicians from Vancouver's pool of exceptional talent. It was fun to work with our old friend Tom Colclough again (the brilliant saxophone and clarinet player on *Bananaphone*, who also played on *Raining Like Magic* in the film *FernGully*). And vocalists Megan Metcalfe and Saffron Henderson added a lively luster to the tracks.

Connie did agree to be Sleido's voice, and it was music to our ears. Michael and I exhorted her to bark in a number of moods and styles, cajoling her to intone the JazzDog's broad canine cacophony. She really got into it. (Results exceeded expectations.) We then sampled the various sounds on a keyboard where Sleido could "speak" to us at the touch of a finger. Connie also played and sang on two traditional songs, one being *Skip to My Lou* and the other a quirky version of *Six Little Ducks*, in which Michael, Connie and I each sang one word at a time, in sequence. It was challenging and great fun.

Four-year-old Julia Graff gave us a charming in-studio bananaphone interview. Twin sisters Shannon and Heather Beaty (aged six) learned and sang their parts so fast we were amazed. Their cheerful voices joined me in the jingle that introduced the Berry Nice News of the Day.

The News had two segments: one on seasons, set to Vivaldi's *Four Seasons*, confirming that "once again this year" the seasons would come in exactly the same order as last year; and the other about money: "In a surprise move, world bankers have announced that, from now on, instead of paying for things with money, people will pay with bananas." It concluded that while "money doesn't grow on trees; think again, bananas do!"

As for the weather on *Raffi Radio*, we presented a *Down by the Bay Weather Report*. This was an ode to the water cycle, set to Michael's piano melody and tracing the circle of evaporation, cloud formation, condensation, rain, groundwater, streams and ocean, "where the sun is about to come up, on another day, down by the bay."

I also created a segment called "Wishing Well," to which we asked kids to contribute. On CBC Radio's *Vicki Gabereau Show*, heard nationwide, we announced a songwriting contest for kids. They had to send in between four and sixteen lines in their own handwriting, starting with the words "I wish," and we would choose three of the entries to be included on this album. For one of those, I would add music and sing the song. We received hundreds of entries on all kinds of subjects, some thoughtful and some very funny. The winner came from twelve-year-old Bailey Rattray of Kamloops, B.C., whose song was called *Whatever You Choose*. She wrote:

> *I wish that everyone could be, exactly who they really are,*
> *No one should have to hide, what they're really like inside.*
> *Everyone's the same, but different, what have you got to lose,*
> *Just be whatever you choose, whatever you choose.*

The other selections were also delightful, and the whole segment opened with Michael's harpsichord version of Robert Schumann's *Arabesque*.

In a way, the trickiest part of the album was the opening sequence that led right into the intro of the title song. I wanted to let kids know what came before the cathode-ray tube. "Once upon a time, way before television, there was a thing called 'radio,' a wooden box, a friend of the family that brought voices out of thin air . . . and it brought music from distant places." In these spots we added short segments of vintage CBC Radio (with the kind permission of the CBC), bringing the opening to life.

TOURING TROUBADORIA

RAFFI RADIO AT RADIO CITY MUSIC HALL IN NEW YORK? Getoutatown! Well, we did it—as part of the Raffi Radio concert tour.

This tour involved the biggest and most complex production I'd ever taken on the road. For a long time, I had wondered what it would be like to mount a show that was theatrically lit, with a number of "specials" and dramatic lighting moves. I was also curious about lamps that could throw moving beams of light in all sorts of colors, the kind rock bands had used for years. I wouldn't use them the way the rockers did, with all manner of fast changes, sometimes several times in one song. But I felt their color-rich flexibility could add an arresting visual element to my concerts that would support and enhance the musical experience.

It took a little time, but we managed to track down gear that would serve the purpose. The lamps we acquired used a small mirror angling around a stationary bulb to create a moving beam, and the beam could be any one of a number of colors and widths at the flick of a switch. And the whole routine could be computerized.

With this in mind, I felt ready to design an all-new show for the Raffi Radio tour. Playing it out in my mind, I saw the audience being invited to spend an evening in Troubadoria, "a place of star magnolias and cherry blossoms, of dogwood and cedar." We would need exquisite photo slides showing the splendor of the natural world and the glory of Troubadoria as the context for the music.

We decided to use two huge slide screens set four feet apart, but angled to look like an open book from a center seat in the audience. Most people would be able to see both, and from either side of a theater they would see the full image of one panel and a bit of the other. Fourteen-foot-high banners on either side of the screens would frame the onstage look of our fantasy place. (The design of the red, yellow and blue banners was inspired by my friend Tania Godoroja's beautiful painting of a troubadour making music.)

All we needed now were the slides. I spent a good part of the summer hunting for them, being really fussy for the images I kept seeing in my mind. Through a couple of sources we managed to acquire dozens of fabulous images: close-ups of flowers and birds, landscapes, sunsets and a variety of magical nature shots.

This show was also going to have a totally new opening. Michael and Connie would come out to center stage with an announcement about the evening, a pretend visit to a magical place called Troubadoria, where "there's even a Radio Station, and we'll be happy to take you there." They would exit as the lights dimmed. Then we'd hear trumpet fanfare from our "helpful guide" (stage manager Greg Marshall, hoisting a long trumpet with a banner hanging from it). With the first images of huge sunflowers projected on the screens and the sounds of chirping birds in the air, I would make my entrance through a black curtain between the screens, a designated beam lighting my way.

It was the lighting that was the trickiest element to work with. While the computer program could have a beam of light pick up my entrance and light my walk forward to my downstage position, it couldn't vary the timing of it. This meant I had to pace the walk the same every time, something I was not used to doing. Synchronizing my moves with the light beams, once learned, need not have been that difficult and, in a theatrical run of several weeks in the same theater, it would become routine. However, we were moving from town to town, and in each new theater it took hours just to get the lights positioned and focused properly.

That wasn't the only challenge. We had thought that we could do our normal "load-in" and "tech" (ensuring all the sound and light gear was on stage and functional) within the usual three hours. But with this show's requirements, including two banks of three slide projectors each and the six new overhead lamps, the whole set-up took about six hours—double the work it had been for the previous year's tour. Before we figured this out, our sound checks got pretty rushed for the first few shows we did, and I was unnerved that things were running so late and down to the wire.

With the show still new to me and the usual little wrinkles to iron out, we were on the road. Sleido was a big hit, Connie bringing her on stage midway through the show to sing a couple of numbers with us. And I hit nearly all of my cues, though I was still nervous about it all. My confidence was boosted in Boston (our second stop) when friends came backstage to sing the show's praises.

A couple of nights later we were in New York.

"Raffi Radio at Radio City" read the 49th Avenue marquee of the famous concert venue. It was a tickle to be sound-checking on the stage of the hall where I had attended my first Grammys a few years ago. Whatever butterflies I had in my stomach settled down by showtime. I realized that I was experiencing growing pains, just like other performers did when tackling something new and stretching artistically to make it work.

As it turned out, the show went without a hitch, and the audience totally tuned in.

* * *

It was this tour that was colored by my mother's fatal illness. Her hospitalization and cancer diagnosis had a double effect on me as I went through the motions of tour preparation and rehearsals.

It threw an extraordinary new stress into the usual mix of details, giving me a new priority—one that cast a surreal veneer over all the others.

The days that followed were filled with phone calls to Toronto and flying there from Pittsburgh and Chicago to visit my frail father in the nursing home and Lucie in the hospital.

Short of canceling the tour, which Lucie wouldn't hear of, there was nothing else I could do but give my best on stage, singing from the same source of love that bound me to my audiences as it did to my family. My parents' physician, Dr. Svadjian, had stated that Lucie's condition could deteriorate quickly or through a period of several weeks. I was fully prepared for the call that would cancel the next few shows and have me on the next flight to Toronto.

What I wasn't prepared for was the unbelievable timing of Lucie's passing—and then Arto's—which came exactly midway through the rest period between two tours. The sudden loss of both my parents was astonishing enough. That it occurred when it did was even harder to fathom.

In a suburb of Chicago, I rejoined my touring family two days after the double funeral. I might have appeared to be functioning normally, but my world was now profoundly different. From the very first song that night in the Coronado Theater, I felt my parents' presence in the hall. And every word I sang I heard as if for the first time, as though time had rearranged itself out of respect for Arto and Lucie to speak to me in this way. Michael and Connie confirmed the feeling that the evening's performance was like none other.

One calming factor during this extraordinary period was the steady presence of our new tour manager, Paul Ryan. Through my most trying personal and professional circumstances, Paul was a gentle strength that smoothed the storms and guided me through the glitches. That I made it through as well as I did is largely due to him.

Near the end of the tour, I was so tired of being away from home that hotel rooms and hallways had an unsettling effect on me. At times I felt quite disoriented. Increasingly, I heard a voice telling me that I had to stay off the road for a long while. I also heard the call to write this book and I knew that would be my next work after this tour was over.

Back on the West Coast in early December, I developed a serious throat ailment that would have meant canceling the Vancouver show had it not been for the effective antibiotics my doctor prescribed as a last resort. Fortunately, my throat held together and I didn't have to disappoint the hometown crowd.

In Victoria, the last show went smoothly enough, right on cue. Among the well-wishers backstage were several teenagers with LP covers from their childhood for me to sign. I was touched.

The wrap-up party at the hotel was rather subdued. Sitting with close friends, I paused to take in the end of the CTV national newscast, which we knew featured a lengthy profile on me, shot in Toronto shortly after my parents' passing. It marked the end of the tour and, for me, the end of an era.

VII

SIMPLE GIFTS

It's a gift to be simple, it's a gift to be free,
It's a gift to come down where we are to be,
And when we find ourselves in a place just right
It will be in the valley of love and delight.

A Shaker hymn

IMMEDIATE LIVING

AT 5 A.M. CHRISTMAS MORNING 1995, SOMETHING WOKE ME from a sound sleep. I was alone and didn't hear anything, but was drawn to the window. In the dark, I made my way over and looked out. I had to rub my eyes: the sky was dotted with pin-light stars that seemed to be pulsating—I had been awakened by starlight. In a breath of marvel, I quickly wrote down a few words, said a prayer, and then stayed up to watch the slow sunrise over the bay. At the island home of my friends Tony and Tania I had begun a ten-day retreat into solitude.

In this rural setting, I tuned into the natural dynamics of a time-less reality. Stoking the fire in the wood stove, watching the play of tides on the bay, I felt the rhythm of the day's passing light. Listening to the fray of emotions within me, the fears and comforts that vied for position, I put the world on hold.

Over the next few days I found myself not wanting to buy a news-paper or turn on the TV, radio or CD player. In the stillness untouched by random voices, images and news from afar, I came to feel an expanding inner self. With my attention not spread so thin, my immediate world—the tranquil beauty of the bay, the clean island air—became very dear to me.

When I returned to the city, I felt so good that I thought about extending this un-mediated state indefinitely. Personal visits and phone calls became newly important. I no longer needed to turn on the car radio for company, and I got very fussy about what sensory input I let in, as though my life was, in a word, complete.

For years I had been a media hound, a keen observer of socio-political events in Canada, the U.S. and the world at large. Now I pretended I had all the information I needed for the time being, at least the kind I was likely to get from commercial media. I was still reading all sorts of books, but something in me had profoundly shifted. I felt a sense of contentment, of having enough, and that fullness didn't want or need petty intrusions.

What began as a brief trial period stretched to six months (before I tuned in to some of the 1996 summer Olympics). After the first month, I noticed how much time I had gained. The absence of jarring news items that each morning used to bring—a gruesome murder, another child abduction, a civil war—gave me a clean start. A positive vibration. Less need to react, more time to initiate.

Abstinence brought other changes, too. Very few commercial messages crossed my path; the shopping impulse, already low in me, dropped even more. Spending less emotional energy on stories that had little to do with me and that I could do nothing about, I now found that the people in my immediate life took center stage.

I started to reflect again about media's impact on our lives, and on children's lives in particular.

It occurred to me that the loud ambient noise drummed by media obscures the real danger signs of our times—the ones deemed "not sexy," like the loss of biodiversity, or ecosystems at risk. I saw our high-fat media diet as a "virtual" reality, a negative feedback loop that reduces the spectrum of being to melodrama with pseudo-crises and shopping solutions, impairing our ability to see a broader picture or respond to deeper issues. I pondered the fiscal values that drive media to spin everything into competitive discord and scandal, increasing anxiety and promoting a scarcity model of life.

On the other hand, it gave me comfort to remember that more and more people from all walks of life appreciate the teeming abundance of our natural world, the interconnected "systems" nature of things that Fritjof Capra described so well in his book *The Web of Life*. We're learning that everything is nested in everything, systems within systems, a collage of ecologies. Everything affects everything and, for humanity, it all starts with the child.

It became apparent to me, in a new way, that if society's problems are also systemic, they cannot be properly addressed without a serious look at the ecology of the child in the formative years. This gave me a new sense of purpose in the writing task I was about to engage.

POSTCARDS

THE WRITING BEGAN WITH THE PURCHASE OF A FOUNTAIN PEN. Smelling the ink on the nib took me back to my Cairo childhood faster than you could say Cavoukian. I cleared my calendar, making room for the book that wanted to be. Putting pen to paper and sitting at the keyboard I delved into the archives of experience, opening mental files and running movies of the early years.

Sure enough, page by page, chapters formed as though by design with one another, and the book acquired a life of its own. As to the craft of writing, there was a steep learning curve, the scale of which I had not anticipated. I threw myself into the project as if it were easy, and this may have been useful. If I'd known at the beginning how difficult telling my life's story was going to be, I might not have gone ahead with it. The initial efforts produced mixed results. But I learned from the early mistakes, regrouped and, with the support of friends, kept on going.

I had figured the book could be written in a year, but that was wishful thinking. It took well over two. And, as creative endeavors go, focusing on one project for that long was something entirely new to me. To say that I learned a lot—both about writing and, through that exacting process, about myself—would be an understatement.

Early in 1996, Paul Ryan took over the reigns of Troubadour and brought with him years of experience in the entertainment field, ranging from tour managing to general management duties. Paul and Bert worked closely together on all matters, focusing on securing new U.S. distribution for Troubadour with a "roots-based" company (in Cambridge, Massachusetts) called Rounder Records. And our new office manager, Nicole Jackson, became a terrific addition to our team. Everything was well in hand. It was time for a change of scenery.

I traveled to Maui for the first time, and then on to Australia to visit friends. It was the first real vacation I'd had in years, and it was wonderful to feel so carefree. After ambling through Sydney's art shops and beaches, I ventured out to Katoomba for a bit of a bush trek, glad to get acquainted with gum trees and kangaroos and to hear the kookaburra's winsome call. By way of a friend, I had a memorable meeting with an urban aboriginal who told me that for thousands of years his people have scanned the Milky Way to know when emus would lay their eggs. In Melbourne I had a lovely visit with Australia's premiere children's entertainer, Franciscus Henri, and his family. Franciscus has long delighted countless children with concerts and recordings, and ever since I recorded his song *Ducks Like Rain* on my *Rise and Shine* album in 1983, we have kept in touch.

I then went on to New Zealand to join my friend Tanis and a small group on a tour of the land of rainbows and mist, or *Aotearoa* as it is known in Maori. We took in some spectacular scenery, learned native lore and soaked up the sun. At a weekend "Festival of Sharing" attended by fifty or so people, I was coaxed into giving an informal evening concert that even included my first song in Maori. The next day we were fortunate to hear archeologist and author Barry Brailsford, who gave us an account of the recent discovery of the Waitaha—the rainbow tribe—a peaceful people who predated the Maori by over a thousand years. (Barry's book *Circle of the Stone* chronicles his remarkable findings.) Also on hand was Rose Pere, a fiery elder who held us spellbound with her brand of traditional Maori wisdom.

I returned home rejuvenated, having gained new friends and perspectives to inspire me.

In the spring, I sang once again at the Vancouver Children's Festival. Doing several performances solo for a change brought me as much pleasure as any of my previous appearances. And in one of those shows, who should share the stage for a couple of songs but Franciscus Henri, who had come to visit me (and the festival) with Liz, his wife and long-time manager.

During the second year of working on this book, I accepted only a few performing opportunities. In April 1997, I gave two concerts in support of a group in Washington, DC, called TV-Free America, who succeed each spring in prompting millions of families to reap the benefits of "no TV" for a week or more. Then, in May, I returned again to bask in the glow of the Vancouver Children's Festival, this time on the occasion of its twentieth birthday.

In late summer, I was invited to sing at the opening night of a conference of North American environmental educators in Vancouver. For part of my performance, I was joined by the Sta'alis Dancers, a group of Native youngsters from a nearby community who danced to my song *First Peoples*; and I sang two songs from *Evergreen Everblue*, accompanied by a choir of forty children.

It just so happened that I, too, was celebrating a twentieth birthday of sorts (at my age, you take these when they come along). It had been twenty years since the release of *Singable Songs for the Very Young*.

The anniversary spawned both my first-ever boxed set of CDs and tapes and a fall concert tour of eighteen cities in Canada and the U.S. I performed solo and the experience brought back the feeling of the early years, with just me and my guitar and kazoo onstage. Well, all right, a couple of bunches of bananas too—and a bright blue umbrella, just for fun.

* * *

It's not often that I see Deb, so when she did visit Troubadour a while ago, I welcomed the opportunity for a chat. Although she too lives in Vancouver, we've met only a few times since we parted and our paths rarely cross. It was good to see her. I was very glad to know she was doing well and I shared the news about my autobiography. We couldn't help but reminisce a while about our work together, and Deb said she felt proud of her contributions to my music and the success of Troubadour. I was happy to hear it. Together we had nurtured my children's entertainment career and, personally, Deb was a great gift of love in my life.

A GIFT OF ART

NOT LONG AFTER MY PARENTS DIED, I INHERITED MANY PIECES of artwork that had been in the family as long as I can remember. They included a number of oil paintings by my father, as well as several by other Armenian painters. A moving company bound them in protective containers and, along with a few boxes of personal effects, shipped them to the West Coast.

What a storehouse of images and memories came alive in my living room as a friend helped me unpack painting after painting, small statues and prized souvenirs of Arto and Lucie's lives. I felt immediate connection. The power of religious icons danced in my mind as I saw and touched each item in the morning light.

Over the next two days, the paintings quite easily arranged themselves on the white walls that seemed to have been waiting for such color. The signatures of many of the works called me to explore the artists' origins. I noticed two still lifes by the great Armenian painter Samsonian, a friend of our family's. From a bookshelf I pulled out a book on Samsonian's work, a present from my parents one Christmas. It was full of the man's brilliant and prolific output of color and form.

My father's own paintings in a robust style—sunflowers in a vase on blue and red, boldly outlined gladiolus, the old Muslim man reading, two sailboats in Nice (1951), his self-portrait which stood in the Cavouk studio for decades, the painting of me at four years old, sleeping on the couch—these gifts now held me breathless, in tears and long sighs.

Out of the boxes of personal effects also came treasures of my childhood that I didn't know Lucie had kept: my very first textbooks from Kalousdian School in Cairo. With great care I leafed through more than a dozen books—history, short stories, songs and plays, the *New Kindergarten* book of reading and writing Armenian, my first "learning English" book.

In among all these I came across a very special volume, a tribute to the man after whom I was named, published in Paris in 1937 to mark the centenary of his birth in 1835. It was entitled *Raffi: Life, Writings, Remembrances*. Inside, on the upper right-hand corner of the title page, was the inscription "2nd Prize, Lucie Papazian, June 26, 1938." I held the book to my heart, I opened and smelled its fragile pages. I turned them gently and found a photo of a bearded and bespectacled Raffi, and further along, photographs of his mother, the family home and the room in which he wrote.

A rush of feelings, hard to describe. Why now? What was this stirring, this sense of discovery, this thrill of something from my early life (and beyond) calling to me with such emotion? I felt the tug of my ancestral roots, a fresh feeling, compelling, in the new inner spaces created by the recent events.

In the coming days and weeks, I opened all the old books, delicately, again and again, mending them with tape wherever possible. Poring over them with hungry hands and eyes, I buried my nose in their tattered pages for the scent of another time, decades old, that paper carries so well. I breathed it in. Tears swelling in my eyes and throat, I called my mother's name. A faint conversation arose, deep and wordless, between a man, the boy he was, his books and the gift-givers, his departed parents.

Intense curiosity led me to review the Armenian alphabet. Although I'd spoken Armenian all my life and could slowly decipher print, my reading and writing of it were largely lost. Slowly, using my first kindergarten book for guidance, I learned once more to write the letters I traced years ago, and to read the text out loud.

The old books containing short stories helped expand my vocabulary, since each story was followed by a list of words and their meanings. Once more I reveled in the folds of the exquisitely beautiful Armenian language, full of animated nuance, a richness in sight and sound. But my eyes also caught a sad notation: the biographies of many of Armenia's most illustrious writers bore the same year of death, 1915, with just one word of explanation—"martyred."

In the history book was a piece on Ancient Armenia's religion, listing the principal gods and goddesses. It was here that I discovered that the Goddess of Purity and Light was named Anahid, my sister's full name. Fascinated by the account of the ancient peoples and their custodial divinities, I was amazed that a schoolbook of such a devout and old Christian culture would include references to a pagan past. I phoned Ani, Onnig and Kristin to share my excitement.

At Onnig's suggestion, I telephoned our old family friend, Albert Noradunkian, to talk about how these childhood books were affecting me. Albert was pleased to hear from me and shared my happiness, saying that even salmon swim home eventually. We made plans to meet in Toronto and go to the Armenian Church to buy a few other Armenian books and a good Armenian-English Dictionary.

Later that month, over Armenian coffee, Albert and his wife, Angel, and I reminisced about our early years in Canada, and told many a Lucie-and-Arto story. (In Cairo, Ohannes Grandpa had taken to Albert, and would drop by his jewelry shop every afternoon for long talks, mostly on spiritual topics.) I learned that Albert himself, in the last ten years, had pursued his own study of Armenian. He showed me his computer (which he uses in a number of languages) and his work on a vast compilation of Armenian phrases. To watch this very active and razor-sharp septuagenarian speak of things Armenian is to revel in a man alive with the roots, trunk and flowers of his culture. I left with lots to chew on.

Swimming home. Perhaps easier for salmon than for a man born in a desert, outside his original cultural environs.

On a little island off Canada's west coast, in a cottage warmed by a wood stove made in Norway, listening to a CD of Armenian folk music recorded in the U.S. and amplified by Japanese electronics, wearing aboriginal moccasins and sipping Armagnac from France, again I contemplated identity.

Once more the question challenged me and I engaged it whole-heartedly.

A chance conversation in Vancouver led me to meet with Robert Semerdjian, a wonderful local Armenian who was born in Egypt. Bob studied at the American University in Beirut before moving to Canada in 1962, eventually settling in Vancouver where he has been a teacher for nearly thirty years. In our far-ranging talks, Bob shared generously about his early life and his parents' narrow escape from the genocide. From this I gained further insights into my own past and felt moved towards a renewed look at the greater Armenian community.

I was making new Armenian friends, renewing acquaintances with old ones, and reading numerous books on Armenia's history and culture, written by Armenian authors and others. The music of the composer Khachaturian and of Father Komitas—the collector and singer of Armenian folk songs whom my father had emulated—now rang in my ears. In solitude I sang the beloved lament *Groong* (crane) and felt the cry of decades of unresolved Armenian sorrow. And I reflected at length on my growing up in the multicultural mosaic that is Canada.

The desert child flew across the ocean to another continent and, after a time, came to live in a temperate rainforest. At age fifty he finally understands that he is the son of holocaust survivors—two children who prevailed against great odds to make their mark in the world. And still, he grapples with the basics: Who am I? *Whose* am I? Where is home?

We have all heard about the importance of knowing our roots. Decades ago, the painter Sarian—father of modern Armenian painting—put it this way: "The earth, like a living thing has its own spirit; and without one's native land, without close touch with one's motherland, it is impossible to find oneself, one's soul." To my mind, although the thought still rings true, in today's world it begs for more. One's "native land" is an idea (and a place) harder than ever to define. Knowledge of our cultural roots—as embodied in our racial lineage and "motherland" environs—no longer offers an adequate context for identity. Today I feel it is not enough to link soul to racial roots and motherland.

One far-out photograph changed all that.

The first "self-portrait" of Mother Earth in 1970 by her NASA astronaut-children, a blue-and-white (unretouched) image of the entire planet from space, was, I believe, an evolutionary step for humankind. Never mind that it took Cold War gadgetry to do it, that single shot has recast the entire context of human identity. Today each one of us, no matter where we were born, is a child of the "whole Earth" image. Our eyes have beheld a vision that we can't unlearn.

However dimly it may reside within us, this nascent consciousness may well constitute a collective re-birthing, or a celestial baptism.

Like the Apollo astronauts gazing upon our borderless Mother, were we also not enchanted seeing her in this new way? From the vantage point of our ancestors, it was right to emphasize connection to a motherland, a country, state or homeland. We, with our widened visual scope, are just as right to broaden the metaphor. And just as individuation is a necessary stage in the recovery process towards a connection with Creation, so the traditional search for one's roots is an essential part of learning to embrace one's planetary heritage.

When my mind scans the footage of millennia, the myriad inter-mingled tribes and cultures appear to me like confluent streams and tributaries that make up the one river of humanity. Trade, industry, food, music and art have swept across the canyons of custom and language in reciprocal cycles between victor and slave—a vast complexity of triumphs, sufferings and accommodations that has spanned the ages. And though we still recognize distinctions of language, peoples and territories, I see in history's pages the blurred and superimposed outlines of but one story: that of simple human grapplings with issues of survival, belonging and fulfillment.

More than all the differences between peoples and all the diverse paths of human enculturation, it is our common song that I hear—the song of the human soul and its incarnations, and of its children, ever leaning out for love.

It is interesting to note that the worldwide environmental movement took form around 1970, the time of Earth's self-portrait. So many global ecological crises have arisen since then, begging us to recognize the borderless reality of the postmodern world where self-interests and group interests—regional and international concerns—converge.

Bit by bit, we are led to the inevitable conclusion that on this crowded planet we serve ourselves best in the transcendent state of caring for each other. In ways we may not yet realize, we *have* become each other's keeper. As never before, in this holographic reality, our own well-being—perhaps our very survival—is linked to everyone else's. Each part of the world indeed reflects and affects the whole.

As ancestors to coming generations, what message will we send to our descendants?

RENAISSANCE

ONE STORY IN AN OLD READER OF MINE (WRITTEN IN THE 1850S) really caught my attention, its message uncannily capturing thoughts that I had held for years. The author was none other than my namesake. His real name was Hagop Melik-Hagopian, but he used the single *nom de plume* Raffi. Here is my translation of his story.

The School of Lord Toteeg

From when I was little my mother cared that I learn how to read and write and turn out to be a good man. I was ten years old when she took me round to our village priest. It was the day of the Pentecost.

"The Pentecost is a good day," my mother would say. "If a youngster enters school on that day, he learns a lot, because the Holy Spirit on that day gave speech to the disciples."

With this belief, my mother handed me to the schoolmaster and said to him, "Lord Father, may I be in service to your holy right hand, I have brought my son so that he may learn to read and write. The meat to you, the bones to me. Do whatever you want, as long as he learns and makes good of himself."

I didn't understand what my mother's words would mean; I only heard that the Lord Father promised to give me good teaching. He also added that my deceased father had been a good friend of his, and out of love for him he would pay special attention to me.

Lord Toteeg—this was my schoolmaster's name—had received his education in the monastery of Aghtamar.

Our school was one of the extra rooms of Lord Toteeg's home, almost adjacent to the animals' pen. In that narrow and dim space were crammed forty or so students.

The lessons would start early in the morning. The schoolmaster would be seated in a corner, like a *koorm* [pagan priest] of olden times. In front of him was a small bookcase. One by one, the students would draw near, kiss the Lord Father's hand, kneel and, placing the textbook on the bookcase, begin to "account for themselves." For every mistake, the student would receive the sharp blow of a narrow cane in the palm of the hand.

There was another punishment . . . which, strange as it was, was equally horrible. The guilty student had to stand on one foot, with two hands holding a huge religious book. For hours he had to keep this thick and heavy book above his head, in both hands. Arms would tire, nerves would unravel, and a fainting feeling would ensue; but, so what? I was so used to this devilish punishment that I could stand for hours on one foot like a duck.

As well, there were other strict measures.

In the mornings we had to enter the classroom totally hungry. The teacher would say that with a full belly you couldn't learn, and if a boy eats too much before the lesson, he loses his wits. We took that advice to heart. So much so that we were afraid in the morning to wash our mouths, lest we lose the tongue's white coating and the schoolmaster think that we had broken our fast.

And so like this, until noon, we would receive instruction on a totally empty stomach. Our heads would spin and we would shake, but what could we do? We were so afraid of the cane, its sharp blows and this situation's harsh punishments.

When I would tell my mother about my trials in school, she would give me her customary reply.

"Son, until you are beaten, until you face hardship, you don't learn a thing."

I wondered why, with all this beating, I was so tortured and still I wasn't learning.

I was not a stupid boy. On the contrary, I was of sharp mind. When my mother would tell me a fairy tale, I would learn it on first hearing, and when a minstrel came to our village and sang songs or told stories, again I would memorize it all. But of the teachings that my schoolmaster gave I understood nothing. It seemed to me that they were not in Armenian.

So weak was I both in spirit and in will, and so diminished were my childhood abilities, that I fully believed my teacher when he would angrily scream in my face, "Devilish dog, no good thing can come from you!"

But with whom lay the blame?

In telling this story, my namesake offers insights rare in his culture. He contrasts his natural learning ability in memorizing his mother's fairy tales and the minstrel's songs to his abject failure to learn through the tyrant priest's torture; he contrasts the open learning of curiosity and attention to the failure of control and coercion.

How curious that the punishments described by Raffi circa 1850 were still used over a hundred years later in the Armenian school I attended in Cairo. Though I was always at the top of my class in marks, I too had to stand in line to get the ruler's sharp crack on my hand for spelling mistakes. For other minor errors my face was slapped and my cheeks painfully twisted in the teacher's hands.

Onnig would tell me about the cruel punishments in the older grades, including the one that made students hold heavy books in outstretched hands for a long time. And in an Armenian school in Toronto in the 1980s, Kristin, in her early years, was subjected to the same pain and shame of the ruler's smack in front of the whole class.

And why were we children being punished? Not for making mistakes. Simply for being children.

Raffi's account of his childhood experience underscored what Alice Miller said about poisonous pedagogy. The tyrannical handling of children by adults bent on giving instruction "for their own good" with little or no regard for the effect on the children was unconsciously passed on from one generation to the next.

When Onnig and I first attended Toronto schools in 1958 we were immensely relieved that teachers didn't hit us for minor errors. But the use of force was still there from time to time. One day my grade six teacher called me to the front of the class, told me to bend over, and took the broad yardstick to my backside for the crime of taking another classmate's seat and pushing her in defense of what I thought was *my* desk. I felt humiliated.

In western schools, progressive educators can no longer justify using force on students. However, it is a sad irony that the level of youth aggression in schools today, especially in the inner city, poses a formidable challenge to the whole issue. I can only believe that this kind of behavior is merely a symptom of the societal violence all around us and from which schools are not immune. Obviously, such aggression cannot be tolerated. Yet, to me, it makes no sense to reply in kind.

Although, by and large, children nowadays are not physically mistreated in school, the advocacy of corporal punishment in education still hangs on in some quarters as reactive elements seek to control aspects of children's anti-social behavior. I would argue that the youth's behavior is likely caused by the very constraints of poisonous pedagogy. Here I mean pedagogy in the broadest sense, since it fashions the social contexts that perpetually shape our lives—psychic, political and economic.

I remember well the kindness of teachers who truly loved the students in their care. In my first couple of years in Toronto, for instance, a very caring woman helped me after school to improve my reading. Thanks to her gentle manner, I felt loved in her presence and didn't want our sessions to end. And I can't forget Mr. Matheson in junior high, who emphasized "auxiliary reading" of publications like *Atlantic Monthly* (which I still read on occasion), and exhorted us, above all else, to read critically. At times, he whacked his desk with a pointer to wake us up, to make sure we got the message. He was on fire on our behalf, and we knew that.

Then there were those classroom teachers who believed they had a divine right to rule. They frightened me, but hardly won my respect; I endured them as best I could. Interestingly enough, I don't remember most of what schoolteachers taught me about curriculum.

There are many hidden lessons in education. It is from my school experiences and my later reflections on learning that I would say *you teach who you are:* your very being is imparted in the interactions within any lesson. As much as any subject a teacher presents, the teacher's tone of voice, disposition and relations with the student are also teaching a lesson in the passing play of life.

* * *

The written words of my ancestor reached me like a faint radio signal from a voice of another age, a message from seven generations ago wanting to be amplified and broadcast to the world. And I wondered what *I* might say to those living seven generations from now.

Volition or violation—the words whispered in my ear. It's about a basic choice we have: either respect and nurture the volitional instincts of children, or risk violating their spirit. If we do not acknowledge and support the intrinsic abilities of the child, we fail in our obligation to that child in one form or another.

And of course, if we neglect the real physical and emotional needs of young children in the early years—especially the first three—we gamble with the very development of the child brain where all the patterns of the body and mind form. Early neglect is a terrible tragedy. Its toll in human misery is incalculable and takes great pains to undo.

That's why finding one's true voice is a boon, not only to oneself, but to all of society. When we help children make that discovery from an early age, we help them find a place in the world, and a purpose in this life. The benefits ripple in all directions.

MERRILY MERRILY

I HAVE LEARNED THAT THE PLAY OF ADULT LIFE, AS IN CHILDHOOD, is messy. Trial and error is the way we sort out our likes and dislikes, what works and what doesn't. In a way, all of it becomes the compost of our emergent growth.

In Nature's complex play, all ingredients are used, nothing is wasted. Decay feeds growth. The biodiversity web in which we live uses all aspects of our learnings and becomings. If we have the courage to periodically turn inward and reflect, we may find changing vistas along the spiral path of time, gates of experience through which to view the familiar with fresh insight. For me the journey is a humbling paradox—at once a broadening of understanding and an appreciation of how little one knows about Creation's unfathomable depths.

The gift of my life has been the weave of its threads, the concert of people and places and times—a tapestry as rich as the Persian rugs my little feet once walked upon, as fine as the hot Cairo sand, as old as the ancient Ararat peaks.

A gift of people is what I carry: a gift of hearts and minds spoken, roads traveled; the gift of our common human song. A potluck offering of riddle and rhyme, stings and triumphs, tests, betrayals, joys and endurance, love lost and found, heroic journeys and everyday healings. The gift of beauty in the dazzling array of sun and surf, flora and fauna on this gleaming planet.

The love of the children and families with whom I've made music—*this* is a gift like no other. The children's faces, eyes alight, darling hands and dancing feet, live forever to recall. Their perennial voices, soft breezes stirring leaves in the garden.

When I remember that I am Creation's child, my eyes close, the mind chatter stops and I take a deep breath. When I remember, I give thanks for each plate of food and ask that all may be fed and that all who thirst find comfort. When I remember, the small pleasures loom large and my smallness of being gives way to the expanded awareness of this vast belonging we call Universe.

Dear Universe, how is it possible that I love children more now than ever? How is it that the life energy of the very young attracts me, that the vibrational aura of the six-month-old, like the subtle energy of buds and flowers, has such a strong pull? I know every child is different, as individual as every grown-up. But is there a child essence I am drawn to, beneath the habits of culture and personality, that is accessible in fleeting moments?

There *are* moments when the trust between two people holds quiet celebration and wonder for both, in a bubble of being, a marvel of love. That's one reason why there is nothing quite like reading to a child. These days, I am lucky that the young friends in my life provide such joy. After all, we need each other.

One afternoon not long ago, I went to visit a four-year-old neighbor down the street. As soon as I entered the cozy apartment and said hello to her parents, the brown-haired, dark-eyed beauty ran over to us announcing, "I'm a flower princess!" and danced circles around us. For a while, the living room with its plants and toys became a whirlwind of floral princess-ness, appreciated and applauded by the grown-ups.

Robin is usually in a state of fantasy play in the nest her parents Lisa and Michael have made. She embraces her surroundings with the confidence of one who has every right to explore and engage all that is new, and she doesn't miss a chance to make the world her own. With tea, I took out the book that brought the princess to the sofa.

Curled up on the couch, Robin and I are reading *Stellaluna*, about a bat who temporarily loses its way. "Stellaluuuna," I say and almost sing the name and she does too. Would she like to turn the page? "Yes." I read in understated tones; she smiles and whispers, turns the page. Soon the story and pictures have us laughing out loud. At the book's close come the familiar words, "Read it again." I do, and leave it with her for a few days.

Next time I see her she's a quacking duck. "Puddleduck, Robin-duck, waddle-duck," we say, "I'm a duck, you're a duck, quack quack." Does she have a hug for me? "Yes." Big hug. "You're too barky to kiss," she says of my bearded face. After we read *Sea Otter Pup*, she is changed. "I'm a seal, a seal."

Five-year-old Sergei was born to my island friends Tony and Tania, and somehow he got called the Beezer, "the Bee" for short. I've known him all his life.

"Hi the Bee!"

"Hi Raffi, hi the Raf."

When he comes to visit, Beezer knows where to find the tiny cars he loves to play with, knows he is allowed to take out one at a given time. On a low shelf in the bookcase are the children's books, with colorful covers that beckon. He loves to go over and choose one for us. (Oh, now he's got two or three!)

"Hey, where's that jumping frog, Raf?"

"You know, in the drawer where you last saw it." He tiptoes over and finds the frog, walking back with the most satisfied look you could ever see on a little boy's face.

The Bee and I have a rich play repertoire. For a while when he was three, his favorite game was "What's That?" Anywhere we were, at the market, for example, he would point to something and ask "What's that?" repeatedly, for what seemed like hours. Such energy, I would think: how does he go on like that? Once, I turned the game around, mimicking him, pointing every which way and saying "What's that?" He opened his eyes wide with surprise and gave a loud chuckle. Had I caught on to his game? Did I understand it was more fun to ask than to know?

Beezer's home—where I like to nap and eat pie—is filled with music, books, maps, paintings and artifacts. The dinosaur books are among his favorites and, though not yet reading, he has near-flawless recall of any dinosaur's name just seeing it on the page. His vocabulary is as wide as his curiosity, enriched by his parents' attention and the occasional word-play with his pal Raf. Instantly he memorizes the little poems he hears, like this one: "The kiss of the sun for pardon / The song of the birds for mirth / You're nearer God's heart in a garden / Than anyplace else on Earth." We don't analyze the poems; we simply enjoy them.

One day, just for fun, I dubbed him "Beezer Dubois, famous French film director." With a French accent, I introduced some words en français that Dubois might use. "Repeat after me, the Bee— *formidable . . . enchanté . . . d'accord!*" I said with great flair, and he said the words right after me, one by one, both of us laughing at every word. "Once more, *encore!*"

Beezer doesn't miss much. When we're out for a walk in the woods, his parents and I are likely to say "Good spotting, Bee!" as he finds yet another slug, worm or tree fungus. He loves spotting things, whether it's the cat in the book *Waves in the Bathtub*, or the string of tiny bells in my big jade plant.

The last time we played "I spy with my little eye . . . ," trying to find various things in the room, I was struck by his generosity. After I called out what I spied and he found it—to our mutual joy and applause—he'd take a turn. Over and over again, if I delayed even a little in moving towards his chosen object, he would let me know in what direction I might likely find it. He wasn't playing to win or to trick me, but for the fun of it.

For the gift of friendship with Robin and the Beezer, my heart abounds with gratitude. But I have only words to convey the wealth our play provides.

TURNING AND TURNING

The future ain't what it used to be.
Yogi Berra

I SOMETIMES WONDER WHAT THE WORLD WILL OFFER MY YOUNG friends when they are my age. So much depends on how we see our planet, and how we respond now to both the promises and the threats to their future. I have felt a responsibility to address some of the issues of our times, and writing this book has given me an opportunity to join the public discourse. And with respect to children, that requires looking at the factors that most affect the world we leave to them. The unprecedented concentrations of corporate capital constitute a global power, a concern that should not be left to economists alone. As a potent force, today's business activity affects every family's health—for better or worse—as never before.

All around the globe, real struggles are under way to safeguard the sanctity of Nature as we used to know her, and perhaps human nature in the process. Consider these examples:

A wide group of toxic chemicals, according to the latest research, so pervades our world that no one—from the Arctic to the Antarctic—can hide from the effects of these pesticides, industrial chemicals and other pollutants. They permeate our environment and our bodies. As authors Colborn, Dumanoski and Myers reveal in *Our Stolen Future*—

a book that many call the sequel to Rachel Carson's *Silent Spring*—
nowhere on Earth is there a "clean, uncontaminated place, nor any
human being who hasn't acquired a considerable load of persistent
hormone-disrupting chemicals."

In just fifty years, the once benign biosphere has turned poisonous,
putting every baby now being born "at risk." Toxic pollutants that linger
insoluble in air, water and soil accumulate in plants, animals and
humans. Despite a frightful legacy that includes disruption of hormonal
activity, distorted sexual development and a staggering 50% drop in
human male potency, more than a thousand new synthetic compounds
are produced and enter the biosphere each year. What's more, the dangers
posed are greatest for the most vulnerable people—our very young.

All this has made "children's environmental health" a growing
focus for physicians and parents alike. While many people still tune
out this kind of news, the U.S. Environmental Protection Agency has
established a Children's Health Office and is planning to open a
number of children's environmental health centers across the country.

The biodiversity of seeds is under the threat of patenting by multi-
nationals, which would claim for the private sector what we used to
consider part of our global commons—Earth's abundance, free for
the taking. Fortunately, there is resistance. Farmers in India, for
example, responded recently to a takeover bid of local seeds (seeds!)
by telling big business where to go.

The genetic altering of foods ought to frighten us to the core, the
way it can blur the species composition of a simple tomato or
cucumber. So little is known about how producing and eating
genetically changed foods might affect human health and the planet's
well-being that, if left unchecked, the cut-and-paste food business
could turn into a dangerous roulette game.

This is not a game, however. The issue at stake is the fundamental right
to know what we're putting into our bodies and feeding our children.
Citizen groups should not have to fight for right-to-know labeling of all
such foods, including irradiated foods and milk containing BGH (bovine

growth hormone). In this basic "freedom of information for health" matter, legislation to put family health first deserves strong support.

The cloning of animals and the threat of human cloning also pose great moral questions. Playing God in this way seems to contradict the yogic teaching that says by the time you have gained the power to move mountains, you would have the wisdom to leave them where they are.

On the up side, I have been excited to learn that a new understanding of the way the human brain develops is profoundly affecting the public's perception of early childhood. The findings of the past decade have brought forth insights into the nature of human intelligence that cannot be overlooked. Much of this we knew intuitively, and now it's supported by science.

It is known, for instance, that how a newborn is held, loved and stimulated in the early months is critical to the child's growing intelligence. What's more, about 90% of the brain's development occurs in the first three years, and neural wiring largely sets a person's emotional parameters for life. This knowledge sparked two fortunate events that deserve mention here.

In his 1995 ground breaking book *Emotional Intelligence*, Harvard graduate and *New York Times* columnist Daniel Goleman presented the latest scientific research on the workings of the brain and their connection to emotional functioning. He explained how one's capacity for emotional understanding and the management of one's emotions are paramount to having a healthy outlook on life. The roots of intelligence, he confirmed, clearly lie in the emotional context of early childhood. Goleman's book spurred *Time* magazine to do a cover story on EQ (emotional quotient), a broader—and more important—measure of intelligence than intellect alone.

Such brain research results also inspired actor-director Rob Reiner to launch a national campaign in the U.S. called *I Am Your Child*, whose slogan is "the first years last forever." In a one-hour TV special shown on ABC in 1997, Reiner's advice to "read, sing and play with your child" was echoed by a number of well-known personalities, including the President and First Lady. Not long after, *Newsweek* magazine came out with an entire special edition focusing on the first three years of life. For the very first time, a national public awareness campaign, highlighting the cost of neglecting children's emotional health, stressed the vital importance of nurture in the early years.

* * *

If only we put as much energy into supporting human potential as we do into pursuits that divert our attention from life's true and enduring blessings.

How ironic that a *digital* mode of creativity as imitation of Creation's numerical designs may appear appropriate at first glance. But users beware. The very precision and separation of bits recorded digitally (thus allowing their easy alteration) also poses the great challenge of synthesis. We may be proficient in taking things apart (as Newtonian science has done in recent centuries), but we aren't so clever in putting them back together again. As Severn Cullis-Suzuki entreated the adult world in Rio, "If you don't know how to fix it, please, stop breaking it."

I know from my experience with digital recording in the studio that the computer screen lets you easily erase or alter anything at will, right down to the tiniest audio blemish, like "lip smacks" that occur when the mouth opens to speak. Of course, digital video imaging allows similar retouching capability—both big and small—to the point that you can create or change images at will. (Examples that come to mind are a *National Geographic* cover photo in which one of the Giza pyramids was moved, the morphing of video images in rock videos and commercials, and special effects in movies.)

We seem to want the power to make alterations on life's constituent parts, to render the world digital for enhanced wealth, influence and control, perhaps the ultimate in divide-and-conquer. But towards what overall good, no one is sure. Does the Earth really need a make-over? Personally, I would much prefer to live with her "before picture" than a techno version. I can't help but wonder if digital isn't just the latest in retouching, for the sake of appearances.

It seems to me that we are at a juncture where it is nearly impossible to trust the images we are presented, and it is just as difficult to know who is behind them. These days, even the colors of a marvelous sunset could have been enhanced—by air pollution. If there is something wrong with this picture, it is fidelity run amok, a crisis of trust.

As we approach the new millennium, I do detect a great deal of fear in people struggling to know what to hold onto.

Many retreat to old beliefs and behaviors in an instinctive reach for something familiar, as often happens in times of personal crisis. Some seek shelter in fundamentalism, others put their faith in computers, and some ride capitalism even harder. It's no wonder. The task at hand is a tall order: integration, both societal and personal, in a fundamental redesign. A cohesion of values—an alignment of heart, mind and soul—is not impossible, but something that most of us have not been taught. With that, a central question for these times becomes, "Who can we trust?" And in the same breath, "What can we believe in?"

The crisis in external authority ultimately leads us back to a central power, to the person we see in the mirror. Do we trust this person? Can we at least trust that the questions we hold are honest, and that the loss of faith in outmoded icons—painful as it is—might be serving a purpose?

If we cannot look to outside experts to rescue us or save the planet, will we accept our part in solution scenarios, or will we shrug and leave it to someone else? Conventional thinking in commerce, media and politics has outstripped its usefulness but not outspent its power. Are we willing to use *our* personal power—in purchasing, voting, at work, in child rearing—in the daily decisions where we can make changes large and small?

With commercial media increasingly under the control of fewer owners, and much of the news broadcast prepared by PR firms employed by corporations, again the question arises: What can we trust? Tobacco companies lying to the public for decades may only be the tip of the iceberg when it comes to the credibility of big corporate enterprise. Can reasonable skeptics steer free of the high-priced and high-powered misinformation that passes for business as usual?

When it comes to such credibility gaps, children are the ones who bear the brunt of the parent society's irresponsibility. I would say that not knowing what to believe from their elders drives them crazy, and they act it out in every conceivable way to get our attention.

Neither young nor old can take much comfort in politics as adversarial sport, and so many of us wonder how we regain our lost confidence in government and, more importantly, in governors who have turned lying into an art. How can even honest public servants pursue long-term sustainability issues if their sights are trained on short-term rewards? And without radical campaign finance reform, how can they keep arm's length of the money interests that elect them?

In this very complex world, I am amazed that the hopelessly outdated words "left," "right," "liberal" and "conservative" are still hurled about. What are young people to make of such foolishness? Surely politicians—and indeed, every one of us—would benefit from a more constructive approach to public service. In the meantime, we would do well to fashion legislation and incentives that spur ethical and far-sighted governance. At the very least, in parliamentary democracies, we might insist that the term "honorable" be earned.

Central to all of this is one fundamental premise that drives human enterprise: *wealth*—its definition, creation—its very notion needs urgent and thorough review.

The way the wealth of nations is currently accounted—tabulated as GNP or GDP—there is less money to be made (and less economic growth) in letting the mountain be than in moving it. Like TV's bias for motion, fast action and quick edits, capital's penchant is to remake the world; its bias is action, not conservation. Unless the notion of riches returns from the symbolic to the real world, I fear we will look for power in all the wrong places.

For the human species, whose true nourishment comes from that immeasurable currency called love, a money-driven global culture that puts a premium on what it can control, measure and sell courts disaster. This destructive controlling impulse, with its delusions of grandeur, begs the question: Is the desire to play God a power we can afford?

In *The Road Ahead* by Bill Gates, there's a chapter called "Friction-free Capitalism." The grand idea here seems to be that we should all have (via the Net) the ability to buy whatever we want, at any time of day or night, from wherever in the world we can get it the cheapest. But that is simply the polar opposite to ecological thinking, which stresses short supply lines, bioregional sufficiency and full-cost accounting.

It stands to reason, then, that in the global economy's ever widening gap between the haves and have-nots, the drive to "have it all" can only come at an inestimable cost. For the have-nots, for those living off-line, for indigenous cultures—in fact, for anyone not playing the Net game—the game gets tougher and they fall farther behind along the way. And those out to win at all costs turn playing fields toxic and strip the garden bare. As Vancouver ecologist Bill Rees has pointed out, for everyone on Earth to live the North American lifestyle, it would take the resources of three-and-a-half such planets.

WALTZ OF POSSIBILITIES

I AM IMPRESSED BY THE WAY YOUNG CHILDREN APPEAR TO GRASP the essential issues quite clearly. A few years ago, for example, Adam Love (aged six) said to his father, "If we stop the cars, the trees can heal the sky." I have noted a similar desire to help protect the Earth expressed in many of the letters sent to me by children in the early grades.

And it's always interested me that in the drawings of the very young, the most commonly recurring image is the sun.

We all knew magic once upon a time. That magic can be reclaimed in the quantum garden where it still plays—where physicists and mystics now meet and bow. It calls out to us to know it again, to hover like hummingbirds and drink its sweet nectar: as near as Creation's floral designs and orgasmic rites each spring, as far as the luminous spiral galaxies, to be kissed through the doors of perception. For free.

In this time of unprecedented opportunity and chaos, I believe we are co-writing a new "grand narrative." Many call it the birth of spiritual new age; others call it an information age. Some see a time of certain disorder and cataclysm, but—fortunately—a growing number see instead a pivotal time in human evolution and thus for all life on Earth.

I am of the "pivotal" mind, and I sense the matter at hand as nothing less than an ecological revolution of epic proportions, not confined to air, water and soil, but centered in the heart, body-mind and soul. It involves a quantum leap to a new paradigm: an identity shift from *homo sapiens* to *homo amans*, the loving human, the magnificent animal now realigning along its higher human nature. Human as relational being, the conscious lover, choosing love.

To my mind, the "unthinkable" disappearing acts of recent years—the Berlin Wall, the Soviet Empire, apartheid—*have* made the 1990s a turnaround decade. All over the world we've seen a new spin on what we think is possible. The dismantling of Soviet communism, the Czech Republic's Velvet Revolution, and Mandela's freedom walk are nothing short of miraculous.

We have witnessed the "impossible."

So why dwell any longer on what "can't be done" when we'd be wrong in a minute? What better time to envision the unthinkable, to fashion desirable pathways outside the sum total of our past experience, along the confluence of our current dreams.

Rapid decay—whether in a flower that has long lost its glory or in the collapse of obsolete social systems—is more readily visible than the emergent growth of seedlings and creative new ideas. For a long time, these nurse out of sight in rich dark soil and in daring hearts. Indeed, such growth is fed by the decay that itself is a part of the cycle of renewal.

We seem to be at a place where past contradictions and contrasting cultures combine for what they offer to this transitional age—a synergy beyond analysis, full of strange reciprocity, complementarity and bracing paradox—in the words of Czech President Václav Havel, "a time of transcendence." As we feel our way through the disarray we see in our communities (both human and wild), we are challenged to keep informed and keep hope alive. It takes some effort to hold a positive vision. All the while, technological innovation outpaces our ability to keep up with it.

The Internet—that lucrative boom in *one* way of keeping informed—has pushed data transfer and time to new speeds, affecting user expectations in the process. But is the Net's seductive allure offering the illusion of another techno-fix to the world's problems, one more distraction from real flesh and blood? From what I have seen, rather than offer altered thinking or a change of heart, the Net expands a user's *existing* inclinations. If it does in fact amplify humanity's unsustainable course—the very model we need to outgrow—would that be a cause for consternation or would it hasten the demise of the obsolete?

Will the democratic possibilities of cyberspace see fruition in tantalizing and unpredictable ways, proving both proponents and critics wrong? Has this technology come along at precisely this time because the world, as some have suggested, needs to be wired to awaken some form of "global brain"? Does it hold the promise, for example, of a mass coming-to-our-senses to expose the questionable activities that transnationals want to pursue with impunity? It's hard to know.

While the impact of the Net on individual, family, community, business and, indeed, on human evolution, continues to be a topic of debate, its potential for democratized communication currently favors those who can afford the service, hardware and all. The larger effect of the Net may be to add to the growing gap in personal incomes in the global economy.

If the Net is with us to stay, the very young are bound to grow up with its images, which they will access through their parents, older siblings, and on their own. One problem here (aside from other concerns about children and computers) is that inappropriate and socially undesirable transmission can't be easily filtered out. The prevalence of cyber-porn or racist propaganda will inadvertently find its most impressionable users to be children—especially those in homes with absent parents and those who feel lost and unconnected.

Like the spread of television and computers, the spread of the Internet has occurred more rapidly than a sober appraisal of its considerable powers might advise. E-mailing 5,000 miles away as easily as across the street and web-page interaction with countless users— such benefits of increased links may be obvious, but the down side of mega-contact is harder to peg. Instant communication often begs instant reply, leaving little time for reflection or verification. For its superb specs as electronic courier, the audiovisual libraries it brings to our fingertips, and the portable lap-top offices it enhances, the Net is promoted as salvation by cyber-gurus touting its near-infinite applications. Yet, I am wary of that rush to judgment—there has been little discussion as to what cyberspace holds for the real world under duress.

NATURE *AND* NURTURE

A GARDEN GROWS A COMMUNITY OF BEING, OF EARTH AND SKY, of roots and cloudbursts, trunks and blooms, and of the creatures it houses. Seasonally, winter's promise is kept, bringing new buds, the faith of seeds made manifest for all to see. Here—and in the inner garden—within the design of millennia, are we too not born to blossom and turn, true to our design? This connection to a process both the same and far greater than oneself can provide roots for being, a secure seat in the rightness of the given moment. For me, that basic faith in life is the heart of partnership, human and beyond.

From my experience, the move from dominance to partnership in human relations starts within, and primary relationship is not so much with another as it is inside: not me and you, but soul and psyche. Inside each of us is the theater where we can enact a new play (the partnership model that Riane Eisler talks about) and then take that experience and move it outward. It's in how we regard ourselves that we can practice the partnership way of supportive, loving being.

For a culture undergoing a profound change in character, healing becomes a universal vocation. And the chains of societal violence melt in as many places as possible when we find ways to wholly love and accept ourselves. This change is not something we do in our heads; it doesn't happen by mere intention or meditation alone. It requires integration at an *emotional* level: to mend where we were broken and move into a new experience of self—one that knows its past and has made peace with those who played their part in it. With that, we can view the world through a stunning new lens.

It has been tremendously encouraging to see once-immovable walls of denial crumble as individuals, communities and even governments engage in sincere processes of reconciliation. There are many recent examples, including the apology of the Canadian government to Japanese citizens forced from their homes and interned during World War II, the drive to free the assets of Holocaust survivors' bank accounts, and the work of South Africa's commission for Truth and Reconciliation.

In August 1997, I was one of many who had the privilege of witnessing a Canadian peace story akin to the dismantling of the Berlin Wall: it was the occasion of the Royal Canadian Mounted Police joining with aboriginal peoples to carve out a new leaf in the history of this land.

An idea conceived in faith, between two friends from previously conflicting cultures—artist Roy Henry Vickers, a Tsimsian from northern British Columbia, and RCMP staff-sergeant Ed Hill—VisionQuest became a healing journey of a thousand miles made by seventy Natives and Mounties in three large canoes. On this sea voyage down the British Columbia coast, the group stopped in more than twenty villages and towns and called out to assembled chiefs and elders, "We come in peace, and respectfully ask permission to come ashore." In communities where, for decades, the force's arrival brought pain and suffering, the RCMP had come to apologize—to heal historical wounds. And the apology, made in full "red serge" uniform, was met with forgiveness every time. Natives walked with Mounties in a rare atmosphere of mutual trust, and children watched with wonder.

At the end of the voyage in Victoria, RCMP Commissioner Phil Murray spoke movingly about the importance of this journey and the change he feels is now at hand. We are, it appears, at the dawn of a new era.

To see the historical significance of this event, one has only to think of the state security forces of countries around the world, and ask which of those agents of colonial powers has ever apologized to the indigenous peoples they have harmed.

Unusual accommodations in a postmodern world: unpredictable healings, no cure too wild to hope for, no miracle untenable. Like magic, they mock despair, disarm cynics and dare us to keep to the high road; they challenge the quality of our every thought and vibration. An alchemy of technology and ancestral dust is at play, as old and new merge in unprecedented alloys. The whole world over, possibility reigns supreme.

* * *

Recently, my young friend Beezer and I were hiking up a wooded hill. All along the way he noticed various plants and rocks and we were both so taken by the different mosses we saw that we decided to name them, both for fun and to better identify them. At one point on our trek Beezer turned around and asked, "Hey Raf, what does 'normal' mean?" We walked a while and I said, "That's what people call whatever they don't consider special." "But one day," I added, "you'll understand there's no such thing as normal." The hike, at its summit, gave us a view of mountains, water, forests and sun, and, in a nearby tree, a bald eagle.

Every week I hear of an exciting idea in sustainable living: ecological architecture, community-supported agriculture, energy-efficient technologies, ethical investment funds, organic cotton, natural learning—the list goes on and on.

The difference between pessimists and optimists, the saying goes, is that pessimists have better information. I'm not so sure; besides, it may be missing the point. To me, anyone who precludes miracles isn't playing with a full deck. And no new paradigm has ever sprung from the cynicism of arrested imagination. It's true: you won't find a five-year-old cynic anywhere.

When I am tempted to despair, and occasionally fall, I remember that pessimism is a form of arrogance. As a fuel for creative action, it's hopeless. And irrational. Just because we can't see what solutions lie around the bend doesn't mean they won't appear. Neither do horrific acts of human desperation cancel out the beauty in the world or the love in our hearts.

Spring's bursting blossoms come without concern for their chances of success. They bloom as is their nature.

In many ways now, we're called to sing, as is our nature.

AFTERWORD

THE TIES THAT BIND US TO THOSE WE LOVE MOVE SO UNEXPECTEDLY, it seems the heavens do work in mysterious ways. Through the twists and turns that inevitably came with losing both parents, it was generosity and love that prevailed in my family, giving our grief the richness it deserved.

Over the course of my writing, I have had many opportunities to talk to my sister and brother about family dynamics. At times I wondered how three siblings could have such different experiences of the same event and such varying recollections of episodes in our family history. But then, I realized, how could it be otherwise? It's gratifying to see how far the three of us have come in understanding each other's perspectives. We have learned to take the time to listen well, and to cherish the enrichment our collective family remembrances provide. And we do keep alive the mother tongue that feeds us still. If our parents only knew.

As busy as Ani has been in her position as Ontario's Information and Privacy Commissioner, she was always there to lend me a word of encouragement or share a memory or two. Since her best-selling book was published in 1995, Dr. Ann Cavoukian (as she is known professionally), has become a privacy expert widely respected not only in Canada, but in international privacy forums where she often speaks.

She works tirelessly to keep up with the latest threats to privacy and the means to protect citizens to the greatest extent possible. The acclaim she receives gives me joy and I am comforted to know so well one who engages the privacy issue so tenaciously.

Onnig, the Cavouk heir, has carried on his photography with a masterful touch, most notably earning the honor of official photographer to His Holiness Karekin I, Catholicos of all Armenians. In recent months, Onnig provided me with dozens of photos, articles and momentos from our parents' home and greatly assisted me in tracing the family history. Our recollections have been heightened by his trip to Cairo and Jerusalem in the fall of 1997, the sites of so many Cavoukian stories.

Returning to the place of his birth gave my brother the opportunity to take part in a reunion at Kalousdian School. His video of the old schoolyard showed it was now only half its original size (an expressway had claimed the other half). Among the very old black-and-white portraits in the administration office, some carried the Cavouk signature, as did the color portrait of Mayrenie Grandma (in prayer) that Arto and Lucie had donated when they visited the school a few years before.

In Jerusalem, Onnig saw the magnificent paintings in the St. James Convent inside the Armenian Quarter—including ones Ohannes Grandpa had restored. He returned saying he was overwhelmed with the great numbers of people who knew our family name (and our parents) and the high regard with which our father's work was held.

Perhaps the biggest surprise for me has been how I have come to love injecting Armenian sayings into nearly every conversation with my family. The more we indulge in that untranslatable, hilarious, absolutely marvelous Armenian humor, the happier I am.

And how wonderful that Kristin and Sevan can join in this as well. After being an honors air cadet, Sevan is pursuing his commercial pilot's license in Calgary. He is a wonderful young man, with a good sense of humor and an infectious laugh. For two years, Kristin has been the assistant manager of a crafts store in Vancouver. She also continues to develop her natural musical talent, playing guitar and fiddle and singing in fine style, as I have heard on the occasions that we have made music together. Best of all, Kristin and I can light up the phone line or a personal visit with the rich vocabulary of Arto and Lucie—the phrases, the voicings, the gestures. In so many ways, their legacy lives on.

* * *

A cassette full of song ideas has gathered over the last two years. In the mornings, with my first cup of coffee or tea, I've slung the guitar over my shoulders and strummed out a few chords and words without even trying—without thinking. Many of these musical tidbits sound surprisingly good to me over repeated listenings and I'm wondering what I'll do with them.

I am also full of ideas for another book, one that would be on the theme of honoring children and the collective good that might come from doing so. The idea plays in my mind as a set of questions at the center of which is something I have been pondering for some time: how would life be in a "child-honoring society"?

In thinking of a bright future for us to look forward to, I feel the time has come to honor the child and thus create a society that would earn the love and allegiance of all its children. It's a book we can write together.

ACKNOWLEDGMENTS

The assistance of those who, in small and large ways, came to my aid in the writing of this book is greatly appreciated.

To Fritjof Capra, June Callwood, Bonnie Simpson, Herb Barbolet, Zenobia Barlow, Herman Daly, Peter Bakalian, Theo Colborn, Ardith Cole, Carol Edgarian, George Tomko, Robert Semerdjian, Gary Hirshberg, Tanis Helliwell, Bob Zievers and Jill Swartz—who, on short notice, read the manuscript and gave me the benefit of their thoughts—I am very grateful.

Readers of portions of early drafts were Tara Cullis, Mary Ferguson, Leone Pippard, Ann Dale, Cath Webb, Kathleen Forsythe, Pille Bunnell, Severn Cullis-Suzuki and Tania Godoroja; Olga Sheehan did timely copy editing for the early text; and Nancy Flight provided sound advice. Tania also created the leaf logo for Homeland Press.

Many thanks to Onnig and Ani for their generous help with the manuscript, to Onnig for the numerous photos he provided, and to Kristin for her feedback.

Troubadour's publication of this book under the Homeland banner meant that suddenly we had to learn to be publishers—I truly appreciate the attention my colleagues paid to the numerous new duties required of us. Along the way, Paul Ryan and Nicole Jackson (with designer Betty Skakum) went to great lengths to make our "organic book" dream come true. Paul was a steadfast support to me throughout the writing, encouraging the work in its various phases. Nicole vigorously tackled the demanding permissions duties required, and we all benefited from Adela Krupich's administrative help.

Special thanks to Bert Simpson, my first writing teacher, for his indispensable part in the making of this book. Bert provided the invaluable perspective of our long years of friendship and working together and, from start to finish, helped guide the work in a number of ways. For his informed contribution to many aspects of the contents, I shall always be grateful.

And to my esteemed editor, Georgina Montgomery, whose unfailing grace and grit finessed the completion of this project, I owe a turn of gratitude. In the end, it was Georgina who pulled it all together, held me to task at every turn and, in the process, taught me a great deal about the craft of writing. *Merci*, Georgina.

To so many who saw me through considerable growing pains and held me in their thoughts and prayers, my heartfelt thanks.

SELECTED READING

Bateson, Mary Catherine. *Peripheral Visions: Learning Along the Way.* New York: HarperCollins, 1994.

Beland, Pierre. *Beluga: A Farewell to Whales.* New York: Lyons & Burford, 1996.

Brailsford, Barry. *Circle of the Stone.* New Zealand: Stoneprint Press, 1995.

Cannon, Janell. *Stellaluna.* New York: Harcourt Brace, 1993.

Capra, Fritjof. *The Tao of Physics.* Berkeley: Shambhala, 1975.

———. *The Web of Life.* New York: Bantam Doubleday Dell, 1996.

Cavoukian, Ann and Don Tapscott. *Who Knows: Safeguarding Your Privacy in a Networked World.* New York: McGraw-Hill, 1997.

Colborn, Theo, Dianne Dumanoski, and John P. Myers. *Our Stolen Future.* New York: Dutton, 1996.

Cullis-Suzuki, Severn. *Tell the World.* Toronto: Doubleday Canada, 1993.

Daly, Herman E. and John B. Cobb. *For the Common Good: Redirecting the Economy Toward Community, the Environment, and a Sustainable Future.* Boston: Beacon Press, 1989.

Doczi, Gyorgy. *The Power of Limits.* Boston: Shambhala, 1994.

Durning, Alan Thein. *This Place on Earth.* Seattle: Sasquatch Books, 1996.

Eisler, Riane. *The Chalice and the Blade: Our History, Our Future.* New York: Harper & Row, 1987.

Fernandes, Eugenie. *Waves in the Bathtub.* Toronto: North Winds, 1993.

Gibran, Kahlil. *The Prophet.* London: Penguin Books, 1992.

Goleman, Daniel. *Emotional Intelligence.* New York: Bantam Books, 1995.

Gore, Al. *Earth in the Balance.* New York: Houghton Mifflin, 1992.

Havel, Václav. *The Art of the Impossible.* New York: Knopf, 1994.

Hawken, Paul. *The Ecology of Commerce.* New York: Harper Business, 1993.

Lang, David Marshall. *Armenia: Cradle of Civilization.* London: George Allen & Unwin, 1956.

Lao Tzu, *Tao Te Ching.* New York: HarperCollins, 1988. (Translated by Stephen Mitchell.)

Leach, Penelope. *Children First.* New York: Alfred A. Knopf, 1994.

Liedloff, Jean. *The Continuum Concept: Allowing Human Nature to Work Successfully.* Reading, Mass.: Addison-Wesley Longman Inc., 1985.

McKibben, Bill. *Hope, Human and Wild.* New York: Little Brown, 1995.

Miles, Victoria. *Sea Otter Pup.* Victoria: Orca, 1993.

Miller, Alice. *For Your Own Good.* New York: Farrar, Strauss & Giroux, 1983.

———. *The Drama of the Gifted Child: The Search for the True Self.* New York: Basic Books, 1981, 1997.

Needleman, Herbert L. and Philip J. Landrigan. *Raising Children Toxic Free: How to Keep Your Child Safe from Lead, Asbestos, Pesticides, and Other Environmental Hazards.* New York: Avon, 1994.

Pearce, Joseph Chilton. *The Magical Child.* New York: Plume, 1977.

Roszak, Theodore. *The Voice of the Earth.* New York: Touchstone, 1992.

———. M.E. Gomes and A.D. Kanner (editors). *Ecopsychology: Restoring the Earth, Healing the Mind.* San Francisco: Sierra Club Books, 1995.

Talbot, Michael. *The Holographic Universe.* New York: HarperCollins, 1991.

Winn, Marie. *Children Without Childhood.* New York: Pantheon, 1981.

Woodman, Marion. *The Pregnant Virgin: A Process of Psychological Transformation.* Toronto: Inner City Books, 1985.

Permissions / Credits

We gratefully acknowledge the following for their kind permission
to display photos and reprint previously published material.

PHOTOS:
1–6 © Cavoukian Family Archives.
7 Public Domain.
8–17 © Cavoukian Family Archives.
18 © 1960 Willy Lobel.
19 © 1963 *The Toronto Telegram*.
20–27 © Cavoukian Family Archives.
28 © Onnig Cavoukian.
29–30 © Cavoukian Family Archives.
31–34 © Troubadour Records Ltd.
35 Drawing by Troy Hedly. Lettering by Chris
Anderson. © 1976 Troubadour Records Ltd.
All rights reserved. Used by permission.
36 © 1974 Dick Darrell.
37 © *Studio Light*, Vol. 2, No. 3. Reprinted with
permission from Eastman Kodak Company.
38–40 © Cavouk Portrait Studio Ltd..
41 © 1973 Onnig Cavoukian.
42 © Cavoukian Family Archives.
43–46 © Cavouk Portrait Studio Ltd..
47 © *Studio Light*, Vol. 2, No. 3. Reprinted with
permission from Eastman Kodak Company.
48–49 © Cavouk Portrait Studio Ltd.
50 © Cavoukian Family Archives.
51–53 © Troubadour Records Ltd.
54 © Raffi Archives.
55 © Cavouk Portrait Studio Ltd.
56 © 1998 Jeffrey Mayer.
57 © 1986 Deborah Pike.
58–61 © Troubadour Records Ltd.
62 © Deborah Pike.
63 © 1989 Gary Gershoff. Used by permission.
64 © Anji Smith.
65–66 © Raffi Archives.
67 © 1993 White House Photo. Used by
permission.
68–69 © Marian Rivman. Used by permission.
70 © 1994 Tracey Page.
71 © 1994 Alan Mayor. Used by permission.
72–73 © 1994 Tracey Page.
74 © Raffi Archives.
75 Courtesy of Michael Maser.
76 © Onnig Cavoukian.
77 © 1997 Tania Godoroja. Used by permission.

REPRINTED:
Pg.6. Troubadour definition. *The New Teachers'
and Pupils' Cyclopaedia*, page 2924. © 1915
Holst Publishing Company. Public Domain.

OVERTURE
Pg. 11. *Suzanne*. Words and music by Leonard
Cohen. © 1967 Sony/ATV Songs LLC. All
rights administered by Sony/ATV Music
Publishing, 8 Music Square West, Nashville,
TN 37203. All rights reserved. Used by
permission.

CHAPTER I
Pg. 15. By Raffi. © 1998 Homeland Press.
All rights reserved. Used by permission.

CHAPTER II
Pg. 45. From *Letters to a Young Poet* by Rainer
Maria Rilke, translated by M.D. Herter Norton. Translation © 1934, 1954 by W.W. Norton & Company, Inc., renewed © 1962,
1982 by M.D. Herter Norton. Reprinted by
permission of W.W. Norton & Company, Inc.

CHAPTER III
Pg. 75. From *Tao Te Ching* by Lao Tzu. Translation
© 1988 by Stephen Mitchell. Reprinted by
permission of HarperCollins. All rights
reserved.
Pg. 78. *It's Alright Ma (I'm Only Bleeding)* by
Bob Dylan. © 1965 Warner Bros. Music,
Copyright renewed 1993 by Special Rider
Music. All rights reserved. International
copyright secured. Reprinted by permission.
Pg. 84. *Going to the Country*. Words and music
by Bruce Cockburn. © August 1969 Bytown
Music Ltd. All rights reserved. Used by
permission. Included on the album "*Waiting
for a Miracle*" by Bruce Cockburn (1987),
True North Records.

Index

Index

MAKING THIS BOOK

Our aim from the start was to produce an "organic book"—one with non–toxic elements—to the fullest extent practicable. In the production of books, the publishing industry, like many others, has in recent years begun to use environmentally benign materials and processes. We made every effort to take advantage of this existing healthy trend, as well as going further to ensure optimal paper quality and durability alongside environmental considerations.

A key decision was to use papers bleached without chlorine, which in its various forms, becomes a persistent pollutant and poses a serious health threat, particularly to children. That's why we used two different papers: the dustjacket and photo pages are Totally Chlorine Free, made from virgin fibers never treated with chlorine; and the text pages, containing post–consumer recycled content, are Processed Chlorine Free, which means that no chlorine was used to bleach their fibers (virgin and recycled) this time around. Our thanks to Archie Beaton and the Chlorine Free Products Association (CFPA) for their guidance. The CFPA logos for both kinds of chlorine–free papers are displayed below. (All the papers we used are acid-free.)

We also opted for vegetable–based inks, non–toxic glues, and a water–based coating on the dustjacket. We're grateful to have found Friesens, a Canadian printer in Manitoba that works with these supplies.

One necessary compromise involved a plastic laminate for the hard cover to ensure strength and durability. In time we hope to find a preferred alternative for this also.

While our commitment to the organic idea has cost significantly more than standard commercial practices, we have chosen to absorb the difference rather than pass it on to book buyers. We see this as an investment in a better future for all of us. As more and more pulp and paper mills and publishers turn to benign alternatives, costs will decrease and the price difference between these and toxic procedures will vanish.

As we work together to create the healthy world our children deserve, the costs of polluting technologies will no longer be hidden and, in such a world, organic processes will be rewarded for all the obvious reasons. In the near future, the burden will not fall on those committed to sustainable means.

There are many ways of doing the right thing. Our choices were guided by alternatives that have been tested and true, and that are widely available. We hope we have acted as a small catalyst towards making the publishing industry truly sustainable.